Comments worked with P

I have known the Rev. Lonnie Branch for more than 40 years as a man of deep faith and love of family. He believes that with God all things are possible. His determination, courage, and confidence has proved that many times.
> *Ida Lockett, parishioner*
> *Holy Family Lutheran Church*
> *Chicago, Illinois*

From the time of Rev. Lonnie Branch's call to ministry, he has shown determination and perseverance. His positive, compassionate outlook and thoughtful listening have made him a strong instrument of faith. On his journey through ministry, this servant of God has deeply touched a wide variety of people and congregations.
> *James R. Harris, parishioner and president*
> *Holy Family Lutheran Church*
> *Chicago, Illinois*

Pastor/Chaplain Lonnie Branch performed a very difficult assignment in his service at the Anamosa State Reformatory. He not only ministered to the young men who were incarcerated, but personally visited their home congregations to help give them positive connections when they returned home. . . . He provided an outstanding ministry with a new component in utilizing the resources in the inmates' home communities, which continued in future years.
> *Pastor Ramon A. Runkel*
> *Director of Chaplaincy Services of Iowa (retired)*
> *Des Moines, Iowa*

This is definitely a book you will want to read. It is warm, inspiring, and filled with compassion. With society's fast and competitive lifestyles, it tells of real life situations and how God has healed and helped restore hope, faith, and unconditional love for one another.
> *Estena Barnes*
> *Martin Luther Lutheran Church*
> *Mobile, Alabama*

Reflections of Light is the compelling and entertaining story of the lifelong journey of Lonnie Branch. A man of great faith, he was eyewitness to, and in the middle of, the tumultuous civil rights struggles. During these decades of change, he survived childhood challenges, created a solid family, and broke color barriers in the Lutheran seminary and church leadership. Readers of this book will view history through the eyes of a remarkable man.

> *Marsha Jarvela, parishioner*
> *Prince of Glory Lutheran Church*
> *Minneapolis, Minnesota*

As church secretary and council president, I worked side by side with Pastor Branch for five years and witnessed first hand how he was able to cope with the many challenges of the congregation with consummate skills, endless patience, and graceful humor.

> *Laura Lindsay, parishioner and president*
> *Lutheran Church of the Atonement*
> *Atlanta, Georgia*

Pastor Lonnie Branch was a special person in my life. He saw something in me that needed to blossom. Pastor Branch encouraged me to create a training series for the deacons [at Lutheran Church of the Atonement]. Sometimes the going was difficult, but Pastor Branch continued to encourage me; the church and I were better off for the effort. It instilled a confidence in me to move forward because it is all God's work. I lost my own father at an earlier age than most, but my Father in heaven provided me with another father on earth.

> *Joseph P. Robnett, parishioner and deacon*
> *Lutheran Church of the Atonement*
> *Atlanta, Georgia*

In my years of working with Lonnie as a correctional chaplain at the work house, I remember his "win them over" model of ministry. He showed radical acceptance to the men, women, and the staff in the prison, while also holding them accountable—a powerful presence of love in his work and words of ministry, and most of all in his relationships of transformation. He modeled tough love and development of sacred ground in relational ministry.

> *Sue Allers Hatlie*
> *Director of Clinical Pastoral Education in Community Justice Ministries*
> *Greater Minneapolis Council of Churches*

Reflections of Light

The Odyssey of a Black American Lutheran Pastor During the Civil Rights Years

Lonnie L. Branch

Kirk House Publishers
Minneapolis, Minnesota

Reflections of Light
The Odyssey of a Black American Lutheran Pastor
During the Civil Rights Years
by Lonnie L. Branch

Copyright 2014 Lonnie L. Branch. All rights reserved. No part of this book may be reproduced or transmitted in any form by any means, electronic, mechanical, recording, or otherwise, without the express permission of the publisher. For information or permission for reprints or excerpts, please contact the publisher.

ISBN-13: 978-1-933794-76-1
ISBN-10: 1-933794-76-3

Kirk House Publishers, PO Box 390750, Minneapolis, MN 55439
www.kirkhouse.com
Manufactured in the United States of America

Dedication

Dedicated to our family matriarchs:

My mother Rebecca,
a single parent, whose encouragement
provided the toughness and determination
to build on our family foundation, to stand tall and
relentlessly persevere in confronting anything
that diminished or threatened our humanity.

My grandmother, Lenora,
who also taught me the importance of family, God's love,
and the church. She succeeded in teaching by example
in her closeness to my mother. They journeyed together.
Under severe restrictions, their tough love, sacrifices, and
discipline established the ground work that shaped
my formative years and family values.

Finally, my wife, Doris,
who did not marry a pastor, but was strengthened by God
to embrace all the changes within our family structure,
to multitask and build a strong foundation for the family.
God indeed has blessed us!

Contents

Foreword 9
Introduction 11
1 Beginnings in Memphis, Tennessee, 1939-1941 14
2 A Negro Child's Heritage, 1932-1941 18
3 Chicago South/North Side, 1942-1949 30
4 Christ's Epiphanal Light, 1949-1953 49
5 Adulthood & Marriage, 1953-1961 56
6 Civil Rights Era & Cabrini Green, 1962-1967 64
7 Theological Education, 1967-1969 93
8 Resolving Conflicts, 1969-1970 126
9 Wartburg Theological Seminary, 1970-1971 133
10 South Park Mission, 1971-1973 145
11 Iowa State Men's Reformatory, 1973-1976 165
12 Prince of Glory Lutheran Church, 1976-1983 196
13 Martin Luther Church, 1983-1989 212
14 Lutheran Church of the Atonement, 1989-1996 234
15 Hennepin County Adult Corrections, 1996-1999 248
16 St. Olaf Lutheran Church, 2000-2002 254
17 A Continuing Odyssey, 2003-2009 257
Epilogue: Glowing Lights 259
Appendix: Researching Family Roots 262
Acknowledgments 263

Foreword

The context of the ministry of Rev. Lonnie Branch, as he gives witness and testimony to the Christian faith, causes me to be reminded once more of the long journey of black people in our brutally radicalized existence in the United States. The existence of black people has been marred by racism. My working definition of racism for this forward, among a multitude of other definitions, is a denial of human personality.

The civil rights movement, during the decade of the 60s, was noted for demonstrations and major racial unrest. As one reads through Rev. Branch's story of unrest, one can see that this unrest existed not merely in the society, but also in the church.

The context of the civil rights movement in the United States church and society is the context in which Rev. Branch's life and ministry has unfolded. Some highlights of the struggle in the society was witnessed in the following ways:

1857:	The Dred Scott Decision (civil rights of black people)
1870:	Thirteenth Amendment to the Constitution (black suffrage)
1896:	Plessy vs. Ferguson (separate but equal)
1920:	Nineteenth Amendment to the constitution (women's suffrage)
1954:	Brown vs. the Board of Education (segregation illegal)
1955-60s:	Martin Luther King movement
1960s:	President John F. Kennedy backed the Civil Rights Act
1964:	President Lyndon B. Johnson signed the Civil Rights Act
1965:	President Johnson signed the Voting Rights Act

The struggle in the church was evident in the following challenges:
- Women were not allowed to be pastors
- Black pastors were pastors only for black congregations/churches
- Many black LCMS pastors were not provided insurance and pensions
- Education was European-oriented
- Churchwide and synod assemblies had little or no voting women and/or persons of color
- Many interracial relationships and marriages were not accepted
- Many Euro-American churches/congregations refused to commune persons of color

Having stated a few of the issues in the context of Rev. Branch's life and ministry, one readily can see how racism was operative in society and church and how his life was a struggle for freedom!

For hundreds of years the Christian church has enjoyed the material benefits of being racist. Many churches have helped to colonize persons of color with its Euro-American interpretation of religion on a global context, provoking the emergence of liberation theologies. Our churches were dominated by Euro-American racist leadership, contradicting the biblical mandate that Christians, both pastor and laity, should ". . . do justice, love mercy and kindness, and walk humbly with God." This mandate of Micah 6:8 is the call of God for justice in a racist society and church, as witnessed by Rev. Branch.

I heartily recommend this book.

Dr. Albert Pero Jr.
Emeritus Professor of Systematic Theology
The Lutheran School of Theology at Chicago

Introduction

This memoir is a condensed, historical account of my loving, blended family and the valued traditions that shaped our lives. It describes my personal odyssey during a time of great societal change. The word *odyssey* is taken from an epic poem by the Roman poet Vergil which comes closest to describing my life's journey. The miseries and struggles of Odysseus approximate my own life as a black man living in America. Through it all, God has been "an ever present help in times of trouble," guiding me in God's love, to become a faithful husband to my wife and parent to my children. However, as a people we have inherited another legacy—that of white racism which continues its omnipresence in our lives. I'm amazed at how we have been able to retain our sanity, define our identities, and maintain family cohesiveness. Born in the South, the oldest of seven siblings, I pause to think about the power of our matriarchal family's sacrificial love. Religious values and traditions of our black culture were the backbone of my parents' strength.

Hopefully, what I've written reflects God's grace in bringing us closer together as God's family. My intention is not to provide a voyeuristic peek into our lives but to affirm and build on our accomplishments, revealing our family roots and our mutual love and faith in God to overcome racism and poverty. Those were miraculous times in which we lived, and I will always look back wondering how we ever "got over." Little or no love was given us by white people and even less affirmation of our humanity. Although our struggles sometimes revealed the worst in us, God's love provided ways for us to "move on up—a little bit higher." I saw the pain in my parents' struggles to protect and develop our physical and mental health. Their lives personified *an* economics of love which helped me to grow into a loving human being in the midst of a dehumanizing white racist environment.

God's love for me began in my mother, Rebecca, and grandmother, Lenora, who were inseparable. They laid the foundation for a family legacy with the future of a new "day of rejoicing that comes in the morning" (Psalm 30:5, NIV). Today, in this time, it is important to unashamedly affirm and rejoice in what they accomplished. They valued education, and I was always told that "education was the Negroes' only way out of poverty and racism." *Other than my wife, Doris, these were the most loving, caring, and mentally tough women I've known.* It was their love that gave me a lasting insight into a truth about life that guided me towards working hard at being a loving family man. We all share the same Godly DNA when it comes to coping with family life today. If we fail to build on their legacy, then we will become deficient and never move forward. Before Moses died, God allowed him to see the Promised Land; before my mother, Rebecca, died God gave her a glimpse of the Lands of Promise in each of us. "We've come this far by faith, leaning on the Lord"—and on Rebecca, Elbert Kershaw Sr., Grandma Lenora and Robert Aycock, our aunts Rebecca Fleming and Ursula Fleming, and uncle Al—all members of a loving, blended family. For me, believing God's promises and moving forward in life are no-brainers; they are not options. So I wrote my memoir to share my experience of God's love in my blended black family.

Today our progress as black people is being measured by our response to the election of our first black president. As responsible black families and citizens, we must continue to pursue a place at the table of socio-economic and political equality. We have not arrived, as some may think, and we must continue defining our own identity, goals, and destiny as Americans. To do less ignores the sacrifices of our forebears and flies in the face of being created in God's image.

Using the descriptive terms *black* and *white* highlights the significant particularities and psychological struggles in the lives of black people. Today, many younger blacks prefer the name African-American to feel that they belong, but the identifying word "black" is still necessary to emphasize equality in partnership. The term African-American can be delusional, potentially spawning psychological deficiencies causing us to forget family and racial heritage. Our children and grandchildren have little knowledge and only muted experience in the struggles our forebears had in defining themselves as human beings. Young black people have no idea of the sacrifices made by black families for their rite of passage through the Red Sea to a new Land of Promise. We must continue to learn how to define African—black—Americans as people created in God's image.

CHAPTER 1

Beginnings in Memphis, Tennessee

1939-1941

We should not try to escape our legacy in being descendants of African slaves. Thankfully, those deep psychological wounds inflicted on the psyche of African Negroes prior to and during the Civil War era will never let us forget our heritage. To forget or ignore our past status dishonors the suffering, sacrifices, and struggles of our black, African ancestors. Blaming the slaves for losing the Civil War, white Southerners vented their pain by hating Negroes and maligning our humanity. The residual effects of their hate resulted in an ideology of white ethno-supremacy, enforced by Jim Crow laws and segregation as a normative relationship between whites and Negroes. The Ku Klux Klan, a white supremacist terror group, recruited its membership in white Christian churches. Symbolic of their diabolical perversion of the Holy Bible was the burning of crosses soaked with kerosene rags in front of Negro homes. Coming at night, faces covered with cloth sacks and wearing white robes, they murdered Negro males and children. Equal protection under the American constitution was non-existent for Negroes, and we were still enslaved. This is the milieu in which I was born and lived.

I clearly remember Sunday, December 7, 1941, in our home at 664 E. Georgia Street. We huddled around a small radio hearing President Franklin Delano Roosevelt say that "a state of war now exists between the United States of America and the Empire of Japan." This declaration of war caused a strange but joyous excitement, with a flurry of activity that I had never seen. I was nine years old and did not fully understand what was happening. Finally, it became clear; I heard my parents say we were going to move north, to Chicago, because "we'll be better off there, where we can work in the defense plants and help win the war. We'll have good paying jobs."

Our family was looking for a better land where life was filled with the promises of a new day. My grandmother's two sisters lived in Chicago and had kept her informed about more opportunities there for Negroes. In retrospect, their conversations sounded as if they were talking about the biblical Promised Land, "a land flowing with milk and honey." These words were never spoken by them, but it was a moot point about Chicago being a better place for Negroes than Memphis. The excitement in our family also was happening in the homes of a many southern Negroes.

My mother and grandmother.

My mother, Rebecca, and I lived with my grandmother, Lenora, who worked as a maid at the Peabody Hotel in downtown Memphis. Occasionally, Mother and Grandmother picked cotton to supplement our family income. Before leaving Memphis, my grandmother shared a dark family secret. She told me Lonnie Branch was not my father and that my "real father" was coming to visit us. His last name was Wilkerson. Can you imagine my confusion? To this day, I cannot remember anyone ever mentioning his first name. My mother only referred to him as "that old Dutchman, Mr. Wilkerson." Grandma Lenora was always angry whenever his name was mentioned. She may have thought that he was not doing enough, if anything, to help support me and my brother George. My mother always remained silent about Mr. Wilkerson and was angry at Grandma for telling us about him. Nevertheless, my mother confirmed that he lived in Memphis saying, "Old Man Wilkerson is a white man, married and living with two daughters, who are school teachers." I believe my father's family roots may have begun in Pennsylvania where a large Dutch population had settled. I do not know if my biological father, Mr. Wilkerson, had other children, but I knew now that he had two Negro sons—Lonnie and George.

Before leaving for Chicago he visited with us. Looking at him was like groping through a fog bank, trying to not only see but understand what was happening. I was shocked to see a white father, the second father that I had never known. I think he only came because Grandma Lenora had, in some way, threatened him if he did not come to say goodbye to his two sons. He was much older than my mother, with a medium build, average height and slightly thinning, dull-grey, straight hair. He didn't stay long, but I could hear him speaking in whispers to my mother in another room. He never spoke to me or George but as he left, he reached down and patted us both on our heads. We never saw or heard from him again. My mother said that if any neighbors asked who he was I should say he was our insurance man. I have always suspected that keeping our paternity secret had more to do with protecting him than us. I became aware of my need to forgive him for not being there for me and George, and I now can pray for God's blessings on our entire family.

After Mr. Wilkerson's visit we continued to prepare for our trip to Chicago. There was a lot of excitement as we looked for a better life in Chicago. I was nine-and-a-half years old when we left Memphis. My sister Lenora was eight, George was six, and Ira Willis Kershaw was two years old. I did not know at the time that my mother was expecting her fifth child.

During the train ride a humorous incident occurred. My mother had killed and cooked a couple of chickens to eat during our trip to Chicago. The remaining chickens and ducks that were not killed had been given to our neighbors, including George's little pet Bantam rooster, Big Red. George had seen my mother killing the chickens, and he did not believe Big Red had been given away. In fact he thought we were eating Big Red, and he refused to eat anything. Finally, when could not resist any longer, he began eating a sandwich, crying as he ate it. After reassuring him that it was not Big Red he was eating, George felt much better and stopped crying. As George calmed down I looked out of the train window at the scenery and enjoyed my first train ride to the Land of Promise.

My grandmother, Lenora Fleming, born sometime between 1895 and 1897, was the youngest of three sisters. She married my grandfather, Horace Carter. Lenora Fleming Carter's oldest sister, Rebecca Fleming, was born on June 12, 1883. Ursula Alyce Fleming was the middle sister, birthday unknown. All three sisters were born in Pine Bluff, Arkansas.

On October 12, 1913, Lenora Fleming Carter, the youngest sister, gave birth to her only child, Rebecca. My grandmother, Lenora, was between sixteen and eighteen years old when my mother was born. She named her daughter, after her oldest sister, Rebecca Fleming. In 1919, my grandmother's two older sisters moved from Pine Bluff to Chicago, where Ursula met and married Allen Bentley. My grandmother and mother remained in Pine Bluff until moving to Memphis sometime between September and November 1931. For whatever reason my grandmother's husband, Horace Carter, remained in Pine Bluff, and I would never come to know him.

CHAPTER 2

A Negro Child's Heritage

1932-1941

Before her marriage to Lonnie Branch, my mother, Rebecca, graduated from Booker T. Washington Senior High School. She was married on November 18, 1931, and at eighteen years old was expecting her first child. Rebecca—a young, beautiful, petite brown-skinned Negro woman—received a bridal booklet and marriage certificate indicating that my grandmother, Lenora Carter, and Ms. Luella Ward, my mother's first cousin, witnessed the marriage. Other witnesses were Haywood Branch, Henry Branch, Willie Branch, Inez Brown, Pearl Stark, Fred Knox, Robert Aycock, and Ethel Rice, who gave the expected baby a kimono gown. My mother's father, Horace Carter, was not there.

On Friday, February 26, 1932, my mother, now nineteen years old, gave birth to a baby boy at 11:00 A.M. in John Gaston General Hospital in Memphis. The hospital has now been renamed Shelby County Regional Medical and Trauma Center. Rebecca named her first child Lonnie Lee Branch Jr. The city of Memphis, named after the capital of ancient Egypt on the Nile River, is located in southwest Tennessee, along the banks of the Mississippi River. At that time, the population of Memphis was 252,000, but has now risen to 1.26 million. The predominant foreign immigrant nationalities were Italian, Russian, and German, including a notable Jewish presence. Memphis had two large daily newspapers, one that I remember was the *Memphis Commercial Appeal*.

When Rebecca married, she and my grandmother were living at 285 South Third Street. Following the marriage, events happened that are open for speculation. Although brief, the marriage resulted in the conception of my sister, Lenora. I believe my mother married Lonnie to have his name on the birth certificate as my father. Lenora, my mother's second child was born on Wednesday, September 6, 1933, at 9:25 a.m. in John Gaston General Hospital. My mother named her after our grandmother, Lenora. Unable to say the word "sister," I called her "Tutta," and to this day her family nickname is Tutta. The following month, on October 12, my mother marked her twentieth birthday. Two years later we moved from Third Street into a two-story tenement house on Turley Street where on Sunday, August 25, 1935, at 5:45 p.m. my mother's third child, George Vanderbilt Branch, was born. During his birth, I was told to go outside and play, but I could not because of my mother screaming. Hearing her cry out in pain I angrily yelled, "Leave my mama alone!"

Two months later, on October 12, my mother had her twenty-second birthday. We moved into a new home on Turley Street. A beer garden (tavern) was located directly in front of our house. On weekends we could hear people screaming and cursing, with sirens blaring from police cars and ambulances. On a very cold night the beer garden burned down. We stood outside on the rickety porch of our second-floor apartment, watching flames and sparks shoot up into the dark, moonlit sky. Standing outside in the cold and smelling the burning wood caused me to shiver and shake. I was scared, but I did not cry because I was not alone. When my mother noticed I was shaking, she took me by the hand and we went inside the house. She said, "I'm glad somebody finally got mad enough to burn down the place." And, as if having an afterthought, she said, "It was probably some drunk."

My mother never worked outside the home because she had to care for her children. I think our only source of income came from my grandmother who worked as a maid at the Peabody Hotel in downtown Memphis. On any clear night my mother would take me to the window of our home and show me where "Grandma Lenora worked." We could faintly see the glowing, bluish-white light on the roof of the Peabody Hotel. Grandma also worked as a part-time maid in the homes of rich white people. She often told us stories about fighting off sexual advances by white men in those families. "It had to be handled very carefully," she said, "because I didn't wanna git fired."

My entire childhood seemed to be filled with physical and mental pain. I was a magnet attracting all kinds of maladies such as chicken pox, measles, mumps, malaria, and yellow jaundice (hepatitis). When I was five years old, I would run to the corner of our street and wait until my grandmother arrived from work on the trolley bus. One day while running to meet her, my left leg suddenly collapsed and I fell down on the concrete sidewalk. What was so unusual is that the left side of my thigh and leg had no feeling. It was as though I did not have a leg. When she realized that I could not walk, Grandma Lenora picked me up and carried me home. The doctors at John Gaston hospital diagnosed me with infantile paralysis, later known as poliomyelitis. This disease usually consisted of a fever, paralysis, and atrophy of muscles with a permanent disability. At that time the only treatment was Sister Kenny's therapy of a diet consisting of cod liver oil, vitamin C, citrus fruits and juices, fluids, and plenty of sunshine. Hot, damp cloths were placed on my affected thigh and leg. Somehow my mother provided the special diet, but we had no medical or hospital insurance for therapy treatments. The only insurance Negroes had was burial insurance—and only if we could afford the premiums. With the love and prayers of my parents I walked again without limping, though with one leg smaller than the other.

I had a bad accident following my recovery from polio. My mother was scrubbing dirty clothing on a metal washboard when I decided to watch her by sitting on the partially closed lid of a tin tub filled with boiling water. As I sat on the lid it tilted, and I fell backward into the tub, scalding my lower buttocks. Earlier my mother had promised to take me downtown to watch a parade, and now we were in an ambulance with sirens wailing, heading to John Gaston Hospital. We were so well known by the hospital staff some might have thought we lived there. My scalded backside was treated using housefly maggots to eat away dead tissue. I was laid on my stomach with my hands tied to the bed to keep me from scratching and clawing at my flesh. However, when my mother arrived to visit me, she found I had freed one hand and was scratching away. When she saw me her screams brought nurses from everywhere, and the maggots were removed. It's been said: "That what doesn't kill you will make you stronger." I don't think I'll ever understand what that means, but I do know that God is always "a very present help in times of trouble." I vividly recall my mother, on bended knees with her hands tightly clasped, crying and praying. All three of us children slept with her on a small bed with a thin mattress laid on top of a skimpy, broken bedspring. Kneeling on the floor beside the bed, we prayed together. My mother taught me that whenever you are hurting, pray the Lord's Prayer! My parents did not have much time to attend church, but in retrospect I will always consider them good Christian people.

Later, Grandma Lenora married Robert Aycock, whose family lived in Lake Charles, Louisiana. I could not pronounce his nickname, "*Bob*," so I called him "Arb." Robert had a striking resemblance to the Indian chief Seattle, whose face is on one side of an old United States buffalo nickel. The city of Seattle, Washington, is named after this Indian Chief. Robert drank a lot of whiskey and was always "slurping down" raw oysters covered in hot sauce. When not eating them with a fork, he placed the pint-sized white cardboard box to his mouth and swallowed them.

A speech impediment caused him to stutter, and when he drank it seemed to make him angry, causing him to cuss and speak in a different language. My grandmother explained, "He has mixed blood," either Creole or "Redbones." Creoles have mixed Spanish, French, and Negro ancestry. Redbones are descendants of Native Americans and runaway slaves who found shelter among Indians in Louisiana. Both racial groups spoke in a mixed dialect that served as their native language. My grandmother said her mother—my great-grandmother—was a full-blooded Creek Indian. I told her she was mistaken, that there were no tribal Indians named Creeks— only the Cree Indians who lived in the northern Canadian territories of Manitoba and Saskatchewan. Nonetheless, she insisted that there were Creek Indians saying, "You don't know what you're talking about!" I forgot about the incident until years later when I drove through Alabama on my way to Mobile, Alabama. I saw a huge signboard with these words printed on it: "You are now entering the Federation of the Creek Indian Nation." My grandmother was correct, I didn't know what I was talking about. The Creeks were American Indians, any of several tribes, mainly Muskogean, but included the Blackfoot tribe, to which my great-grandmother belonged. For survival, these Indians had formed a tribal league called the Creek Indian Confederacy, and they lived in Georgia, Alabama, and Florida. They were named Creek by white frontiersmen because of the many creeks and tributaries located in their tribal territory.

The time following the birth of my brother George was a time of strange, terrifying memories. We no longer lived with my grandmother, and our new house was really scary. My mother's boyfriend, Buster, would occasionally come to spend the night with us. One night, when he was not there, my mother and I were in the bed with my little sister and brother. As I looked up at the dark ceiling I saw how the light from our kerosene lamp had formed a circle of light. We had no electricity, and my mother had shortened the wick in the lamp to use as a nightlight. As I stared at the ceiling something strange happened. Suddenly, a distinct dark shadow slowly emerged from the circle of light and moved out into the darkness of the ceiling. The shadow was shaped like the footprint of a small baby. As it moved further outside the lamp light, another small shadow shaped like a baby's footprint slowly emerged. Although amazed at what was happening, I was not frightened. I gently nudged my mother to wake her and, without speaking, I pointed to the ceiling. When she saw the footprints she raised the lamp's wick for more light. She checked our window shades to eliminate any outside light that might be coming in the house. As we watched, the little footprints became more energized, gliding across the ceiling, walls, kitchen table, and the window shades. They quickly moved away whenever we tried to touch them. Although they seemed quite harmless and playful, my mother became frightened. We watched the little dark footprints all night until they disappeared. In the morning, thinking we had seen the last of them, they suddenly reappeared. At this point, my mother contacted our landlord who called in others to help with the problem. After tearing down wood and plaster walls in the house nothing was found. Covering the shades and windows with tightly taped newspaper changed nothing. The little dark footprints continued their playful ways of "catch me if you can." Finally, our landlord suggested we find another place to live. But before moving my mother shared our experience with a friend who suggested she read selected Bible verses from the Acts of the Apostles. Even now, I can see her at our kitchen table, praying and reading from the Bible. My mother's prayers were answered; the playful little footprints finally disappeared.

My mother's boyfriend, Buster, was abusive in many ways. I will never forget that horrifying night when he hit her in the head with a hammer. Earlier, he had tried to poison us by putting something in the oatmeal my mother had cooked for breakfast. If she had not smelled the strong odor of Lysol disinfectant we might have gotten sick and died. The night he brutalized my mother, They were cussing and shouting about a "bloody diaper" and the little girl who lived next door. I heard my little sister's name mentioned. Later, I was told that Buster had sexually molested both girls and was running from the police. It was during this argument that he hit my mother with a hammer. Blood streamed down from her scalp, eyes, and face before it finally dripped onto the floor. As she wrestled with him, my mother grabbed a lit kerosene lamp and hit him on the head. Glass shattered everywhere, and kerosene spilled on his clothing, setting him afire. The house became filled with the pungent odor of kerosene and smoke. I was so terrified I could not speak or scream. I did not know what to do until my mother shouted at me to get my little brother, George, and run. With blood still dripping from her face, she picked up my sister, Lenora, and ran out of the house with me following close behind. The night was dark, cold, and scary, with only a full moon and the stars to light our way. As we ran toward my grandmother's house, I began shaking like a leaf. Looking back, my mother saw a clump of bushes moving and shouted that Buster was chasing us. We ran faster! I held onto my little brother's hand as best I could, but lost my grip and he fell, hitting his head on the sidewalk. George began crying as he saw blood running down into his face. What a bloody mess—my mother and now my little brother! When we finally reached my grandmother's home, she was not there, but Grandfather Robert (Arb) was. Hearing our screams and banging on the front door, he let us in. Once inside, we saw a large dark shadow slowly move across the window shades. My mother was right—Buster had followed us! Seeing the shadow, my grandfather went into his bedroom and came out with the biggest pistol I have ever seen. Walking to the front door, he unlocked it and backed away. Cussing and stuttering as usual, he shouted, "The door is unlocked, come on in; I've got what you're looking for!" Thank God Buster never came in. I had seen enough blood that night! Eventually, Buster was arrested and sentenced to eight years in prison for molesting the two little girls. In the midst of this ugliness, somewhere in my young mind a beautiful thing happened—I knew this was not the way a family should be.

Following our horrifying experience we moved into a federally funded public housing complex, named Foote Homes, built only for Negroes.

My grandparents moved with us. My mother was her only child, and they had always lived together or somewhere in close proximity.

One evening, while standing on the front porch of our new home, I looked up into the sky and saw a beautiful sunset. There were clouds in the sky and flashes of lightning. Sensing something bad was about to happen I told my mother, "There's going to be a big storm tonight." And, that night a tornado hit the Foote public housing complex. Lightning struck our home, and wind ripped off the roof. Rain poured down from the ceiling and ran down the walls. Flashes of lightning came inside the house creating a lot of static electricity. These shimmering waves of multicolored electricity, with hues of red, orange, yellow, and bluish-green, stopped in front of my sister and little brother's bed. Terrified and screaming we ran into another room and jumped into my mother's bed, with these electrical fireworks following closely behind. They stopped momentarily in front of my mother's bed and then slowly left the same way they had come in. Later, my grandmother, the only other person at home with us, said that when the storm rolled in, she had gone into the kitchen to close a window, when a bolt of lightning flashed through the window barely missing her. As water cascaded down the walls firemen put tarpaulin on what was left of our roof. We were blessed again—no one was killed or hurt and we were still a family. Later, we heard about an old Negro man who lived in a dilapidated make-shift shack at a nearby junkyard; he slept through the entire tornado, and his little shack was still standing.

Following this terrifying storm we moved from public housing into another home at 664 East Georgia Street. We could smell the sweet aroma of flowers from magnolia trees on both sides of the street. These fairly large duplex homes were similar to "shotgun" homes with thin plastered drywall separating us from our neighbor. Our back porch had two adjoining, somewhat private outhouse toilets. We flushed them with buckets of water poured into a deep hole below the commodes. The homes stood on top of brick pillars approximately three feet off the ground under which I would crawl, looking for chicken eggs. Occasionally, hens would get out of the chicken coop and lay eggs under the house. The chickens and ducks were given to us children as Easter pets.

A large bayou, located across the street, was a favorite play area in spite of warnings from our parents not to play there. A peach and fig tree stood inside a nearby fenced-in yard, and its limbs hung over the fence, making it easy for us to get peaches. My grandmother always reminded us to not eat green peaches because they would give us the "botts" (botulism, diarrhea). Needless to say we found out what it meant to have the "botts."

There was a large wooden swing on our front porch, hanging by links of chain fastened to a wooden beam on the ceiling. I really enjoyed playing on that swing! In the summer bees and hummingbirds darted around honeysuckle flowers growing from a trellis attached to the outside of a porch railing. We knew why the hummingbirds hovered around the flowers, because we had learned how to suck the sweet nectar from the flowers.

The interior of our home had a long hallway extending from the front to the back where three bedrooms were located. A wood-burning cook stove and a sink with a small water pump for well water stood in the kitchen. A large galvanized tin tub was used for baths and washing clothes. Occasionally, my mother used another small fireplace in the living room for cooking. Kerosene lamps were used in some areas of our home because the electrical wiring had not been completed. However, a couple of electrical outlets were available, and we could listen to a small radio. My favorite programs were the "Adventures of Captain Midnight," "Jack Armstrong, the All-American Boy," and "The Shadow."

Thanksgiving and Christmas were joyful times because my grandfather's family, from Lake Charles, Louisiana, always mailed us gift boxes filled with dried shrimp, okra, hot peppers, and pecans. My grandmother made pecan pies and cooked the best seafood gumbo you have ever tasted. Her two sisters who lived in Chicago, Rebecca Fleming and Ursula Bentley, also sent Christmas gifts. One Christmas I received a little Western Flyer red wagon. This was the best toy I'd ever received.

My sister, Lenora (Tutta), was accidentally scalded when she was four years old. My mother was cooking spareribs over a small fireplace when Tutta and I ran into her with a tricycle and a frying pan full of boiling water spilled all over my little sister. I'll never forget their screams and cries of pain. Even now, I can smell the distinctive, sweet odor of linseed oil my mother poured all over her as she wrapped her little body in white bandages torn from clean bed sheets. Tutta looked like a little Egyptian mummy. She was hospitalized for six months and three weeks with third degree burns. God is always good; my little sister came back home.

Five years later, on June 3, 1940, when she was twenty-seven, my mother married Elbert Kershaw in Crittenden County, Arkansas. He was a handsome, brown-skinned Negro man of medium height and a muscular build. Elbert was born on December 2, 1904, in Oxford, Mississippi; he was nine years older than my mother. My second brother, Ira Willis Kershaw, was born at 11:05 p.m., Tuesday, October 8, 1940, at John Gaston Hospital. Now I had two brothers and a sister.

Education was very important to Negroes, and I am reminded of a story my stepfather, Elbert, told me about looking for a job before marrying my mother. He did not have any money and needed a job. Walking into an employment office he asked a white man standing nearby where he should go to apply for a job and was directed to another white man behind a small window. When he reached the window he asked if there were any jobs available. Looking at him, the man nodded his head as though saying yes and wrote something on a piece of paper. Assuring him that he would be helped, he folded the paper, gave it to him, and told him to take it to another man at the next window. After giving him the note, my stepfather was told that he had mistakenly been sent to the wrong window and should give the note to another man at the window directly across the room. Still hoping for a job, my stepfather did as he was told; he went to the window and gave it to that white man. After reading it, the man said the same thing: "You're not at the right window; take the note to the man behind the window near the front door, and I'm sure he'll take care of you." Again, he walked over and gave the note to that white man. After reading it he returned it to my stepfather, saying that there were no jobs available. Disappointed and hurt, still clutching the note in his hand, my stepfather went outside and handed the note to a black friend who read it to him. The note read: "Keep this 'nigga' moving from window to window 'til he gits his ass the hell outta here!" My stepfather never forgot this humiliating experience.

I did not know then that he had dropped out of school and could not read or write. His hurt and anger caused him to go back to school to learn how to read and write. Eventually he joined a church, taught Sunday school, and met my mother. His story reminds me of what my mother always said: "No matter what, even if you never get a chance to use it, get an education! You'll never get out of poverty and be free from segregation without it; and remember all work is honorable. If you have to dig a ditch, be the best damn ditch digger there is!" However, remembering that I had been diagnosed as a chronic asthmatic she added: "But you'll have to work harder at an education because you have to work inside an office doing some kind of clerical work."

At five years old, my mother enrolled me in the first grade at Porter Elementary School on Wellington Street which is now Danny Thomas Boulevard. Booker T. Washington High School, from which my mother graduated, was near Porter school. The school teachers were mostly female. State segregationist laws restricted them to living only in Negro neighborhoods. The school principal, Ms. Flagg, had a light complexion and was short and stocky. She had an intimidating, authoritarian persona and frequently visited our home.

She always allowed me to ring the school tardy bell. The bronze bell was large and heavy with a big clapper inside, and I had to use both hands to ring it. Ms. Flagg had a special way of handling problem students; she was also the disciplinarian. She used a large ruler and sometimes a leather razor strop to hit the palms of our hands. When she thought that one hand had toughened enough to take the pain, she used the other hand. And, when she thought you were faking the pain, she had you open both hands and turn your palms down; then she would hit you on your knuckles. Eventually, we all realized who was in charge and rarely created a disturbance in class or anywhere else in the school. You might get away with bad behavior at home but not at Porter Elementary School. My mother always welcomed Ms. Flagg into our home. She was considered a trusted family friend, and my parents accepted her harsh teaching discipline. Discipline of this nature wasn't used in high-school.

Ms. Lorraine Hansbrough, another teacher at the school, deeply influenced my life. *I was nine years old when I fell in love with her.* When it was time to leave Memphis to go to Chicago I pulled a small sapling tree out of the ground to give Ms. Hansbrough. With her help the tree was planted in the front yard of her home. This was my way of saying, "I love you, so please don't forget me." This is when I realized that I would marry a woman just like her. I've told my wife, Doris, this story many times, because she reminds me of this pretty little school teacher.

Both teachers were light complexioned, but Ms. Hansbrough was taller with a slender build. It was her pleasing smile and personality that impressed me. Ms. Flagg was not a mean person, but her authoritarian demeanor made me uncomfortable. My mother allowed me to go on many excursions with Ms. Hansbrough. Handy's Park was one of few public parks available to Negroes. We never went to the park, only to movies. The New Daisy movie theater accommodated Negroes, but whites could go there and sit wherever they wanted. Whatever her reason, Ms. Hansbrough never took me to the New Daisy Theater. The Malco Theater was built for whites, but Negroes could watch movies there. However, Jim Crow State laws prohibited us from watching movies on the main floor. We had to watch movies from the balcony while seated in white theatres. The unique personalities of Ms. Flagg and Ms. Hansbrough provided me with an early well-balanced academically and culturally balanced education.

At eight years old, my mother thought I had a common cold. She used a lot of home remedies but could not get rid of a lingering cough and shortness of breath. Just when it seemed that I was getting better, the coughing and wheezing flared up again. She finally took me to John Gaston General Hospital where, following allergy tests and chest x-rays, I was diagnosed as having hay-fever and chronic asthma. I was found to be allergic to rag-weed (highly allergic pollen), household dust, pet dander, poultry feathers, mold, mildew, and egg whites. It seemed as though I was allergic to living. I was given allergy shots and placed on a special diet. The prescribed medication, Tedral, provided only short-term relief. I inhaled smoke from medicinal powders such as Green Mountain and Asthmador, sold in drug stores. These powders came from the belladonna plant whose berries, roots, and leaves produce atropine. Inhaling the smoke from these powders provided temporary relief. The stinking odor made my bed covers and clothing smell like marijuana.

There were happier memories, especially when I went fishing on the Mississippi River with my mother. The river landscape was beautiful, dotted with trees and small islands called deltas. Over time, these islands were formed by clay, silt, sand, and gravel accumulated during numerous floods. A large bridge spanned the river where we fished while several barges floated on the river. Barges were used to transport consumer products and other materials up and down the river. My grandmother told a story of my grandfather, Arb, who bet his friends that he could swim from one of the deltas to the river shore. Knowing he could not swim, his friends readily accepted his bet. Taking off his shoes and stripping down to his underwear, my grandfather stepped into the river and while holding his breath, walked underwater until he reached the other shore and won his wager.

Land near the river was used for more than fishing. Several gardens were planted on land near the river, and we planted our own vegetable garden. One day after returning from the garden Grandma left me at home alone. Soon afterwards, my grandfather, Robert, came in "stinking drunk," smelling like a whiskey distillery. He began vomiting blood and had "messy" blood seeping through his pants. After cussing and staggering around for awhile he fell out on the floor unconscious. Not knowing what to do, I was terrified. He was too heavy for me to move, so I went to the kitchen sink and pumped some cool water into a pan. Splashing water everywhere, I was able to raise his head enough to place it into the pan. Finding a rag, I used it to bathe his head and face. I will never know why I did not cry or leave him to go find my mother. When she returned and saw the bloody water, with vomit and feces everywhere, she thought I had drowned him in the pan of water. Realizing he was still alive, she ran for help and he was taken to the hospital. He was only in the hospital for a brief time, leaving without officially being discharged. Later, we were told that he had a stroke and, to no one's surprise, was suffering from bleeding ulcers. Our neighbors called me a hero for saving my grandfather's life. Although I did not know what a hero was, I felt very proud in helping him. Yes, God is good all the time! We were still family and our journey to a Land of Promise was just beginning!

CHAPTER 3

Chicago South/North Side
1942-1949

From a biblical perspective our leaving Memphis had similarities to the Israelites' departure from Egypt. We, too, felt as though we had been freed from slavery and saw God's Land of Promise as north in Chicago. When we left Memphis I was ten years old and my youngest brother, Ira Willis Kershaw, was almost two years old. I was excited and wanted to meet those family members who had sent me a little red wagon for Christmas. We arrived at Chicago's Union Station in March 1942. Temporary housing arrangements had been made to live with my grandmother's two sisters, Rebecca Fleming and Ursula Alyce Fleming-Bentley. When my aunts left Pine Bluff in 1919, they moved into an apartment on Chicago's Southside at 5616 South Prairie Avenue. Ursula had married Allen Bentley who worked downtown at the main U.S. Post Office. Twenty-three years had passed since my grandmother and her sisters had been together. Aunt Rebecca appeared more educated, outspoken, and influential in managing family affairs. Aunt Ursula was soft spoken, with a pleasing personality. My aunts had lighter complexions than Grandma Lenora.

I reference skin color because of white racist color differences that influenced Negro families. The economics of Slavery was grounded in genocidal, psychological, and socially engineered concepts of inferiority in darker skin people. As Negroes we consistently have had to define our social identities for survival within a racist system of color and caste. The psychological stigma of inferiority attached to black skin continues, to this day, to destroy black family cohesiveness. Negroes have constantly resisted preconceived notions of black inferiority. However, segregationist laws tended to make our unique and gifted humanity almost nonexistent.

Aunt Rebecca got my grandmother a job at the Palmer House Hotel where she worked as a maid. The Palmer House, one of the better-known landmark hotels, was located in downtown Chicago. Nine of us lived in my aunt's home that had three bedrooms and one bathroom with a large enameled tub and face bowl. I had never seen a bathroom with a bathtub. We children did not know how to use the bathroom in a timely manner, resulting in a lot of wet spots on my aunt's carpets, which none of us had ever seen in a home. The wheezing, coughing, spitting, and crying during my asthma attacks was very stressful for Aunt Rebecca. She could not sleep and had to get up early every morning to go to work.

A movie theater was located near my aunt's home. My sister Lenora, George, and I would go to there to see movies. Our first effort to go to the movie theater ended abruptly when a group of bigger Negro boys forced us to give them our money. Whenever we went to the movies they were waiting for us. Being the oldest, and realizing that seeing a movie was going to be a challenge, I came up with a plan. We hid the money in our shoes and waited for the boys to leave before buying movie tickets. It was not long before they caught on to what we were doing, but by the time they did we were preparing to move to the North Side. My stepfather, Elbert, did not come to Chicago with us because he had to make arrangements for his elderly mother to come with him. I am certain he felt added pressure in having to find adequate housing for his pregnant wife. As my mother's time drew nearer for the birth of Loyal David, the more anxious she grew in not wanting to burden her aunts with a new baby in their home. Our journey to Chicago, the Land of Promise, seemed to be derailed. Employment opportunities were good, but our family was too large to find a decent home in which to live. The Hebrew people had no free train rides in their odyssey to the Promised Land, and the Sinai Desert challenged their determination. The same was true of our odyssey in the Sinai Desert of Chicago! Two months later Elbert arrived in Chicago, having made arrangements with a nursing home in Memphis to care for his mother until he relocated in Chicago. Soon he found a job as a freight handler for the Pennsylvania Railroad where he worked ten years until he was laid off. Later, he worked at the Lifshultz Fast Freight Trucking Company until his retirement.

Finding affordable rental housing was practically impossible, so when my parents found it, they lied about the number of children in our family. The home was a three-story apartment building located on the North Side at 1454 Clybourn Avenue. My grandparents moved into the first-floor apartment, and we moved upstairs on the second floor. Shortly after the move, my mother gave birth to her third son, Loyal David Kershaw, on May 1, 1942, at Henrotin Hospital.

My stepfather sent for his mother, Ms. Birdie Kershaw-Jones-Reno. When she arrived we saw a frail elderly, slightly mentally challenged, brown-skinned Negro woman. My mother told me that she had been physically abused by a number of men and was not in the best of health. She suffered from diabetes and foot problems, eventually having two of her toes amputated. Eventually, the increasing need for professional medical care necessitated placing her in a nursing home where she later died.

One day I had a *kairos (Godly)* moment when I saw something special about my stepfather, Elbert. Sometimes when he did not have money to ride the streetcar home from work, a friend with a car dropped him off near home. It was one of those days when I saw him walking home. He was in a hurry and was oblivious to anyone watching him. It was if this was the first time I had really noticed him and the old faded coveralls covered with patches sewn on by my mother. He wore a heavy shirt underneath the coveralls that were held up with large suspenders draped over his muscular shoulders. His shoes were big and heavy with the leather partially torn exposing a layer of steel to protect his feet. Suddenly, "the eyes of my heart were opened." For the first time I saw my stepfather's weariness and patched clothing as a badge of honor, and he became more than a stepfather. He had assumed responsibility to care and love three children who were biologically not his own. I loved him, but I do not remember telling him—perhaps he already knew.

A number of large wooden sheds were in back of the 1454/1456 Clybourn Avenue apartments. Coal was stored in these sheds to be burned in a large cast iron potbelly stove as fuel to heat our home in the winter. A flexible pipe with a damper to adjust the flow of smoke extended to the chimney. The coal was sold to us from large trucks in sacks or by the truckload. I did not mind shoveling coal into our shed but hated hauling heavy buckets of coal up to our third floor apartment. An ice house was located across the street, and late at night we could smell the pungent odor of ammonia used in making the ice. Trucks loaded ice behind the ice house. We had electricity and natural gas for a cooking stove but could not afford a refrigerator, so we bought blocks of ice for our ice box. Two small Italian owned groceries were located near our home, but we shopped at the one that allowed us to buy groceries on credit.

Noisy streetcars, powered by electricity from overhead wires, ran north and south on Clybourn Avenue. They ran all the way to Riverview Amusement Park, a well-known Chicago landmark. I used this streetcar to get to Waller High School which since has been renamed Lincoln Park Magnet High School. Nearby Ogden Avenue ran east and west. The west Ogden Avenue overpass crossed over Halsted and Division Street, and the Chicago River. At night my friends and I walked up the overpass and rolled automobile tires down into oncoming traffic. It was hilarious, hearing the sound of shrieking brakes, blaring car horns, and see cars turning sharply to avoid hitting the tires. We stopped these pranks when we saw how dangerous they were and that people could be killed.

East North Avenue led to Lake Michigan. Larrabee Street and North Avenue intersected at East Ogden Avenue where the Keno movie theater was located. Later it was renovated and replaced by the Ideal Theater. Montgomery Ward Mail Order Catalogue Store was located south on Larrabee Street at Chicago Avenue. The building stands alongside the Chicago River and has been converted into new condominium apartments. The Plaza movie theater was east on North Avenue, in the middle of a white business area. St. Michael's Catholic Church was located nearby. Clothing stores, butcher shops, Del Farm Foods, and Northern Home Furnishings, a large furniture store, were on North Avenue. My grandmother worked at Northern Home Furnishings as a custodian and eventually as a maid in the owner's home. Most of the businesses were owned by Jews and Italians.

Lincoln Park, Lake Shore Drive, and the "Gold Coast," with its high-rise luxurious apartments, meandered along Lake Michigan's shoreline. Pedestrian bridges crossed over the Lake Shore Drive traffic into the beach area. Baseball diamonds, tennis courts, picnic areas, and a large zoo with a flower conservatory was part of the park's attraction.

However, people usually came to see the zoo's main attraction, a large gorilla named Bushman.

An upscale movie theater, The Windsor, was located on the Gold Coast. Near the theater was a shooting gallery/penny arcade and bowling alley. My friend Jimmie (James King) and I worked as pin boys in the bowling alley. There were no automatic setup machines for bowling pins and we earned only a penny per line. To earn more money pins had to be setup for two bowling lanes. Jimmie, who was two years older than me, was able to handle an extra bowling lane. During the summer months we delivered newspapers, usually around four in the morning. Before "throwing papers" on our routes, we waited for a local bakery to open and bought sweet rolls and donuts. I learned to earn money for what I wanted by working for it, and Jimmie was a positive role model.

The One Fifty-Two Movie Theater was located on 152 West Division Street as was the Negro-owned Johnson's Funeral Home. Funeral homes and mortuary schools were de facto segregated which in some ways was more insidious than white racism in Memphis. Oscar Mayer Meat Company and Washburn Trade School were located at the intersection of Sedgwick and Division Streets. These streets, landscapes, and venues were very significant because of the people who lived there and whose memories I will never forget.

In September 1942, my mother enrolled me, Lenora, and George in Frederick Von Schiller Elementary School. I was ten years old, Lenora was nine, and my brother George was seven. Schiller was centrally located near Clybourn and Ogden Avenues, between Evergreen and Scott Streets. A small wading pool for younger children, or "baby pool" as we called it, was on the school playground.

Following academic tests at Schiller School, I was placed in the sixth grade. The majority of the students were Italian. The tests were usually required of students moving to Chicago from other states, especially those coming from southern states. The academic tests qualified me for a double grade promotion, capable of reading and learning at a high school level. In spite of a segregated education I was academically ahead of my northern peers. Nevertheless, I was not given the double promotion because of my age and their concern that I would not be able to handle peer group pressure. Although experiencing some difficulty in adjusting to a new multicultural environment, it was good to have a white teacher with blacks and whites in the same classroom learning together. There were racial confrontations, but I could fight back without expecting a nighttime visit from the Klan. Discrimination in educational achievement was more subtle in elementary school but became more open and frequent in high school. Perhaps Chicago did have promise for Negroes, but why should living in the Land of Promise, flowing with milk and honey (namely, resources and opportunities) mean there would be no more racism?

A small Catholic Church on Evergreen Street was within walking distance of Schiller School. Annually, local Catholics cordoned off the street for carnival—festival games, Italian foods, pizza, frozen lemonade, crabs, and snails. Carnival rides, games of chance (gambling), and food sales served as church fund raisers. Lenora, George, and I always hung out at these feasts, as we called them, enjoying foreign food and playing gambling games, hoping to win money and prizes. The dominant ethnic groups in our neighborhood were Italian, Polish, German, and Jewish emigrants. A favorite pastime in Stanton Park for older Italians was playing Bocce ball, a game similar to lawn bowling. Stanton Park had a large baseball field, two softball diamonds, and a field-house with offices and a small gymnasium and a large swimming pool. Whites and Negroes used the same facilities, but boys and girls did not swim together. White lifeguards patrolled the pool; only later did the Chicago Park District hire Negro lifeguards. I took swimming lessons at the pool but did not learn to swim until after nearly drowning at the all-Negro Belknap Boy Scout Camp in Whitehall, Michigan.

The 1454 Clybourn Avenue building was located next door to the Chris Paschen Construction Company. In fact, living on the second floor we could almost step from our window onto the roof of the construction company. We lived there for about five months until the building was sold to Chris Paschen, and he had us evicted. We were hurt and fearful because we had no place to go—so much for Chicago being a Land of Promise! But God blessed us in another way. When my baby brother Loyal David was almost a year old we discovered that another building owned by Chris Paschen was available. We were successful in having him rent us two apartments, one for my family and the other for my grandparents. The first floor was occupied by a single parent, Ms. Harris, who had two small children. Later I delivered ice to her in my little red wagon to earn money. My mother's second cousin, Louise, moved in with my grandparents on the second floor, and we moved into the third floor apartment.

Luella Ward, my mother's first cousin, who was present at her marriage, had left Memphis earlier, moving about ninety miles northeast of Chicago to Milwaukee, Wisconsin. Louise worked at the North Chicago Laundry until she was badly burned. One of her hands was accidentally caught between the rollers of a steam press called a mangle. The mangle was used to iron damp clothing passed between steam-heated rollers. Her hand and arm were so badly burned she wore a shoulder brace and could not work, which led to her being fired. She filed a lawsuit and won a financial settlement against the laundry company. The money was shared with my grandmother who used it to buy the only refrigerator I had ever seen. She was also able to purchase an old second-hand piano on which I learned to play several tunes including the "boogie woogie." My grandmother's two sisters, Rebecca and Ursula, moved to the North Side for a brief time until purchasing a home on south Sangamon Avenue.

George and I always had our hair cut at the Dreamland Barber Shop on Oak Street. The shop was owned and operated by a Negro named Antonio Derr. White racism in Chicago was more subtle. Although there were no signs restricting patronage, barber shops as well as barber schools were covertly segregated. My mother took us to the barber shop until we were older, always giving special instructions on how our hair was to be cut. Mr. Derr was very obliging and was the only barber allowed to cut our hair. Tony, as he was called, had three barbers in the shop, including his son. Bad language was not allowed in the shop, and the ladies were well respected. I am certain my grandfather, who managed a pool hall (billiards) down the street, had directed my mother to the barber shop. I am fully aware of the many ways in which my grandfather loved us. Whenever we came to the pool hall he always gave us movie money and never allowed cussing or fighting; if anything happened he made them apologize. The apologies came, not so much out of respect for us, but because he carried a gun. My grandfather's behavior at the pool hall was in stark contrast to what he demonstrated at home where he continued to drink and cuss.

Following demolition of our home at 1454 Clyborn, the land was never developed. We used the land to plant a vegetable garden, and I built a small clubhouse there. After moving into the 1456 building, I had a horrible nightmare. In it I saw a small human foot with what looked like a wasp's nest imbedded in the arch area of the foot. The nightmare continued night after night until the day George, who was now seven, came home limping on his left foot with his pants covered in blood. In taking his own form of revenge on Chris Paschen for evicting us, he decided to use his new box-toe style shoes to kick out a glass window pane in the vacant 1454 building. When the window pane shattered, a piece of glass became embedded in his foot. George's wound was in the exact location as the wasp's nest was in the foot in the nightmare. Blood was spurting everywhere as my mother franticly wrapped a tight bandage around his foot, covering it with a thick towel. She called a taxicab, and I went with them to the doctor's office. This was my first taxi ride because we usually did not have money to hire a taxi. George had severed an artery, requiring five stitches to close his wounded foot. The doctor's wife, a registered nurse, paid his medical bill. I think she was deeply touched by George's ordeal and our financial situation. My mother knew Dr. Davis because of frequent trips to his office for my asthma attacks. Later, another doctor on his staff, Dr. Harry Louren, became the only one to make home visits and, although he told us he was not afraid, we always provided an escort whenever he came. Following George's injury I had no further nightmares.

Another unusual experience occurred in our new home; we were overwhelmed by bedbugs or "chinches." After careful assessment of our problem, never having bedbugs, we concluded the entire house was already infested with these tiny parasites. They feasted on our blood at night hiding in beds, mattresses, and behind wallpaper. To rid ourselves of these nighttime bloodsuckers, my stepfather removed all the wallpaper in our home, then painted the walls and wherever he thought they might be hiding. He said, "If the paint and turpentine doesn't kill them, nothing will!" Fumigating beds and mattresses, then painting the interior of the house worked—no more bed bugs! My stepfather's innovative extermination technique was successful.

On a lighter note, my brother George was given a beautiful German shepherd male puppy. He named the puppy Rinny, from the name of the famous movie dog, Rin Tin Tin. We had Rinny for only a short time because he got out of the house and was killed by a car. After Rinny's death we took in a stray cat who we named Furry. My mother loved pets but was reluctant to have this cat. Later we came to understood why she preferred a male cat. Furry was a female and had five kittens and she needed help to complete the birthing process. My mother took her to a veterinarian to help to deliver her last kitten. But a time came when Furry saved all our lives. One dark, very cold winter morning when we were asleep, Furry, who was sleeping with me, began clawing at the bed covers and getting in my face until she woke me. The pipe damper on the potbelly stove had become stuck, and smoke was everywhere. The stove pipes were glowing bright red, and I thought they were going to explode. Now, fully awake and choking from the smoke, I began screaming. While we were all opening windows, my stepfather poured water inside the stove and finally got the fire under control. If Furry had not awakened me we might have suffocated from smoke inhalation or died in a fire. There was a narrow wooden fire escape attached to our next-door neighbor's home but I was glad we didn't have to use it. Again, God had blessed us and we were still a family!

Our next-door neighbor was a widowed, elderly white woman. We called her the "dog and cat lady" because her home was full of cats and dogs. We had never lived this close to a white person, and she may have given us our pets, Rinny and Furry. Soon George and I began to notice pigeons roosting on her rooftop. We decided to catch a couple of pigeons as pets. At times my mother must have thought we were trying to turn our home into a zoo! We succeeded in luring two pigeons inside an open window of our home with kernels of corn, peanuts, and bread. My mother would not let us keep them because she wanted no part in cleaning up pigeon mess. However, sensing how much we wanted them, my stepfather asked "the dog and cat lady" for permission to build a pigeon house on top of her roof. He assured her that he would build it so it did not damage the roof. In one way or another, we all helped build that pigeon house. It was beautiful, with ten cubicles—large enough for two pigeons and a nest. The pigeons we had caught were put inside one of the cubicles, but they eventually flew away. We thought we would not see them again, but they returned, bringing other pigeons with them. This became an educational adventure for George and me. We thumbed through several library books looking at pictures to identify the pigeons. We had a couple of homing pigeons, completely white with slightly longer necks. George named the male pigeon Snowball. There was another beautiful multicolored pigeon we could not match to any pictures in our books. George named him Bully because he was always fighting the other pigeons. They all fought a lot, especially when mating and defending territorial space. When fighting, they made peculiar noises, using their wings as a shield to avoid being pecked in the eye. The young or baby pigeons, three or four weeks old, were called squabs. Infrequently, my mother prepared us a meal of squabs which were really tender and tasted like chicken.

George and I enjoyed fishing for bluegills and bullheads (smaller catfish) in Lincoln Park Lagoon and perch in Lake Michigan from the North Avenue pier. We always looked for better fishing spots, and one day I decided to go to the Jackson Park Lagoon on the South Side. We rode the Subway and El (elevated) trains to get to the park—which took nearly two hours. The subway train ran underground, avoiding downtown traffic, and surfacing again as the elevated train. After arriving at Jackson Park we found a good fishing spot, a small lagoon where several people were catching fish. We caught a lot of fish and on our way home decided to explore the park, eventually finding a place where the lagoon led directly into Lake Michigan. George pulled off his shoes and began wading in the water. I had not paid attention to the huge waves coming in and waited on shore, watching George and the fish we had caught. Suddenly I became aware that he was getting farther away from shore. All this time he had been struggling to come back on shore but had not said anything; the current was pulling him out into Lake Michigan. I shouted at him to come out of the water because it was time to go home. Looking helpless, he finally shouted that he could not because the waves were pulling him out into deeper water. I was terrified because neither of us could swim and if I went to help him we might both drown. Then another frightening thought came to mind: I hadn't told my mother that we were going to fish on the South Side. If I did not drown and George did, she would hold me responsible. No one was there to help and all I could do was watch George drift farther away from shore.

I wasn't completely in a state of panic because I noticed something peculiar about the waves. When one came in, there was a pause before the next wave came in which might give me enough time to grab George's hand. Shouting loudly at George, I pleaded with him to look at me, not the waves, and do everything I said. Wading into the water as far as I could go, I demonstrated how to jump up in the water as high as he could while moving toward me, whenever I told him. He did as I said, coming closer each time, until I finally grabbed his hand and pulled him ashore. While helping George come ashore, his shoes and our fish had floated away. We were really scared and soaking wet but glad to have lost only his shoes and our fish! Returning home on the subway train, people laughed at George when he walked barefooted to his seat with water dripping from his wet clothing. We never told our mother, who was expecting her fifth child, about George's near-drowning. Yes, God is good! We were blessed again and still a family! On November 16, 1944, my mother gave birth, at home, to her fifth son, Elbert Kershaw Jr., nicknamed Stuffy.

Around this time I met two new friends, Jack Smith and his younger brother Burnette, nicknamed Dumpty, who lived across the street on Clybourn Avenue. I believe their parents may have been divorced because they lived with their grandmother, Ms. Moore, who owned her home. Mother Moore, as we called her, was a Christian evangelist who conducted worship and prayer services in the basement of her home. Negroes as well as a small number of white people attended the services. My parents had a problem with Ms. Moore being a woman minister and told us not to attend the services. But George and I did attend the services. Mother Moore was a good piano player and singer; we learned to sing church hymns and pray. Jack and Dumpty were good swimmers and Jack was also an excellent springboard diver. Joseph Saffold and his younger brother, Howard, nicknamed Rabbit, also lived across the street. Joe eventually became a catcher on our baseball team.

James (Jimmie) King, my closest friend, also lived across the street. His mother, Willa King, a divorced single parent and former schoolteacher, had an older daughter who did not live with them. Ms. King loved solving jigsaw puzzles. After completing a puzzle she would glue it on cardboard and hang it on the wall. One of her puzzles, a beautiful galleon sailing ship, was placed on her living room wall. It caught my attention because I had never seen a jigsaw puzzle or galleon sailing ship.

In 1944 Jimmie and I joined Boy Scout Troop Number 71. We had to be twelve years old. Jimmie was thirteen and I was eleven-and-a-half years old but joined the troop because my twelfth birthday was near the end of that year. We became Tenderfoot Scouts and were required to memorize the Boy Scout oath. Charles Tousaint, a Negro, was our first Boy Scout master. He was what I would call a wise and compassionate disciplinarian who impressed me with his knowledge of the scouting program. Mr. Tousaint (we always called him mister) was married and had a son and daughter. His wife, Hazel, an extremely understanding person, allowed us the use of their home for Scout meetings. Later, the owner of a local black funeral home provided us another meeting place. This is when I first became aware of segregated morticians and funeral homes. There were no signs reading, "Colored" or "White;" it was an implied taboo for Negroes and whites to not build true relationships. The divisiveness of covert racism became firmly crystallized in my mind.

Jimmie and I finally became second-class Scouts, qualifying us to purchase scout uniforms. I will always remember my mother buying my Scout uniform downtown at Goldblatt's department store. We were very poor, and I don't know how she was able to pay for the uniform. One night, on the way home, following a Scout meeting, four young white boys turned their flashlights on me and began shouting and screaming, calling me a "nigger" and threatening to beat me up. Jimmie had not been at the meeting, and I was outnumbered and scared. I did not know if they were jealous at seeing me in my Scout uniform or had other reasons for calling me a "nigger." Maybe they didn't know themselves, but this was the first time I had been racially threatened in this way. I never had this experience in Memphis, a city well-known for its racism. Terrified, and with the sound of rocks whizzing past my head, I ran home as fast as I could. Jimmie and I never became first-class scouts because we could not earn merit badges unless we worked on them at a scout camp, and we did not have the money to go to scout camp.

In 1945, Mr. Tousaint informed us that he could no longer be our scoutmaster because he needed to spend more time with his family. His replacement was Mr. Speights, another Negro scoutmaster. Mr. Speights was a great guy whom we respected, but he did not measure up to Mr. Tousaint. He was the head chef for a large hotel in downtown Chicago, experienced in cooking for large banquets. He also worked for the Boy Scout Council, cooking at white Scout camps during spring time camping. At these camps, white Scouts prepared camp grounds, equipment and trails to qualify for merit badges required for higher ranks in scouting. The Scout camps were segregated and, as Negroes, our opportunities to work on merit badges were limited.

Finally, Jimmie and I had an opportunity to work on merit badges when Mr. Speights recruited us to work at a white Scout camp during the spring. We could earn money for summer camp while working on our merit badge qualifications. Social Security cards were needed in order to work at the camp, and I was thirteen years old when I received my Social Security card. Jimmie and I worked early morning hours into late night, washing dishes, sweeping and mopping floors, and setting tables for over 100 white Boy Scouts. We washed so many pots, pans, and dishes that by bedtime we were soaking wet. We did whatever Mr. Speights asked of us to prepare meals for the next day. As long as we did not waste any food, we ate as much as we wanted. One night Jimmie ate so much bread pudding that he became sick and vomited all over our tent cabin. I will never forget the smell of sour bread pudding and raisins on our blankets and cabin floors. Believe me, there is no fun cleaning up smelly vomit!

Working at the camp earned enough money to attend Camp Belknap, a historical Negro Scout camp, now abandoned, was affiliated with the Owasippe Boy Scout Council of Chicago and was one of the oldest in the United States. Being away from home and sleeping in a tent with an asthmatic condition greatly concerned my mother. Even so, she allowed me to be away at the camp in Whitehall, Michigan, for two weeks. I never thought about homesickness but, wow, did I get homesick! Although camping was a fun-filled learning experience I could hardly make it through the second week. Jimmie and I decided to go on a wilderness canoe base trip. We had to pass a swimming test with our clothing on, including shoes, to qualify for the trip—able to swim in clothing if a canoe overturned. Jimmie passed the test but I did not; in fact I almost drowned. I felt terrible and was embarrassed but was happy to see Jimmie going on the trip.

World War II ended in 1945 with the historic atomic bombing of Japan. In June, at thirteen years old, I graduated from Schiller School, second in a class of about fifty students. I was disappointed at not being academically first in my graduating class. A quiet but smart young Negro girl named Margaret Lane graduated with that honor. No matter how hard I tried, I could not keep pace with Margaret's scholastic abilities. I was a bit jealous, but this incident helped me rethink my earlier feelings of being so much smarter than my classmates. Regardless, Margaret and I gained mutual respect for one another and were the best of friends. In September 1945, after graduating from Schiller School, I enrolled in Robert A. Waller High School on Orchard Avenue. The school is now named Lincoln Park Magnet High School. I enjoyed high school with two exceptions. The first involved my English teacher, Ms. Burns. In the first semester she gave me a failing grade. The second semester I worked harder and received passing grades on all midterm tests and papers. When it was time for final grades, Ms. Burns asked all students who had received failing grades the first semester to form a line and come to her desk for final grades. I stood in line waiting my turn with other students, mostly Negroes, for my final grade. As I neared her desk I heard students grumbling about her giving them another failing grade. Everyone in the line received failing grades. Realizing what she was doing, I returned to my seat and refused to accept the grade. My mother was asked to come to school because of my refusal to accept another failing grade. After meeting with my mother the grade was changed to reflect the grade I had earned. It was not as high as I deserved, but it was better than being failed again.

The second incident was in a history class. My teacher gave us an account of the creation story, specifically how God created the various races. She said: "God took some clay and shaped it to look like a human being and placed it in an oven. After a short time God removed the clay from the oven but discovered that he had taken it out too soon and it was undercooked. Therefore God said, 'This clay represents white people.' Then God took another piece of clay and shaped it to look like a human and placed it in the oven. He left the clay in the oven too long and it overcooked, turning black. And God said, 'This clay represents Negro people.'" She continued: "Because God wanted to get it right, he took more pieces of clay, shaping them to look like a human beings, baking them in the oven until he got all the other races and colors." What a history lesson! Or was this a class in religion? Not only was God a bad cook but he had a poor sense of timing. The human clay images he shaped were inanimate objects without the breath of life, which he had obviously forgotten. Nevertheless, white or Negro, we all had something in common: God leveled the playing field by making us from the same clay. When I told my mother about this experience she visited Waller High School, confronting my teacher with her lack of knowledge and racial insensitivity. Mama was always interested in knowing what was happening at school. It seemed as though I was the only student who challenged racial inequities. Perhaps this is what made me a loner in school.

My closest friend, Jimmie King, being two years older, graduated ahead of me. However, there was another Negro friend, Bingham Powell, who had a deep religious influence on me. We became friends the day I saw him standing near one of the doorways at Waller High School. I noticed he was crying and seemed to be talking to someone, but there was no one with him. After looking at him for awhile I decided to go inside. Moving closer I heard God's name and realized that he was praying and crying. Occasionally he said something I could not understand because the words were garbled and made no sense to me. When I walked up to him he stopped praying but continued to cry. I asked what was wrong and he told me that other students had verbally abused him—made fun of him and said he was crazy because of hearing him pray in tongues (glossalia). I listened intently, sensing that he, too, was a loner. Following our conversation, Bingham and I became friends until after my graduation from Waller High School.

On February 8, 1947, my mother gave birth to twins, Robert and Roberta. Now there were eight children in the family, six boys and two girls who were born at home. Now, Lenora (Tutta) had a little sister. On the night the twins were born, my mother had been fretting about the twin's birth. Frustrated by their projected birth being two weeks late, she screamed, jumped up as high as she could, and landed bare-footed on the hardwood floor of our living room. We all saw what she did. Afterwards, water streamed down her legs from under her gown and I thought she was urinating. I didn't realize that her water had broken. When this happened she shouted, "Call the doctor," and made all of us leave the room.

Following the twin's birth, my grandfather died while working in the pool hall he managed. Chicago Fire Department paramedics kicked in a locked toilet door to get in and take him to the hospital. My mother and grandmother went to the hospital and, with no other adults available, I was left to care for my brothers and sisters. It seemed a very long time before the phone rang and I was told that my grandfather had died from a stroke complicated by acute alcoholism. This time I was not around to help him, as was the case in Memphis. At fifteen years old I did not know what to say to my brothers and sisters, but somehow they knew the phone call was bad news and they began crying. There had been no deaths in the family until now. How could I explain everything to them when I also needed explanations? Later, while sitting on my bed looking out the window I noticed the sun was setting and it was getting dark outside. And it was even darker inside. The lights were not on, and I was acutely aware of the absence of noise and talking. I felt empty inside, as though something had been cut out of my chest. My grandpa had died, and no one was there to explain things to me.

His funeral was held at Johnson's Mortuary (Negro-owned). The funeral ended with the traditional repast meal at our home. I became angry when I saw everyone seemingly having fun eating and talking. My only grandfather had just died, and I did not know how they could be eating and laughing as though nothing had happened. Crying and angry, I ran into my bedroom.

Later, my grandmother found bank receipts of financial transactions made by my grandfather. She believed he had made deposits into some kind of savings account at the LaSalle Street Bank. She and my mother went to the bank inquiring about the transactions presumably made by him. In spite of the receipts, the bank manager denied my grandfather ever having an account there. My mother pursued the issue by asking about a safe deposit box and was told that kind of information could not be given out by the bank. My grandmother always believed the bank manager had lied and cheated her out of her husband's money. It seems that my grandparents did not share information about family finances. We did not have the resources to legally pursue the truth about my grandfather's finances, and the matter was dropped. I learned a valuable lesson from this experience: I would rather have any member of my family have my money than have it taken away by a bank. Nevertheless, in our loss and grief God was good and we were still a family.

Shortly before our second eviction in 1948 from 1456 Clybourn Avenue, my friends and I began to play sandlot baseball. We thought we were good enough to play in an organized baseball league. We looked to my former scoutmaster, Charles Tousaint, for help because he had played on a semi-pro baseball team, the Chicago Blue Sox. With his help we organized our baseball team and selected the name Cobras for the team. Members of the team were Lonnie Lee Branch, George Vanderbilt Branch, Joseph Clark, Patrick Creer, Charles Giviens, Jerry Knapp (our only white player), Joseph Gould, Sherman Hicks, Solomon Hicks Jr., Joseph Mims, Joseph Mitchell, Joseph Saffold, Jack Smith, and Johnnie Lee Webb. Mr. Tousaint was our manager and coach, with me as assistant manager and player-coach. I acted in place of Mr. Tousaint when he was not available. Again, Mr. Tousaint's wife was very gracious in allowing us to meet in their home. We held raffles and hustled money wherever we could find it to buy baseball uniforms and equipment. Our home games were played in the Chicago Park District, Stanton Park League, from which we solicited baseball equipment. Additional equipment and baseballs were given to us by Mr. Tousaint's former semi-pro baseball team.

In one of our games Mr. Tousaint demonstrated his baseball managerial skills. The opposing pitcher of the other team seemed un-hittable, and we had gone several innings without a hit. Looking at the situation, Mr. Tousaint said he wanted to test the opposing team's infield, so when we were at bat he told everyone to bunt the ball. There were no exceptions, including our heavy hitters. We followed instructions and found that the opposing team had terrible fielders and we won the game. That day our strength to win was in defense and the ability to outthink the other team.

Jerry Knapp, the only white member of our team, was a terrific shortstop and gutsy little hitter. Jerry was either Polish or German, but we considered him black. At one of our games playing against an all-white team Jerry was at shortstop when suddenly he was called a "nigger lover." Yelling and crying, he threw his glove down and ran toward the white player who had called him the name. We all ran to help him, and the game was temporarily stopped. When it resumed we won the game. Team meetings followed every game to discuss concerns, areas for improvement and upcoming game schedules. My brother George was the best first baseman on our team which got him elected as the team captain. He was not a big hitter, but whenever he got on base he was a terror at stealing bases. I was the first string catcher on the team with the ability to play more than one position. Sol Hicks, Joe Mims, and I became exceptionally good pitchers.

Another game worth noting is a time Mr. Tousaint absent and we were playing a road game against an all-white team. Without Mr. Tousaint, we were all a little nervous. Joe Mims, our best pitcher, was upset because his best pitches were being hit hard for extra bases. This is when one of the white players at bat shouted, "Come on, Sunshine, throw the ball over the plate!" Joe was really upset and lost his cool. Mr. Tousaint's absence made this an important game to win, so I made a trip to the pitcher's mound to calm Joe down. I told him that he had to ignore the name calling and throw his pitches the way I called them. I had spotted a weakness in the batters and, following my pitch calls, Joe threw one of his best games; in addition, our timely hitting caused the opposing pitcher to leave the game and we won. Before disbanding our baseball team we had an opportunity to play Mr. Tousaint's former semi-pro team, the Chicago Blue Sox. What a surprise, we won that game! Joe Mims was a good pitcher and was drafted by a minor league baseball club but eventually blew out his arm and could no longer pitch. I tried out as a catcher with the Chicago Cubs but chickened out after seeing bigger and stronger white catchers play and hit the ball.

At Waller High School my asthma attacks became more frequent and created absentee problems. In my senior year I was absent twenty-one days and had to make up classes to earn enough graduation credits. I would not have made it without the assistance and patience of my senior counselor and teachers who found ways for me to accumulate the required graduation credits. Another unexpected but Godly blessing occurred: My asthma attacks suddenly decreased, and I was able to attend classes and graduate with my senior class in June 1949.

My close friend Jimmie King had graduated earlier, and we no longer hung out together because he was not interested in baseball. He did not care much for sports, but we often swam together in the tank (pool) at the Stanton Park. We played basketball for awhile, but it seemed as though we no longer had anything in common. Struggling to hold onto our friendship, I began partying and drinking with Jimmie, even smoking cigarettes, but realized I could not handle his new lifestyle. I didn't know it but sex, alcohol, marijuana, heroin, and eventually prison were on the horizon for my very best friend! And it became hopeless to maintain our closeness when Jimmie became hooked on heroin. This is when he told me that if I did not smoke marijuana with him we could not be friends. My response was: "You said it, I didn't! You'll always be my friend no matter what happens, but I'm not going to do drugs with you." Jimmie had challenged me to make more positive decisions than he probably will ever know, and this was one of them. Jimmie's heroin addiction resulted in tremendous weight loss and a host of other health problems. He was in and out of jail before finally being incarcerated for three years. His mother, affected by all of this, no doubt felt helpless, and she died during his incarceration. Jimmie was not violent nor was he a drug dealer; he was the nicest young man you would want to meet—but he made the wrong choices. It was twenty years later when Jimmie appeared out of nowhere. He had seen an article in a Chicago newspaper announcing my ordination in the American Lutheran Church and wanted to be present at the ordination service.

CHAPTER 4

Christ's Epiphanal Light

1949-1953

It seemed like the weather was always bad when we had to move, and in the winter of 1949 we were evicted again. The Korean War had begun, and I was a seventeen-year-old pre-med student at Roosevelt University. Chris Paschen Construction Company was demolishing all of their apartments. The Chicago city court would not extend our eviction notice, and finding a place to move was extremely hard. It was snowing when the movers came and removed our household belongings out onto Clybourn Avenue. One of the movers extinguished the fire inside our potbelly stove with water and placed it on top of his back which he had covered with thick padding. You could see thick smoke and steam coming from the stove as he carried it down three flights of stairs and set it on the sidewalk. Our family situation was beyond embarrassing; it was absolutely terrifying. As snow continued falling I looked at my stepfather's face and saw desperation. Miraculously, that same day he found us another home and we moved into an apartment at 1645 Clybourn Avenue. As always my grandmother moved in with us—and we were still a family.

The apartment was a two-story building where two children had died in the fire of a burned-out storefront. It included two bedrooms, a dining room, small bathroom, and a small kitchen. The storefront had not been repaired and was sealed tight to keep the house warm. We used the space to store boxed household goods and a couple of large trunks. The apartment on the second floor had not been damaged, and another family lived there. Circumstances and lack of resources in Chicago had again forced us to live under less than ideal situations. One of my brothers and I slept on a small folding roll-away bed.

My sister Lenora married Harry Effinger when she was sixteen years old, and they moved into another home. Reluctantly, my mother signed the marriage license, saying, "Harry is older and may bring a little stability into your life."

With no financial help for college tuition, I worked as a busboy clearing tables and washing dishes at a Hardy's Restaurant in Goldblatt's downtown department store. I left there and began working full-time nights at Del Farm Foods supermarket while I attended classes during the day. The stress became so much that I could only complete one year at Roosevelt University. I remained at the supermarket but immediately enrolled in Herzl City Junior College (Malcolm X Community College). The supermarket work was physically strenuous, and my aspirations of a promotion to assistant store manager ended with disappointment. A young white man who had been stealing from the store for some time was given the position. Nevertheless, I did not give up and persisted until I was promoted to a new position of stock inventory manager. I had to work in the store's basement, receiving deliveries, ordering stock and inventorying grocery products. Constant exposure to soap, detergents, dust, and other irritants triggered allergic reactions that caused asthma attacks. Illness and physically hard full-time night work took its toll causing me to leave Herzl College after one year. Before leaving Herzl I had a learning experience that had a lifelong impact. I failed my chemistry class, a requirement for all pre-medical students. Humiliated and defeated, I went to my white chemistry professor who said, "Why didn't you ask questions or come to me before it was too late?"

I said, "I was ashamed to ask questions or come to you for help because I didn't want anyone to think I was dumb."

He said, "You were dumb because you didn't ask questions. You learn by asking questions and asking for help!" His response was harsh and it hurt, but I will never forget the truth in what he said.

In 1950, as required by the federal government's Selective Service Act, at the age of eighteen, I registered at the draft board for military service. Immediately, I was called to have a physical examination. Six months prior to my physical I had been hospitalized with a severe asthma attack. Based on proof of that hospitalization, I was classified as 4F, "unfit for military service." Several amusing incidents occurred during my physical examination. The first was when twelve of us took an elevator up to the fourth floor to be examined. It was a large freight elevator that was in some ways similar to a railroad cattle car. After reaching the fourth floor, the last floor of the building, one young man shouted out to the elevator operator, "Fifth floor, please!" Other amusing responses happened when inductees had ear, eye, and rectal examinations. Many who complained of hearing problems had their ears flushed. When optometrists asked some to read eye charts they quipped, "What chart, doc?" And of course rectal exams and flat feet were other sources of humorous remarks. My friend Jimmie King had earlier been rejected for military service because of his flat feet and classified as 4F. An older friend, R. L. Brewer, a semi-professional boxer, whom I occasionally sparred with, passed his physical and was immediately sent to Korea. Six months later he returned home with a Purple Heart and a leg wound that ended his promising boxing career.

This same year I met a very attractive girl, with a captivating smile, named Doris Jean Hayes, who had a distinct bluish color in her eyes. I had never seen this color in the eyes of another Negro. Although I had a girlfriend, for some unexplainable reason I was immediately attracted to Doris. Perhaps it was her eyes, but I think it was more—it was the captivating smile and her bubbling personality. I first met her when visiting the home of my baseball teammates Solomon (Sol) and his brother Sherman Hicks. Their mother, Jeanette Hayes-Hicks, was Doris's sister, which also caught my attention because I thought she was too young to be someone's aunt.

Doris was the youngest of twelve children of Charles Martin and Nevada Hazel Hayes, born on Christmas Eve, December 24, 1934, in Cairo, Illinois. Doris lived with her parents in the Altgeld Gardens public housing project located on Chicago's far South Side. It was not long before I broke off with my girlfriend and began dating Doris, going to movies and eating popcorn.

Discovering that Doris had never been to Riverview Amusement Park, I asked her parent's permission to let us spend a day together at the park. It made me feel like a grown

Doris and I at Riverview Amusement Park.

man to be financially able to treat Doris to a day at the park. However, my manhood was quickly deflated when she insisted on riding The Parachute. I had ridden every roller-coaster ride in the park but was afraid to go up as high as The Parachute. I didn't tell her how I felt but she knew it—and I was really embarrassed when she decided to take the ride alone. I just didn't have the courage to go on the ride with Doris. However, during one of our frequent phone calls I suddenly found another kind of courage, and I told her, "I think I'm falling in love with you." Doris's sister Jeanette and her husband Solomon Hicks Sr. often drove to Altgeld Gardens to visit her parents. Whenever I did not ride with them I rode the streetcar and took a Trail Ways suburban bus to her home.

After dropping out of college I fell into a deep state of depression accompanied by asthma attacks which resulted in my hospitalization. Conditions for patients at Cook County General Hospital were deplorable. Overcrowding necessitated placing beds in the hallways. When my parents discovered that I was not in the intensive care unit, they brought me home. Placing my arms around my mother and grandmother's shoulders I was walked out of the hospital into a waiting taxicab. My mother angrily said, "I'd rather see you die at home than in a hospital hallway." I quickly recovered after a lot of tender loving care and some good home cooking. Cook County Hospital has excellent doctors and nurses but seemingly has always been underfunded, resulting in understaffing and overcrowding. My friends Solomon and Sherman told Doris how sick I was, and she came to visit me at home. I was really glad to see her!

After recovering from my illness I joined my grandmother's church, Union Missionary Baptist Church, at 940 North Orleans Street. I have no idea how Bingham Powell, my friend from Waller High School, became involved but he also joined the church. My brother George and I, Solomon Hicks and his brother Sherman were all baptized on February 17, 1952, by Rev. R. Marvin Mays.

One Sunday morning when worshipping with the Baptist Young Peoples Union in the basement of the church, I had a strange and frightening experience. It happened as my friend Bingham preached. Young people in the Baptist tradition, when approved, were allowed to preach. There had been an intense struggle going on inside me for some time to believe in God and I wanted proof of God's existence. Closing my eyes, I prayed in whispers, the same prayer over and over: "Lord, show me your light, Lord, show me your light, Lord, please, show me your light!" I needed to know that God was real, and I pleaded with God to give me a sign—God's light! What happened next I cannot understand or clearly describe. As I prayed, my head down and eyes closed, a strange light with a muted purplish hue slowly appeared. I had never seen a light like this. As it came closer the purplish glow became brighter, similar to that of a fluorescent bulb. But there were no fluorescent lights in the church basement, only regular light bulbs hanging from the basement ceiling. The light became eerily disturbing when it began to surround me and my chair. My head had been in my lap during this time, but now I sat straight up, tightly gripping the sides of my chair with both hands. My eyes were closed so I knew I was not seeing any other light. Seemingly frozen in time, I saw myself sitting in the chair surrounded by this strange light. I heard no other sounds in the room and had become totally unaware of my surroundings. God answered my prayer and I was terrified. In fact I thought I was dying until I realized that I was still breathing. I struggled to stop what was happening but could not. I panicked when I knew that I could not control the situation. The light responded to my heightened fear by slowly fading away. Then a voice said: "O ye of little faith, you're not dying. Your prayer has been answered, and you will serve me and witness to my reality!" Instead of being blinded by the light, the eyes of my heart had been opened! I was so afraid of what others might say or think that I only told my brother George, Bingham, Solomon, and Sherman about my experience. I would never again need proof of God's existence. Bingham, looking very pleased, smiled and said that God had spoken to me. My attendance at worship services increased with participation in the youth choir and other church activities. My two favorite hymns became "God Answers Prayer" and "Yes, God Is Real."

    Soon after his baptism my brother George dropped out of high school and, on February 27, 1952, he and Solomon Hicks Jr. joined the U.S. Air Force. When they left Solomon's brother, Sherman, no longer came to church.

    Soon Bingham suggested we join the Sanctified Church (Pentecostal). Listening to him, I felt as if he was saying that becoming sanctified and speaking in tongues would bring me closer to God. We left Union Missionary Baptist Church and began worshipping in a storefront Sanctified Church. Listening to the worshippers speak in tongues made me want to be like them. Why? I don't know. God had shown me his light and this was the only gift I needed! But I wanted to be like everyone else and speak in tongues, so one evening I was asked to sit in a chair for prayer to speak in tongues. A small group of people formed a circle around me, placed their hands on my head, shoulders, and arms and prayed. I could not understand what they were saying or the chanting. My eyes were closed, and I listened intently to the repetitive prayers that strongly suggested I had to make something happen. What no one knew, not even my friend Bingham, was that I had prayed, asking God to keep me from pretending because I thought that some people were not truthful.

After a while the prayers ended when I did not speak in tongues. The group sternly rebuked me and said, "There's something wrong with you that's keeping you from speaking. You're holding back because there's something you're not ready to give up!" I was intimidated and hurt, failing again to measure up to someone's expectations. I felt abandoned by my friend Bingham and decided to return to Union Missionary Baptist Church because, it was the church where I was baptized and my grandmother was a member. For some inexplicable reason I did not feel abandoned by God when I did not receive the gift of tongues. Perhaps, I had already received everything I needed from God. Bingham and I remained friends, but he never returned to Union Missionary Baptist Church.

I began prioritizing what I thought was needed to marry Doris, but did not tell my mother anything about my plans. I needed a full-time job, and on April 14, 1952, one year before our marriage, I interviewed for an office position at International Harvester. The McCormick Works and Tractor Works plant were located on Cermak Road (22nd) and Western Avenue. The company had a turbulent history in labor disputes with the AFL/CIO and IBEW unions. Strikes had created huge profit losses that would eventually result in relocation of the plant. I was given a pre-employment test by a white psychologist from the University of Chicago who told me it was a personality profile to see if I could work with other employees. Later, I discovered that white employees were not required to take the tests. On April 16, 1952, I was hired as a foundry time clerk.

In December 1952 Doris and I became engaged. I had been able to get her ring size and purchase a matching engagement and wedding ring, telling her, "I intend to marry you and saved money by purchasing both rings." I had not told my mother about Doris' pregnancy or purchasing the rings because I did not want her to tell me that I was too young to get married. After signing a marriage license for my sister, my mother had said she was not going to sign any more. However, she relented when I said: "In five days I'll be twenty-one years old and will get the license myself." Realizing I was determined, my mother signed the marriage license. I loved my mother, but our conversation helped me lay a solid foundation for many future distractions and threats to my family life. God had given me the wisdom and faith to live out of an expanded love, not a constricted love.

Doris was eighteen years old and did not need her parent's signature on the marriage license. However, I am sure that Mr. and Mrs. Hayes felt as my mother did and were disappointed about the circumstances of their daughter's early marriage. Unmarried, pregnant, and still in school, even after my awkward attempt at a marriage proposal, Doris accepted the rings. She was embarrassed and did not want anyone to know what was happening. However, she received an unexpected blessing when she risked telling her high school science teacher, Mrs. Walters, about her pregnancy. She encouraged Doris to complete her studies and graduate. Doris' pregnancy was very untimely because her brother Charles Hayes Sr. had planned to help her with her college tuition. I knew it was not entirely my fault, but I accepted the fact that if I had not been around so much she might have been able to attend college. Even so, after sixty years of marriage, I know that God has brought us to where we are today.

CHAPTER 5

Adulthood & Marriage

1953–1961

White and Negro laborers worked in the McCormick Works foundry, but I worked in the Timekeepers Office. This new environment created some uncharacteristic feelings. It was as if, in being approved and accepted by whites to work in an office with them, I had become better than the Negro and white foundry workers. These feelings made me uncomfortable because I could not reconcile them with how my mother had raised me. I'll call it neo-Negro classism—a psychological distortion that education and opportunity had given me a false sense of economic security and status. Whites had let me in, and I was in danger of becoming unquestionably selfish and socially delusional—and worst of all forgetting about those of my own racial heritage. Without "the whole package"—that is, complete privileges of citizenship—I became psychologically vulnerable in my new environment of working with whites. Nevertheless, it was gratifying, for the first time, to experience some success in upward mobility and a modicum of acceptance from whites.

But one day, when walking through the foundry collecting time cards, I looked around and suddenly realized the dangerous work performed by factory laborers. I empathized with their hard work and appreciated how they earned their money. And, more importantly, I realized that without them I was nobody! This *kairos* moment "opened the eyes of my heart" again to see God in the faces of all those factory workers. This moment was heightened as I continued walking through the foundry. Metal sparks from dross and slag flew around me from an overhead cupola—a cylindrical furnace—-pouring molten iron into oven-baked, hardened sand molds handled by laborers on the foundry floor below. They wore asbestos leggings and overalls that provided only minimal protection. Many had scars on their hands, arms, and legs from multiple burns. Although there was a registered nurse and dentist for emergency care, numerous accidents caused foundry laborers to be hospitalized. Soon, the smoke-filled, acrid foundry air began agitating my asthma, causing me to make frequent visits to the nursing office. I could not continue working under these conditions so, being cautiously assertive, I took advantage of every opportunity for a promotion. My determination spurred me on to be promoted to a foundry scale clerk. However, I was not satisfied with the pay or position. My determination to move ahead helped to get a higher paying position in the accounting and payroll office which was located outside the main factory. A noticeable peculiarity in the placement of workers at International Harvester was that white males and Negro women worked together in the accounting office. However, Negro males held no office positions until much later—that is, unless they were janitors. Although the company was unionized it did not make sense that there were no Negro men in the accounting office. Negro representation by the union was only in so far as our labor was needed in particular jobs. Soon, I was promoted as an IBM operator, one of three Negro males who became IBM 360 RPG programmers and worked in the accounting office.

Doris and I were married on February 21, 1953, at Union Missionary Baptist Church with the wedding officiated by Rev. R. Marvin Mays. A private ceremony was held in the pastor's office with Solomon Hicks Jr., Doris's nephew, and Charlie Giviens, a member of our baseball team, witnessing the marriage. We celebrated our marriage at the home of Doris's sister, Jeanette Hicks. My mother and another one of Doris's sisters, Nadine White, who lived on the west side, gave us their blessings. Although encouraged by their presence, our joy was subdued because of so many unanswered questions about the future. Later, I introduced Doris to my aunts Rebecca and Ursula who were now living on the North Side.

Initially, my job did not pay that much, and we were as poor as the proverbial church mice. I am sure that is why Doris's parents welcomed us to live with them in their home in the Altgeld Gardens public housing projects. Marriage responsibilities had rearranged my priorities, making it impossible for me to attend Union Missionary Baptist Church. Although there were churches in Altgeld Gardens I preferred attending the church where my grandmother was a member. Although pregnant, Doris was determined to complete her final year at George Washington Carver High School. In fact she graduated on the honor roll as salutatorian of her senior class. Being pregnant, she was uncomfortable in having that honor but was encouraged and supported by her teacher, Mrs. Walters, who said, "You've earned it!" I was there to hear her welcoming presentation to the graduates and was really proud of her.

Six months later God blessed us with our first child, Patricia Lynn Branch, who was born on August 18, 1953, at St. Luke's Hospital. Patricia was a full-term baby but being underweight she was placed in an incubator, which was a frightening new experience for both of us. I will always remember signing papers responsible for the payment of doctor bills and hospital care for Doris and Patricia. The maturation process of being responsible for a family accelerated when I was laid off from International Harvester. I quickly found fulltime employment at the Container Corporation of America where three members of Doris's family worked. Container Corporation was an industrial paper factory that manufactured containers for various commercial packaging products. It was not long before paper dust, printing ink odors, and poor factory ventilation exacerbated my allergies and asthma, resulting in prolonged illness and absences from work.

In 1955 my mother and stepfather purchased a new home on the North Side of Chicago at 666 West Blackhawk Street. My grandmother, now married to Albert Thomas, was living in the second floor apartment. After living with her parents for one year, Doris and I left Altgeld Gardens and moved in with my grandmother and her new husband. My sister Lenora lived with her husband, Harry Effinger, on Blackhawk Street about three blocks away.

Doris went to work at the Social Security Administration to supplement our family income but had to take a pregnancy leave because of the birth of our second child. Terrance Branch was born on March 19, 1955, at St. Luke's Hospital.

I continued working at the Container Corporation of America, but poor ventilation in the factory triggered many asthma attacks. Finally after being sick in bed for three weeks the company sent me a telegram terminating my employment. I was overcome with grief. Everything seemed hopeless, and I became depressed, wondering what kind of a husband I was. I felt less than a man for not being a good provider for my family. Doris and others in my family did what they could to ease my asthma attack by placing hot towels on my chest and rubbing me with Vicks VapoRub. Earlier, Dr. Harry Louren had made a visit and secured an oxygen tank from a medical supply house. Gasping for breath and listening to the creaking, crackling sounds in my chest I felt as if I were dying. Glancing at my infant son Terry, sleeping in a crib next to me, I prayed, asking God to help me live long enough to see him grow up and spare Doris the grief of becoming a young widow. My family thought I was dying, and my mother asked Ms. Porter, a neighbor living down the street, to come and pray for me. She sat next to me and read from the Bible and prayed. Suddenly she stood up and stared directly into my eyes and in a loud commanding voice said, "In the name of Jesus Christ, get up and walk!"

Struggling to breathe, I slowly got up out of bed and whispered, "Call an ambulance. I want to go to the hospital!" Like me, my family had given up hope for my recovery and was unable or afraid to make a decision to get me to the hospital. Perhaps my mother and grandmother had remembered what had happened earlier at Cook County Hospital. As usual, I had no idea of how the hospital bills would be paid, but soon an ambulance arrived. I silently prayed, as the ambulance attendants struggled to maneuver my stretcher around the narrow twisting stairway leading down from our second-floor apartment. I was taken to Alexian Brothers Catholic Hospital where Dr. Louren was on the hospital staff. The doctors said that my asthma attack was complicated by pneumonia and I would have died without hospitalization. The oxygen I was using at home had dried out my lungs. I vaguely remember kicking and screaming at the doctors and nurses until I was immobilized by some kind of injection in my backside. Oxygen therapy was continued but was now passed through a small jar filled with a liquid that bubbled as the oxygen passed through. Overnight my bronchial tubes cleared, and I ate breakfast that morning. I hadn't eaten a good meal for days and now eating breakfast was a personal signal to me that my asthma attack had ended. I was in the hospital for six days, including New Year's

Eve. Looking out from a window on the top floor of the hospital into a moonlit sky on New Year's Eve I will always remember my feelings of loneliness, hurt, mental anguish, and defeat. Listening to the sirens and whistles coming from people celebrating New Year's Eve, I wept. But suddenly I was aware of being alive and breathing in the air of a New Year, and I felt an overwhelming sense of renewed hope. "For I know the plans I have for you," declares the Lord, "plans to prosper you and not to harm you, plans to give you hope and a future" (Jeremiah 29:11, NIV). With eternal love and mercy, God had healed me and given me eyes to see a new day and breathe in the fresh air of a new year. I had not died and was never alone; God was with us, and we were still together as a family.

Our lives continued to be a continuous roller-coaster ride filled with many ups and downs. It had to be our mutual love, hard work, and determination not to give up that kept our little family together. We were on strike at International Harvester, living on unemployment compensation and food vouchers, when we moved in with my grandmother. God blessed us to make good decisions in our rapidly changing family conditions, carefully making moves that would not adversely affect our children. Soon our little family, four of us now, had to move from my grandmother's home. Doris's brother, Harold Hayes, rented a trailer to move us into our own apartment at 3617 West Grenshaw Street. Again, a feeling of helplessness came over me because I was unable even to help load the trailer because of my recent illness. Doris handled the entire move while taking care of me and the children. This was the first time we had our own apartment, and it became available because Doris's friend, Albertine Irwin. Albertine's parents had bought a home, modified an apartment, and rented it to us. The apartment had separate bathrooms and could accommodate two families. Albertine's sister, Alma, her husband, John Smith, and their baby son occupied the front apartment. We had the rear apartment which included a kitchen and two bedrooms, one that we used as a small living room.

In our move to the West Side the roller-coaster ride went up instead of down. The timing was perfect; the long labor union strike at International Harvester was over. I returned to work and was soon promoted to a principal tabulating operator/supervisor. I had to work as supervisor on the night shift with five other IBM operators—two other Negroes and three white men. In my new position one of the white men named Andy K., a union steward, whom I thought was a friend, refused to accept assignments from me, saying: "You're not my supervisor and never will be!" Andy's seniority with the company was over ten years, and he told me that he would only accept jobs assigned to him by Ed P., a higher-ranking white supervisor who worked on the day shift. I believe Andy's seniority had made him think that he would never have to take work assignments from a Negro supervisor. Whatever his reason, the issue was quickly resolved when Ed P. told Andy K. that as long as he worked the night shift I was his supervisor and he would receive work assignments from me, not him. I was shocked and pleasantly surprised by Ed's response because I did not expect him to do the right thing. Northern racism was covert and had been condoned by the company and tolerated by the union for some time. The AFL/CIO union had never proactively demonstrated fair and equal employment opportunities for Negroes. Ironically, Andy was a union steward and one of the white men who had never been required, as I was, to take a personality profile test to see if he was qualified to work with others before being hired. As a principal tabulating operator supervisor, I was trained at an IBM school to move up to programming a 360 Report Program Generator processor.

Following pregnancy leave, Doris returned to work at the Social Security Administration. Shortly, Federal Bureau of Investigation agents met with her, seeking information about her brother, Charles (Bubba) Hayes, who had a leadership position in the AFL/CIO United Meat Cutter's and Packing House Workers Union. Because of his active participation in the union the FBI considered him a person of interest. Doris underwent a long period of intimidating interrogation that frightened and caused her to cry. This was a shock for both of us, and I was angry because I had not been there with her. Doris was much younger than her brother and had no knowledge of his personal life. However, life is full of inexplicable twists and turns which was especially true for Charles Hayes. Following his sister's scathing interview by the FBI, Charles went on to become the second black man elected to the United States Congress from District One in the State of Illinois. He served in that position from 1983 through 1993.

Doris continued working at the Social Security Administration for the next two years. However, feeling a deep need to spend more time at home raising our two older children, Patricia and Terrance, Doris resigned from her job. Michael Anthony Branch was born on May 18, 1958, at St. Luke's Presbyterian Hospital, and we needed an additional bedroom. Four months later, in September 1958, we moved into a larger apartment on 3849 West Van Buren Street. Doris's sister Maxine and her husband Ernest McShan were home owners and lived nearby at 3343 West Monroe Street. Charles and Nevada Hayes had moved from Altgeld Gardens into an apartment at their daughter's home. This move brought us geographically closer to our families. When we moved to 3849 West Van Buren Street, Frederick Hayes, Doris' brother, was serving at a U.S. Air Force base in Tripoli, Libya, North Africa. Housing was unavailable for military families in Tripoli so Freddie's English wife Margaret had to live with us for a short time.

After eight years at International Harvester my job abruptly ended. The company's manufacturing plant was relocated to Memphis for higher profits and no labor unions. Job transfers were offered to all employees, but those who did not transfer were terminated and given severance pay. The Land of Promise, Chicago, had now played a trick on me, making a u-turn and calling me back to Tennessee. Family ties were vitally important to us so we never considered moving to Memphis. I received 600 dollars severance pay, prorated on my seniority of eight years with the company. This was the largest lump sum of money I had ever received and was used to purchase our first new car, a 1957 Chevrolet.

In November 1959 my grandmother, Lenora Carter-Aycock-Thomas, died from high blood pressure and kidney disease. This was an extremely sad time for me, and any memories of her funeral have been erased. First it was my grandfather Robert and now my grandmother. My brother George was home following his honorable discharge from the U.S. Air Force. He and my grandmother were very close, and her death was twice as hard on him.

Cheryl Elaine, our second daughter, was born on December 8, 1959, at St. Luke's Presbyterian Hospital. Keith soon followed, born on October 26, 1960, at the same hospital. We lived at 3849 West Van Buren Street for the next three years until International Harvester's factory relocation.

With the factory's closing I had to begin working in an entry level job at the Veteran's Administration. This lower income job limited our choices of affordable housing so we decided to move into the Cabrini-Green public housing apartments. Despite numerous setbacks and economic roller-coaster rides, God strengthened my determination to maintain a family, struggling but unbroken and making the necessary sacrifices to survive. I believe Doris and I were on the same page, convinced that "faith is not the absence of doubt but the confirmation of God's promises that we shall overcome someday."

CHAPTER 6

Civil Rights Era & Cabrini-Green
1962-1967

The decade of the sixties was a difficult time for us to make good choices while living in the midst of confusion, chaos, and danger in Cabrini-Green public housing. Our faith in God's promises challenged the sin of institutional racism through the non-violence of the civil rights movement. The original population of the Cabrini-Green area consisted of poor Italians, Irish, and Puerto Rican families but now poor Negroes were living there among war veterans and factory workers. The Swedes who had previously lived in the area had gone elsewhere. When we moved into Cabrini-Green, a more insidious ghetto had developed—

One building in Cabrini-Green.

racism, Negro segregation, and poverty. Concrete apartment buildings, twenty stories high, with eight apartments on each floor, now stood in the area—each with 160 apartments, totaling approximately 1,300 people. Poor budget planning by the Chicago Housing Authority placed too many families in this housing complex without adequate janitorial services and maintenance. My aunt Rebecca Fleming, who had now moved to the North Side, referred to the buildings as "over-crowded high-rise slums, built by white folks to get the stink of poverty out of sight by hiding all of us in one area, twenty stories high!"

When we moved into Cabrini-Green, my parents had bought a home and moved to the South Side of Chicago, at 1536 West Marquette Road. It was strange moving back to the North Side without them living nearby. Stranger yet was how the Chicago Housing Authority qualified us with an unusual choice of living in another federally funded public housing complex. We were given an opportunity to live in the Trumbull Park Homes, an all-white federal housing complex. Extensive media coverage highlighted the racist picketing at shopping malls and schools by white demonstrators threatening violence against Negroes moving into the Trumbull Park homes. We were given an opportunity to live there because the Housing Authority was selecting "qualified Negroes," and our family was "qualified" because of our "light complexion." They said our skin color would make us more palatable to whites living in the area. We were assured of police protection by Housing Authority security patrols and special Chicago police officers assigned to bus stops while we sent our children to school. After discussing the impact it would have on our children, especially with me working nights, we decided to move into the Cabrini-Green complex, apartment 307, at 624 West Division Street. My sister Lenora, who was now married to Willie Battle Jr., moved into the 1340 North Larrabee Street building. A Chicago Fire Department Station was located east of us at the corner of Division and Larrabee Streets. Doris' sister, Jeanette Hicks, had an apartment on Division Street but did not live in the housing complex. The 624 building was located directly in front of a neighborhood tavern. Drunken knife fights and shootings kept the police busy at the tavern on the weekends. This was *déjà-vu*, because when I lived in Memphis there was a beer garden (tavern) directly in front of our home.

We were allowed to have a three-bedroom apartment with a kitchen, dining area, and living room. The interior walls of our home were constructed of painted concrete cinder blocks. The noise and conversations of next door neighbors could easily be heard. Electrical coils installed underneath the concrete tiled floors provided heat. We had lots of heat when sleeping on mattresses until we could afford to buy beds. There were no thermostats or air conditioners, so we could not control temperatures in the apartment. Windows were opened in winter whenever the heat was too high. Entryways and exits on the upper floors had concrete walkways or ramps with railings that were partially fenced to provide minimal safety. But everyone had to be alert when approaching our building because various objects were often thrown from the ramp. Elevators were available when they were not broken, but they ran slowly and you could always smell the distinct odor of urine. The apartment stairways had similar odors, and the walls were covered with filthy graffiti. There were not enough janitors to keep our building adequately clean. Instinctively we knew that the future for our children was not based on food and a roof over their heads but in our awareness of the destructive extra-curricular education they were receiving in Cabrini-Green. We were filled with a constant fear of how this environment was influencing our children, and their security and education became our first priority. Doris enrolled them in Schiller Elementary School, from which I had graduated in 1945. She also found a part-time job at the Jewish-owned Maremont Dry Goods Store located in the building where her sister Jeanette lived. It was miraculous to see how well she managed our meager resources. Most of us see miracles differently and perhaps not as simplistically, but she was the epitome of a multi-tasking wife and loving mother of six children. During our four years in Cabrini-Green, Doris had two health issues that greatly concerned me. She became anemic, diagnosed by the doctor as having a previously existing condition which was exacerbated by her pregnancy. A diet high in iron content and vitamin supplements were prescribed by the doctor. The other illness was very alarming; she developed stomach ulcers. I believe the ulcers resulted from our stressful living environment and the constant struggle for financial stability. Eventually Doris's anemia and ulcers were healed using doctor-prescribed medications and a special diet. My family doctor, Harry Louren, provided medical care for our family in his office and by making home visits to Cabrini-Green.

Working at the Veteran's Hospital was extremely difficult because it was located west of Chicago in suburban Hines, Illinois. We did not have a car, and so I used public transportation as well as a suburban bus from Maywood, Illinois, to get to work. It took close to four hours round trip to get to work, and it is impossible to count the times I fell asleep during my ride. This was my first time working for the federal government, and both my supervisors were white with higher pay grades. I soon became aware of having more knowledge and experience than both in applying IBM processing techniques to hospital accounting. Instead of learning *from* them I had to teach both how to do the job more efficiently. My work environment quickly deteriorated as I complained bitterly. If we were going to leave Cabrini-Green, I needed more income. I was not going to be denied, and I insisted on a salary commensurate with my knowledge and experience. I met with the technical supervisor who said, "I like working with a man who's after my job. You're doing good work and I don't want to lose you, but I can't promote you too fast." His response made me feel as though I was now a threat to both men. I soon received several certificates of recognition and appreciation for integration of new data processing techniques into hospital accounting. But I needed money, not certificates! Nevertheless, this spurred me on to submit additional data to the U.S. Civil Service Commission, hoping that updating my qualifications would eventually increase my pay grade levels. The director of accounting/payroll who had oversight for all of us in the data processing center assured me that he would personally get me promoted. In less than a year I moved from a level GS-4 to a GS-6.

In two years I resigned to take a GS-7 position at the Veteran's Administration Research Hospital on Huron Street near Michigan Avenue and Lake Shore Drive. I became the hospital's first IBM project manager, developing IBM applications to facilitate accounting and payroll procedures.

When President John F. Kennedy was assassinated I was working at the hospital. The shock and gravity of the events that day caused an eerie quietness and fearful looks on everyone's face. Telephone circuits at the hospital had become overloaded, and I was extremely worried because I was not able to call Doris to check on our family. What a sad time! Although I did not personally know the president, I cried, feeling that he was assassinated because of trying to help Negroes and move our country towards a more just socio-economic system.

I left the Veteran's Administration Research Hospital in 1965 and returned to Hines Hospital supply depot, promoted to a GS-9 360 RPG computer programmer. During my three years working at the supply depot, the U.S. Civil Service Commission reclassified me as a GS-11 computer programmer supervisor. When I discussed this reclassification with my white supervisor he said that I would have a better chance to get the position if I secured a political sponsor. What a surprise! Naively, I thought the position was based on qualifications, not who I knew! But where was I to go? I didn't know much about politics and certainly did not know a politician from whom to curry favors. However, I would have no need to explore that possibility because God was guiding me in another direction. I resigned in the spring of 1968 and enrolled in the Lutheran School of Theology at Chicago.

Our apartment neighbors, the Baxters and the Boyds, lived on the third floor of our building. Doris and Evelyn Boyd, who lived with her husband, Leonard, and their six children, became close friends. Although Doris and I were married in Union Missionary Baptist Church, we did not worship there. Doris never joined the congregation, and I left because of how some members had mistreated Rev. Mays in what they called "his gross lack of indiscretion." He was asked to leave because of kissing a woman on the cheek following a worship service. For me, there was a gross lack of tolerance in trying to understand the situation—and it did not warrant his dismissal. However, it was an opportunity for dissidents to say, "Now, we've got you!" Doris was now interested in joining a church. The Jehovah's Witnesses constantly knocked on our door, inviting us to attend their local Kingdom Hall. Finally she attended one of their worship services which answered most of her questions, and she decided not to go back.

Later, Doris' friend, Evelyn Boyd, invited her to go with her to worship at Holy Family Lutheran Church. Evelyn's children Carmella, Vickie, and Leonard Jr. were similar in age to our children, and they also attended the church. Holy Family Lutheran Church was located at 542 West Hobbie

Street, near Larrabee and Division Streets. Doris and Evelyn invited me to go with them, and I told them I was no longer interested in church. One Sunday morning Doris decided to go to the church with Evelyn. She enjoyed her new worship experience and went to other services. Doris and Evelyn constantly told me about Holy Family and how spiritually refreshing the worship service was. In fact Doris said she had invited the pastor of the church, Rev. Downing, to visit our home.

Early in 1963, before the pastor's visit, I was alone in bed when something inexplicably strange happened. This time it was not a light but it was an epiphany (manifestation of a divine being). Initially, being in bed, I thought I might be dreaming, but what confused me was that I was awake—so how could I be dreaming? And if I was awake, why couldn't I speak or move? I have no idea where I was, but from a distance I saw a tall, slender, handsome, brown-skinned young man with long, straight, black hair which was gently blowing in the wind and flowing down onto his shoulders. He wore a long white robe and had on leather sandals. It was peaceful, and I was not frightened, but I had no idea where I was. He began to walk toward me with gentle rippling waves splashing against the sandy seashore but never touching him. Suddenly he stopped and beckoned with his right hand, speaking softly, almost inaudibly: "Come to me, and I will make you a fisher of men." Now I recognized the young man was Jesus, and I knew that he was inviting me to come to him and learn how to be a "fisher of men." I knew that I had to make a decision, but I hesitated, not speaking or walking toward him. I could not speak or move and became frightened. Finally, I was able to get up out of bed, knowing that Christ Jesus had made the same request of me as he did to the fisherman Peter. I did not talk to anyone about the vision.

When the time came for Pastor Downing's visit, I told Doris that when he came I would leave. She looked disappointed and sad, which made me feel terrible. The pastor knocked on our door around 7:00 p.m.; I grabbed my jacket, answered the door, and greeted him. I told him that I was leaving but he was welcome to stay and talk with Doris. But was I in for a surprise! This white man stepped in front of the door to keep me from leaving. During this brief but tense encounter, I thought he should be more careful because this was my home and he had a lot of nerve to block my doorway. However, something about his demeanor helped the situation. He spoke in a soft, non-threatening voice, honestly saying, "I really came to visit you, not your wife. I want to tell you why Holy Family Lutheran Church is here in the projects."

Still simmering with anger at the nerve of this white guy blocking my doorway, I said, "Why now? Why the sudden concern about people in this neighborhood? There was a big Lutheran church down on LaSalle Street, a few blocks east of Cabrini-Green, with 'A Mighty Fortress is Our God,' engraved on its cornerstone; but when Negroes moved in, the fortress crumbled. Whites left the neighborhood and relocated in the suburbs. Maybe I should be a Roman Catholic; they didn't move when the neighborhood changed."

Apparently Pastor Downing had done his homework, and he knew the history of the Lutheran Church in our neighborhood. This white guy who was blocking my front doorway admitted that the church's past failures and lack of faith in ministry with Negroes was deplorable. He asked me to forgive him and the Lutheran church. His confession annihilated my defensiveness and really got my attention. Nothing like this had ever happened to me—having a white man confess his wrongs and ask me, a Negro, to forgive him. As the pastor moved away from the front door he said, "Your wife invited me to visit because she's looking for a church and would like you and the children to come to church with her. She thought you might come if I gave you a personal invitation. There's no obligation-—just come and see what's happening. Come and see if there's anything we can do together to change things!"

It seemed as if I was hearing Jesus speak again: "Come-—and I will make you a fisher of men!" Putting my jacket back in the closet I invited Pastor Downing to come inside. He gave a brief historical overview of the American Lutheran Church's new mission in the neighborhood at Holy Family Lutheran Church. I felt needed as he continued to share a liberating vision of the church's mission. After the pastor's visit, my eyes were opened to see the meaning of my Epiphanal vision. This white man had unwittingly provided an explanation. I knew God was giving me an opportunity to follow him and help Holy Family Church's mission in our neighborhood. One thing is certain: I needed to be needed by someone greater than myself—-a purpose in life. Equally apparent was that I realized my wife and children needed me to go to church with them. Shortly after Pastor Downing's visit we became members of our first Lutheran church, Holy Family.

The American Lutheran Church (ALC), a Protestant Christian denomination, was organized in 1960 with membership largely located in the Upper Midwest. The church's constituting convention was held that same year in Minneapolis, which also served as its demographic center and headquarters. Immigrants from Germany, Norway, Sweden, and Denmark formed the white ethnic heritage and nucleus of the Church. Most congregations were segregated, but with the Civil Rights Movement beginning, the old era of Negro Lutheranism and evangelical outreach was changing. In the 1960s, three of the larger American Lutheran denominations—the American Lutheran Church, the Lutheran Church in America, and the Lutheran Church—Missouri Synod—began to push

The Holy Family congregation in the 1960s (right) and in more recent times (above).

for integrated congregations with increased Negro church membership. As a result, delegates of the newly formed American Lutheran Church passed a resolution to begin three new mission congregations. One of these mission starts was to serve Negroes in our region, and the Rev. Fred J. Downing was chosen as mission developer (a term not used at the time) for the unnamed Lutheran congregation in Chicago. The church building was small and was purchased from Italian Catholics who used the building for religious gatherings and fellowship. In March 1963, during worship services, the first members of Holy Family were received as a congregation. Additional land was purchased for a building annex, which included a new sanctuary and multipurpose classrooms.

In 1964, an ALC Illinois District newsletter, "The Lutheran Messenger," stated: "We thank God for the new members given His Church in Holy Baptism—Mrs. Doris Branch, Patricia Lynn Branch, Terrance Branch, Michael Anthony Branch, Cheryl Elaine Branch, and Keith Branch." Doris and I completed adult confirmation classes and on July 5, 1964, became confirmed members of the congregation. A close family friend, John Stumme, a seminary intern at Holy Family, was received into membership that same day through transfer from his church in Waverly, Iowa. Pastor Fred Downing's home town was Waverly, and during his pastorate it seemed as though he had taken in the entire city of Waverly as members of Holy Family. Pastor Downing was a year older than me and prior to his ordination had served on a U.S. Navy aircraft carrier. He served during the Korean War, when I had been classified as 4F by the selective service administration.

Our congregation was mostly made up of Negroes living in Cabrini-Green. However, a significant number of white members, mostly professionals, lived outside of the public housing area. Some came from Lutheran backgrounds, but I believe most were spiritually motivated to share in the reciprocal nature of Holy Family's ministry. Patricia Noble, a lawyer, and Rev. Charles Christiansen lived in the Gold Coast apartments on Clark and LaSalle Streets, a few miles east of Cabrini-Green. Dr. Olga Jonasson and William (Bill) Clover and his wife, Carol, lived on the South Side of Chicago. Robert L. Thompson, a retired Chicago fireman was one of two Negro professionals in our congregation; he owned a local insurance business and served as an Illinois state representative.

Samuel L. Richardson was a graduate of Tuskegee University in Alabama with roots in the Lutheran Church—Missouri Synod. They did not live in Cabrini-Green, but no matter where each one lived, something had caught the attention of those belonging to our congregation.

Holy Family Church seemed to be a magnet attracting people, black and white, from everywhere. I believe they saw that we were on a mission from God, identifying and empowering indigenous Negro leadership in our church and neighborhood. Our witness was to Christ Jesus' spiritually liberating mandate to be one family with all baptized Christians, white and black. Yes, problems were always present in giving witness to a spiritually liberating mandate of empowerment. Nevertheless, Christ Jesus' words were alive in our hearts: "Be in the world but not of the world" (John 17:16-18)—*be faithful in your mission to liberate oppressed people everywhere.*

Becoming official members of the Illinois District and the national American Lutheran Church required us to form a steering committee, elect a council and officers, and call our own pastor. Holy Family's Sunday morning worship service was liturgically different than Union Missionary Baptist Church but very similar to the Roman Catholic Church. We used worship bulletins with rubrics (guidelines) and sang hymns from the Lutheran, red *Service Book and Hymnal*. The service was chanted, followed by chanted responses from the congregation.

On May 3, 1965, Doris's father, Charles Martin Hayes, died from lung cancer. I will never forget the gentle manner in which Doris's brother, Freddie, shared the news of their father's death with his sister. Five months later, following my father-in-law's death, I was elected and installed on October 10, 1965 as the first church council president of Holy Family Lutheran Church. My election as council president followed a tense meeting where two Negro men whom I respected and admired had aspirations of becoming council president. I was not interested in being a leader in the church and felt that both men were better qualified. Reluctantly, I allowed my name to be placed in nomination, resulting in several tie-breaking votes. When the final vote was cast, I did not vote for myself, but evidently both men voted for me, because I was elected church council president with one of them becoming vice president. The man with the least number of votes became the church council secretary. In our first official act we called the Rev. Fred J. Downing as our pastor.

Shortly afterward, ground was broken for the new church sanctuary building annex, and Holy Family began a rapid growth in membership. On February 1966 we celebrated our first official worship service as an organized congregation of the American Lutheran Church. Three months later, on April 9, 1966, our youngest son, David Alan Branch, was baptized in the old sanctuary, and our neighbor Evelyn Boyd became his godmother. On July 2, 1967, our new church building annex, sanctuary, and classrooms were completed. The new sanctuary was complemented by a beautiful dark bronze metal sculpture on the wall above the altar with a matching bronze crucifix in front of the altar. The sculpture's significance was apparent in its representation of the Holy Family of God in Joseph, Mary, and the baby Jesus, each having Negroid features. It was the most deeply moving piece of religious art work I had ever seen. A matching bronze baptismal font was appropriately placed at the entrance of the sanctuary. Its placement reminded us each time we entered the sanctuary that we were baptized members of God's Family.

Gangs, violence, and street crime became a daily threat in Cabrini-Green. On weekends we constantly heard the shrill sounds of police sirens. Early one night, hearing sirens, I went to the window to see what was happening and saw flashes of light from a gun fired from an eighth-floor apartment window in the adjacent building. In the dark apartment above, the silhouetted shooter could easily be seen by the flashes of gunfire. In looking down below our apartment window, in the direction of the gunfire, I saw a young man limping away, apparently shot. This was not an isolated occurrence; these incidents happened every weekend. Doris and I felt vulnerable and feared for our children's safety. We knew it was time to leave Cabrini-Green. Its reputation for crime and gangs had now rivaled that of Swede Town's Little Hell. Residents living in Cabrini-Green lives might be seen as people "perishing for lack of a vision (Proverbs 29:18)—" with little hope of a future.

Holy Family lacked adequate financial resources and political clout. Money was an obvious, need but there were more complex social evils at work in Cabrini-Green. Disunity among residents was reinforced by racist institutional and church bureaucracy. Pastor Downing recognized and agonized over these deeply rooted problems and became black like us—without losing his whiteness! His heart had been opened to see a renaissance taking place in the lives of black people. This spiritual insight made him seem strange to some and an outsider to others. The eyes and hearts of most whites in the congregation had been opened by God to embrace our brotherhood and sisterhood. This healing began in our homes, strengthening and guiding us to confront the evils of institutional racism. The goal of Christ Jesus' missional mandate was reconciliation with God and with one another, irrespective of race and/or social status.

We committed ourselves to Christ's call to become a counter-cultural congregation. Can there be any other mission than one that faithfully acts on the mandate given us by Christ Jesus? Our unified congregational witness demonstrated our rebirth for mission. This was our time—perhaps, the only time we would have to give witness to God's redemptive love: "And the Lord said, I have surely seen the affliction of my people which are in Egypt, and have heard their cry by reason of their taskmaster; for I know their sorrows" (Exodus 3:7 KJV, Acts 7:34 NIV). Cabrini-Green was our Egypt, and God had seen the afflictions caused by the powers and principalities. God knew our sorrows and helped us become articulate in advocating for socio-economic and political justice. We adamantly insisted that there could be no Christian love without justice.

To this end we perceived that it was not only society in need of demonstrating love and justice but also the church of Christ Jesus. If socio-economic justice for the poor and oppressed did not begin in the Body of Christ, God's church, where and when would it begin? "However, when the Son of Man comes, will he find faith on the earth?" (Luke 18:6-8, NIV). Seemingly, Pastor Downing was a risk-taker, tireless and patient in his determination to move toward God's missional mandate. He was gifted in his ability to bring diverse racial groups together to partnership in Christ's mission in the world. Because of this he paid the price—but Christ Jesus paid a greater price! Being a change maker requires peace with God amidst pain and suffering. Pastor Downing's wife, Janelle, was very supportive, but I'm sure that at times she had her share of pain and suffering. I can only imagine that both she and Pastor Downing were overwhelmed by the complex needs of their Negro brothers and sisters.

An old adage says "Charity (namely love) begins at home." And home is where the heart is-—and hearts are transformed by the love of God. Its truth can be illustrated in an abbreviated quote from a poem called "Mother Love," written by a Christian friend, L. G. Thomas, whose wife is a Minneapolis pastor:

>Mine wuz yours, yours wuz mine.
>All I needed ta be wuz a good child.
>Mine wuz yours, yours wuz mine!
>The peace that wuz—wuz kept!

Jesus' prayer for his family of disciples was: "All I have is yours, and all you have is mine, and glory has come to me through them" (John, 17:10). Slavery and racism are satanic and have weakened our ability, as Negroes, to love ourselves——almost making it impossible to love one another. Holy Family's greatest neighborhood witness was that we were "one holy family of God," irrespective of occupation, social status, or racial identity.

Martin Luther, a Roman Catholic priest and church reformer, emphasized the spirituality in one's calling was as a servant to others—*all others.* He spoke of our call to discipleship as a life-long Christian vocation in mission—not religious volunteerism. Holy Family Church's witness in the ALC Illinois District was our call to address poverty and racial oppression. Jesus said, "All authority in heaven and on earth has been given to me, therefore, go and make disciples of all nations, baptizing them in the name of the Father and of the Son and of the Holy Spirit, *teaching them to obey everything I have commanded you.* And surely I will be with you always, to the very end of the age!'" (Matthew 28:18-20, NIV). This statement inextricably binds us together in our baptism as a holy family, obligated to follow Christ Jesus' call: "The Spirit of the Lord is upon me," said Jesus, "because the Lord God has anointed me to preach good news to the poor! He has sent me to proclaim freedom for the prisoners and recovery of sight for the blind, to release the oppressed and to proclaim the year of the Lord's favor" (Luke 4:18-19, NIV).

Our congregation could not separate the love of Jesus Christ from his concern about justice for those in our neighborhood. The Spirit of the Living God had "fallen afresh" upon all, anointing and reminding us with "*power from on high"* to walk in God's counter-cultural ways, putting flesh on the meaning of our baptism in Christ Jesus. Are the words of Jesus only found somewhere in an old and *yet always new book,* the Bible? Where is its relevance for us today, and how can the power of God's love become the "good news?" Can the words mandated by Christ Jesus become flesh in us? Who are the poor and where can they to be found? Are they too far away from us to recognize in our own mad rush toward upward mobility in a merchandising society? In the midst of unholy alliances, it is almost impossible to effect change. If your perspective is spiritual, these people are us! Jesus begins his counter-cultural mission: "To proclaim freedom for prisoners, recovery of sight to the blind and release of the oppressed." What if any parameters or time lines are there for us to "proclaim the year of the Lord's favor"? Isn't it every day and place where we live? How important is it for our church's response to Jesus' call to a "counter-cultural" mission? Isn't Jesus Lord of the church? Didn't he shed His blood for the Body of Christ?

Seeking answers for our counter-cultural mission began with prayers that moved us outside of our comfort zones to the reality of being faithful, living witnesses as Christian history makers. Our baptismal promises had firmly grounded us to be faithful in obeying Christ Jesus. The Lord's Supper became a "spiritual rock," quenching our thirst for purpose and providing food for the strength we needed in mission. Noticeably, our children grew spiritually, following parental examples to participate in Jesus' call to justice. Confronting the principalities and powers of poverty and racism became a family affair! Mission clarity blossomed within a crucible of faith, grounded in our congregational life. Our people were transformed from being just another Negro Lutheran congregation into the family of Christ, following Christ's counter-cultural mission.

We knew our foundation was grounded on the life, death, and resurrection of Christ Jesus. We learned to love the work of sharing the stories of our transformation. Indeed, our lives reflected the light of God's powerful love—one Holy Family in Christ Jesus! Advocating for justice in the lives of black people increased our congregational membership. Cabrini-Green residents recognized something different about us; they saw a caring congregation united by prophetic voices, black and white, creating social change in the neighborhood. We did not compete with indigenous church denominations to recruit Negroes into Holy Family church. Our mission was to initiate change that promoted social justice for all living in Cabrini-Green. We challenged the American Lutheran Church to manifest its biblical rhetoric in freeing the oppressed poor. Our congregation itself was faith-challenged—giving in unaccustomed ways of our love, time, and talents. We struggled to obey and reflect Christ Jesus' missional mandate. Our strategies to initiate change were so effective that we became a threat to the ALC Illinois District.

Nevertheless, this time was *God's kairos* moment for black people to move towards a new day. In this Godly moment we denounced the racial stigma of being called "Negroes," "coloreds," and in some cases "niggras." We embraced a powerful new understanding of what it meant to be created in God's black image. We shouted loudly, "Black is beautiful. I'm "black and I'm proud!" The word *black* is not always about skin color, but can become a psychological weapon against those whites who pejoratively use darker skin to define and diminish the humanity of black people. The psychological evils of slavery and myth of racial superiority have always been used to justify the separation of blacks and whites. At Holy Family, white brothers and sisters knew better, and they became one in blackness, confronting racism in all of its forms.

The church's unified witness powerfully influenced our families and the people of Cabrini-Green. A miraculous Pentecostal event happened, and we spoke in "new tongues," saying: "We're all black, and we're all proud!" White brothers and sisters embraced a new Christian understanding of blackness—without losing their own whiteness! Speaking of miracles, when and how does this kind of Pentecostal event of redemptive love happen? What is church growth if it is not the place where Christ Jesus revives a powerful new Pentecostal freedom from slavery, black and white, in our lives?

After years of psychological stigma of death attached to the word *black*, some Negroes found it difficult to accept our blackness, and they decided to remain enslaved as second-class citizens. I empathized with their hopelessness—a fear to move from powerlessness and self-hate to new life in Christ Jesus. Nevertheless, our unified will to "seize the day" and live now for Christ's mission, led Holy Family congregation to support a nationwide, non-violent protest for civil/human rights. We recognized, encouraged, and supported our congregational leaders to confront all oppressive powers that placed the stench of death on black people. We became spiritually grounded in our faith, convinced that the power of Christ Jesus would sustain our witness.

Struggling to be faithful to Christ's mission moved us from being dreamers of a new day into witnessing that new day. Our congregation's participation in the ALC Conference of Inner City Ministries (CICM) strengthened our witness with other Christians. This was a major blessing initiated by the American Lutheran Church (ALC), the Lutheran Church in America (LCA), Lutheran Church—Missouri Synod (LCMS), and Lutheran Social Services of Illinois (LSSI). Holy Family Church's involvement in CICM created a broader regional representation of mission, showcasing the spiritual gifts of black people. Holy Family's evangelism was avant-garde in that it involved more than recruiting critical masses of blacks for statistical purposes in the national church. For us, evangelism was more than membership recruitment It was our obedience to Christ Jesus' commandment. Holy Family's willingness to become partners with neighborhood black churches and suburban white churches helped us realize that our salvation was not grounded in being Lutheran but in witnessing with other Christians in mission!

Holy Family Church adamantly refused to build on any foundation requiring support and maintenance of existing ethnocentric white institutions. Instead we faithfully remained a new revelatory witness to the promises of Christ Jesus to follow his marching orders! Soon we became a threat to the hierarchal all-white Lutheran church. As followers of Jesus Christ we, at Holy Family, worked at reflecting the love of Jesus in mission. However, this was not the case for some in the ALC Illinois District. Their racial blindness, lack of love, and fear of losing control caused them to react in negative ways. For us to be partners with them in mission challenged their leadership. It must have seemed to them as though the tail was wagging the dog; they were not having any of that.

In 1969, Following Pastor Downing's resignation, The ALC Illinois District's heavy-handed approach to working with our congregation became more verbally threatening and oppressive. I received several letters (with copies sent to church leaders) threatening withdrawal of financial support if we did not follow the ALC guidelines for mission congregations. Ironically, it was the Illinois District who was not following the ALC constitutional guidelines for congregations. One letter stated:

"Pastor Downing's ministry has led you in the wrong direction." I was deeply hurt and angered by the district's determination to disrespect us as partners in mission and instead relate to us with paternalism and condescension. They were blinded by their past experiences in working with blacks, or lack thereof, and refused to accept our help.

One afternoon, prior to Pastor Downing's resignation, while walking to church, I looked up and saw him getting his hair cut at the black barber shop across the street. I was surprised but glad to see him there because he was breaking one of many covert racial taboos of that time—stay in your place and do business with your own race. I had never seen a white man getting his hair cut in a black barber shop before. In various ways Pastor Downing learned much from us and shared his experiences with other white Lutheran congregations.

Empowered by Martin Luther's comments on the "priesthood of all believers," our congregation enriched mission work in the ALC Illinois District. We shared our gifts and knowledge with district officials as we worked responsibly to reflect the true needs of a Christ-centered mission in Cabrini-Green. However, the fear of losing traditionally structured control blocked every attempt at partnership. The ALC Illinois District condemned the unique approach of Pastor Downing's leadership that was built on mutual respect and reciprocity. Pastor Downing recognized mutuality in learning. He knew we needed one another, and he was aware that he needed to be a learner-teacher. What he learned from us enabled him to see our common humanity and mission. He recognized strength in our differences as essential to our successful partnership in Christ Jesus' mission. And we recognized that his knowledge assisted us in opening socio-economic and political doors that we might never have been able to enter, especially in the Lutheran church.

I believe that most white Lutherans helped blacks, motivated by guilt or paternalism, not love. Many denied God's transforming love by creating condescending and paternalistic relationships. Most white Lutherans had no idea of what it meant to be black and even less knowledge of how God had connected us through our common blood in Christ Jesus. Where was the hope for change in our lives if the deep spiritual mandate inherent in our Christian baptism was not rooted in the hearts of our white brothers and sisters? Many suburban white

Lutheran churches could not see that they needed us too—perhaps more than we needed them.

It is morally wrong to place any economically deprived ethnic group in geographical areas of containment that quickly deteriorate into oppressed economic and political concentration camps. The building of the Cabrini-Green public housing was a cheap, quick political fix to keep poor, uneducated blacks in their place, out of sight and therefore out of mind. We are all created in God's image and human needs are reciprocal, making us all black, poor, and hopeless until we embrace our common need for justice and economic parity. The church had lost its faithfulness to witness to God's liberating gospel of justice for the poor and oppressed of the land. The common mission for blacks and whites in following Christ Jesus' call should not be based so much on racial integration but on political and economic justice. The real issue has never been based on racial separation but on human-created sinful pride and economic greed. The containment and control of people through racial and demographic disparity, black-white/urban-suburban, competing for socio-economic and political advantage, has been with us forever. Holy Family's congregation consistently confronted the church's lack of will to follow Christ's command to free the oppressed poor. Our mission to follow Christ's mandate, as we understood it, threatened many white Lutherans, fearful of losing their positions of power and prestige in the church. Not much has changed, because this same fear and resistance to black leadership and what we bring to the table exists even today.

As black people, we should acknowledge our own greed and the need to act responsibly to change. We have followed the sound of the Pied Piper of Hamelin far too long. For our Godly aspirations to bear fruit, we must affirm our gifts as black people and echo Jesus' call for all to be free from poverty and oppression. Our history is as important as that of any other racial group of oppressed people. Many young blacks fail to see or, perhaps, they even ignore the continuing need to revisit freedom struggles of the past against racism. For some, education has been like the Pied Piper, deluding them into believing the tune being played means that they have arrived and finally reached the American Dream. And that's all it is—a dream! Integration and financial security is good, but blind and reckless assimilation must be resisted and confronted. At Holy Family Lutheran Church faithfulness to Christ Jesus meant our priority was his priority—to share the miracle of our common humanity in Christ's love for all people. The racial, socio-economic, and political diversity in our congregation, with its complex human problems, created the perfect crucible to experience our common humanity. After so many years of clinging to traditions cultivated by ethno-centric fears, most white Lutheran congregations were not so blessed. But where and how should we begin to effectively reflect the light of Christ Jesus? It has to begin where God has called us to be—that is, as part of God's Church—and God will take care of the how!

Although our congregation was politically limited and economically deprived, we became miracle workers in identifying our needs and surviving. We thanked God for the love and blessings that so miraculously yoked us together as a racially diverse Body of Christ!

One day as I sat and chatted with Pastor Downing in his office, I suddenly became extremely nervous, because I wanted to say something to him that was very embarrassing. Actually, I knew what I wanted to say, but did not know how to put it into words. Squirming and moving from side to side in my chair, I finally blurted out, "I love you. I really love you!" And in the same breath I said, "But don't get the wrong idea. I love you in a different way!" Pastor Downing, as always, calmly and softly responded, saying: "I love you too!" Who would have guessed the first person to elicit these words from me would be a white man. There had never been any significant men in my childhood other than my step-grandfather and my stepfather. I loved them but had never said, "I love you" to either of them.

Later, I shared my biracial background with Pastor Downing and explained my intense dislike for his using the word *mulatto*. I hated the word because it had been used by whites to define and separate black people from one another. The dictionary defines mulatto as "the first-generation offspring of a 'Negro' and a 'white' person." I asked the pastor to keep our conversation confidential, not because I was ashamed of my family heritage—I had experienced the destructive way in which the word had been used. I had seen the hurt and pain of an active caste system in my own family. Actually, I was most concerned about the manipulative socio-economic and political effect the caste system had caused in the lives of black people.

Holy Family Church's dedication to a strong Bible-based discipleship slowly began to challenge old missional models existing in the ALC Illinois District. We became effective in networking with other black Lutheran clergy in the American Lutheran Church, the Lutheran Church in America, and the Lutheran Church—Missouri Synod. This enabled us to have a larger group of black clergy with the leverage to demand full and equal participation in all aspects of the Lutheran church's mission. However, at the same time, we had increasingly become a threat to some leaders in the church. As members of the body of Christ, Holy Family Church believed that we could no longer accept our status as mere Negro statistics on the membership lists of the Lutheran church. We demanded a seat at the "Lord's table" where decisions were made about a mission relevancy to the priceless lives, traditions, values, and gifts of all people. True representation for black congregations was non-existent in the ALC Illinois District and national church, and white leadership was held accountable for this disparity.

Our ability to articulate and change our own situation shocked some, causing us to be perceived as not doing evangelism "the traditional Lutheran way." All of which meant waiting until we were qualified to be leaders in our congregations. I spoke with many whites whose criteria for the church's work (separate from Christ's mandate) in black communities was based solely on their solutions to our problems. They could not see that they were the problem, and they needed our help to free them from the idolatry of whiteness. Most blacks, in my day and time, had heard *ad nauseam* the words, "Slow down, you're moving too fast," and "We can't find any qualified black people." I was fed this message all my life and was sick and tired of being politically programmed and packaged in this way. Nevertheless, we at Holy Family Lutheran Church grasped this moment as *our* time, a *kairos* moment to grow in our biblical faith to reflect the light of Jesus in ministry.

Holy Family's first attempt to partner in mission with other black Lutheran churches was with Community Lutheran Church on the West Side of Chicago. Like Holy Family it was a black congregation with a white pastor. I will never forget the reason they gave not to co-sponsor a resolution with us at the Illinois District convention. The ALC Illinois District had spread all kinds of rumors about Holy Family Church being radicals and a bunch of communists. Believing these rumors, they feared getting involved with us, thinking it would be transgressing against the "Lutheran way of doing things." When it came to being Lutherans they had quickly forgotten that Jesus Christ died for the church, not Martin Luther. Their faith seemed to be grounded in Lutheranism instead of in Christ Jesus, and the mission goals of their congregation were non-existent. They feared losing financial support of the mother church. They adamantly stated that our interpretation of Christ's missional mandate was in error, or we would not be in trouble with the ALC Illinois District office. It seemed as though they were saying that "whatever was white made it right." For many blacks, being accepted by whites into the Lutheran church deluded them into feeling as though they had arrived and were therefore accepted. Many times my heart ached for those blacks who lost their identity to belong at any cost. This was and still is the "identity theft" of slavery and racism, and it is unwittingly as destructive to the psyche of whites. As blacks our goal is to obey and follow Christ Jesus, and that begins in the household of faith.

Community Lutheran Church's reluctance to engage in a missional partnership was fueled by their desire to be accepted by a prestigious white church. Most white pastors in black congregations feared involvement in the civil rights movement, and that blinded them to see the civil rights struggle's connection to the Lutheran Reformation. Unlike Pastor Downing, many white pastors failed to see the church's mission beyond their white institutional training, cultural traditions, and social milieu. Most were not called to be in mission anywhere and were afraid of failing, while others were satisfied to create little groups of elite black Lutherans. Essentially, this kind of discipleship resulted in the blind leading the blind. Black congregations like these sold their birthright in exchange for a continuing paternalistic relationship with whites. Their pastor and congregational mission became self-serving with their only goal being to "move on up a little higher" even if it meant leaving other blacks behind. This was the good old American way; they could not confront inequality and injustice against the poor and black oppressed. The members of Holy Family embraced discipleship—first in our church and families and then to poor and oppressed everywhere. This isn't an indictment against anyone and I'm not being judgmental; that's God's call! In many ways, blacks are a unique people endowed in God's blessings with a rich history of overcoming much adversity and with a responsibility to continue struggling against the clinging stench of physical and psychological slavery. Our spiritual vision at Holy Family Lutheran Church was realized in being yoked with whites in solidarity of mission.

Our second attempt to partner was at Good Shepherd Lutheran Church in south suburban Robbins, Illinois. This was another black Lutheran congregation with a white pastor whose response was lukewarm. Although Holy Family Church carried the stigma of "not toeing the line," we became history makers by carrying out Christ Jesus' mission from Cabrini-Green to God's church everywhere. As with Community Lutheran Church, we sought Good Shepherd's co-sponsorship to present a resolution at the Illinois District convention to establish a black student seminary education fund. They agreed to support our proposal but unfortunately, after talking with the district president at the convention they deserted us, saying that we had deceived them. These two congregations and their pastors had never questioned the inequities in mission within the ALC Illinois District and, perhaps for other reasons, were afraid. Surprisingly with the support of two delegates from Westside Community Lutheran Church, Murray Kelly and his father, the resolution was passed. Later, the black delegate from Good Shepherd asked for forgiveness, explaining that he was talked out of supporting the resolution by ALC Illinois District leaders. God is good, and forgiveness healed and reconciled us all! But what a painful experience, of being castigated, charged with "creating waves" because of engaging Christian brothers and sisters in a partnership of Christ's mandated mission! Our censure at the ALC Illinois District convention reinforced the negative perception of being the unclean lepers of our time. We were *persona non grata* members of the ALC Illinois District. Personally, I was exhausted and wanted more involvement by black leaders from other Lutheran congregations.

The ALC Illinois District continued to threaten black mission congregations with financial sanctions, strongly advising them not to partnership with Holy Family. In retrospect, it seems there was no true missional mandate unless it came from the top down and only from whites. Community Lutheran Church in Chicago and Good Shepherd Lutheran in suburbia initially rejected our methodology as fraught with confrontation, risk, and failure because it wasn't the "Lutheran way." They couldn't see that their financial support by the ALC Illinois District had a very different approach—the smell of paternalism, not partnership. These continuing threats tended to cause difficulty in our efforts to join with other black congregations. The closest we came to realizing solidarity was in our partnership with the ALC Conference of Inner City Ministries. Pastor Downing, usually soft-spoken and compassionate was always mentally tough in understanding, articulating, and witnessing to Christ's call to free the oppressed poor. He was a partner with those living in Cabrini-Green, and this frightened those who wanted to control others and make choices for them. Nevertheless, he was determined to persuade whomever he met, white or black, to look at what Christ Jesus did and was doing now to transform the lives of oppressed people. Whenever I listened to Pastor Downing preach, I sensed a call to take ownership and responsibility in God's *unconditional love for all people*. The congregation's mission was grounded in Matthew 28:18 and Luke 4:17-21. As baptized disciples of the resurrected Christ we are held accountable to Christ in mission.

Although our family now commuted from the West Side of Chicago, God's blessings remained. We rarely missed celebrating worship and Holy Communion at Holy Family. The more we experienced Christ's transformational word, the more we took ownership to live lives of witness and discipleship. It was God's word and prayer that blessed us with an increase in church membership and worship attendance. Our congregation's Christian witness to reconciliation was essential to how our mission was perceived by the people in Cabrini-Green. Whenever the Branch family missed worship services it was like we no longer belonged to the neighborhood and were not part of what God was doing in the lives of His people. We weren't called out of slavery to become isolated from the oppression and needs of others. Those biblical concepts of had strong implications for the future of our family as we became more articulate in our Christian witness. For me, this began a spiritual quest to move our family towards a new Land of Promise. What God did in our congregation was to give blacks and whites more freedom to change the inequalities in our socio-economic and political lives. We didn't just *feel* we were making a difference—we knew we were!

The most effective communication tool for Pastor Downing in teaching and initiating leadership development was the use of a "Sermon Talk Back" during coffee break after Sunday worship services. We felt free to question and even challenge the implications and relevancy of his sermon to congregational and neighborhood needs. Attendance and participation was always voluntary, and visitors were welcome, including those who might be suspicious of white Lutherans in the Cabrini-Green neighborhood. This openness and transparency created lively discussion with many challenges and opportunities. I'm certain that he listened closely to monitor our understanding of mission and it consequences while affirming mutual congregational respect and unity. After all, the call in our baptism first had to be grounded and lived out of our household of faith here—at Holy Family Lutheran Church.

Our children became immersed in the educational programs of the congregation, such as Sunday school, youth confirmation classes, Luther League, "Friendly Town Vacations," and summer Vacation Bible School. Education was stressed and valued as a priority in whatever activity we participated. Pastor Downing purposely chose difficult religious curriculum, teaching in a way that challenged adults and youth to learn and apply their knowledge to family, church, and neighborhood. The "Friendly Town" programs gave our children an opportunity to enroll in Lutheran schools, colleges, and other educational institutions.

During the Civil Rights movement the federal government funded the Operation Head Start program which offered access to a quality early educational start in school. These programs were usually sponsored by neighborhood faith-based organizations to improve educational opportunities for our children. Our congregation received a federal grant and in cooperation with nearby public schools provided space in the church for a Head Start program. Cynthia Jackson was its first director. One of the strong points of the Head Start program was that most of the staff members were volunteers and parents of children in the program. The Head Start program was only one of several programs demonstrating our deep concern for the children of our neighborhood. We also provided space our church for an early school release religious program. Because of its focus on Christian education and contact with our church, I envisioned the early school release program as having the potential for outreach in the neighborhood.

I remember very well Roman Catholic churches in our neighborhood actively involved in using early school release programs for Roman Catholic evangelical outreach. However, Holy Family's outreach programs were never used to recruit new church members but as a way to address the socio-economic and political injustices those in our neighborhood faced. This is what opened the door for our increased membership. A case in point was our congregation's Legal Guidance and Support Clinic. This innovative ministry consisted of a small group of Christian lawyers from white suburban Lutheran congregations who met once a week at our church with anyone from the congregation or from the neighborhood needing free legal assistance. Initially, the program offered assistance only to those having financial problems. However, these Christian lawyers immediately saw a pressing need to expand their legal representation to help with criminal cases.

One such case involved Nehemiah Russell, the young leader of a neighborhood gang called "T.H.E. B.L.A.C.K.S." (I've forgotten what these initials meant.) Nehemiah had been frequently harassed and arrested on various charges by the police, and his mother finally sought help from our congregation's Legal Guidance Clinic. She wasn't a member of Holy Family or connected in any way to our church, although she attended a church somewhere in the neighborhood. I don't know the reasons for Nehemiah's multiple arrests, but he often said the police had been attempting to "turn him into a snitch." Pastor Downing and I made several trips to visit Nehemiah while he was incarcerated in the Cook County Jail. This case became a pivotal opportunity for our Christian witness and outreach and for the white lawyers involved in the Legal Guidance Clinic program. Realizing a need for building more effective relationships with people in Cabrini-Green, our lawyers decided to recruit criminal lawyers from their congregations and law firms to represent *pro bono publico* (free for the good of the public) in Nehemiah's legal defense. After one of our lawyers made a simple request for a change of venue, Nehemiah went to trial and was immediately released because of time served. This witness of support by our congregation and white suburban lawyers for Nehemiah ended his harassment and arrests by the police. Following his release from jail, Nehemiah personally thanked everyone for helping him and asked for an opportunity to express his thanks to members of our congregational council. I'll never forget the deeply emotional and Christian testimony he gave of his transformation and his need to confess and ask for our forgiveness. The eyes of his heart had been opened to see beyond his own suffering and pain! He admitted to doing many things wrong and shared some of the "evil thoughts" he had about our racially diverse congregation.

He did question why it was necessary for us to have a white man as our pastor. He admitted to thinking this way even while Pastor Downing and I were working hard to get him released from jail. He wasted no kind words on me and my relationship with Pastor Downing, thinking of me as a "token nigger" with no mind of my own, following whatever this white man, Pastor Downing, said or did. It hurt me deeply to hear Nehemiah hurl these allegations against me, and my eyes quickly filled with tears as I became aware that others in our neighborhood might have similar thoughts. But as Nehemiah spoke he began to cry, saying, "I was wrong. This pastor, white or not, cares about this neighborhood. With the exception of my mother, Pastor Downing and Brother Branch were the only ones who visited me while I was in jail. My so-called friends never came to visit me! In fact, there's no other church in our neighborhood, black or white, challenging the oppression of black people the way Holy Family Church is doing! And, by the way, I've watched Brother Branch for some time now, and I know he's not only supportive of what this church does but is well able to think and speak on his own!"

Because of Nehemiah's earlier negative remarks about me, I was completely surprised. I felt weepy inside, but no tears came. As we continued to listen, we discovered that he was more knowledgeable of the Bible than many of us had thought. We felt that much of what he had learned came from his mother. Even though she maintained membership in her own congregation, she came to us for help with her son. I will always remember what Nehemiah read to us from Isaiah 64:6: "But we are all as an unclean thing, and each of our righteousness are as filthy rags; and we all do fade as a leaf and our iniquities, like the wind, have taken us away" (KJV). Following his reading, Nehemiah asked us to forgive him for how he thought we were being been duped by whites who should be working in their own churches to fight racial injustices. What a blessing for all of us, especially as to how this young man became a witness to the transformative power of Jesus' redemption and salvation!

Our faith in Christ's work in our lives resulted in a win-win partnership with our white Christian lawyers' legal assistance outreach program. But we're winners only so far as we understand that our success was in obedience to God, and that catalyst built an understanding of mutuality in the reciprocity of blessings in partnership outreach. For Holy Family Lutheran Church's congregation, it was never a matter of receiving much-needed financial support but creating an awareness of the equal value and reciprocity in all God-given gifts to build Christian relationships. We perceived true partnerships as those happening through risk-taking, faith-challenged work. Holy Family's determined efforts at evangelism were not only a time of hurt, pain, and setbacks but also of healing, refreshment, and even times of celebrating tangible victories.

"Friendly Town" vacations, for our children living in inner-city public housing, connected Holy Family Lutheran Church families with Lutheran families from small towns, cities, and farms in an attempt to build meaningful, racially diverse Christian relationships. Arrangements for these vacations were made with churches in suburban and rural Illinois; Waverly, Iowa; and Madison, Milwaukee, and Whitewater, Wisconsin. Children from our congregation lived with white families in the aforementioned cities. The only problem we encountered in the "Friendly Town" program arose when children from white families were invited by members of Holy Family to live with Negro families in the Cabrini-Green public housing apartments. The fears of these white families for the safety of their children in Cabrini-Green were valid. But if where we lived was unsafe for their children, it was also unsafe for our children. When our invitations were refused, the Friendly Town program almost failed because some of our families became very angry. Nevertheless, we saw this as an opportunity to confront them with the truth of the reality in which we lived. The concern for the safety of these white children was legitimate insofar as everyone acknowledged that its reality was influenced by latent racial fears as well as the ever-present reality of violence in Cabrini-Green. Most members of our congregation continued their participation in the Friendly Town program. And not only did the program survive, but it also thrived, serving as a conduit to relocate some members of our congregation who desperately needed to leave Cabrini-Green. Two families of the congregation moved into the smaller cities of Iowa and some to Minneapolis.

Our congregation's partnership with the Lutheran Church—Missouri Synod in the Prince of Peace Volunteers (POPV) was, in many ways, avant garde. Volunteers consisted of white college students from Valparaiso University in Indiana. The director was Rev. Walter (Walt) Reiner, chaplain at Valparaiso. The program was developed by Chaplain Reiner, Pastor Downing, and our church council. It provided white students with an opportunity to discover what life was like for economically and racially oppressed Negroes in Cabrini-Green. The students lived in housing provided by the Chicago Public Housing Authority, although some chose to live with families in our congregation. They participated in worship, youth activities, and supervised church administration, engaging in discussions of their experiences with members of the congregation. They attended council and congregation meetings as observers. It was an excellent educational experience of urban immersion for the students. But it was far more than that; it was an experiment in building racial awareness and communication with a missional mandate. Another, albeit short-lived, program of the congregation brought young white people from suburban or small-town Lutheran congregations to Holy Family so they could learn how to become "Listening Witnesses," for their own communities. Because of the brevity of the program, I can only remember one thing: Pastor Downing sent them all back home, saying, "Maybe they were listening, but they were certainly not witnessing!" I can only assume that he meant they were not giving witness to their home congregations about their learning experiences in our neighborhood or about Holy Family Lutheran Church's ministry. Our congregation was also involved in sending members out as "Ambassadors of Christ" to local, suburban, and out-of-town white congregations, conducting "telling it like it is" forums. Our forum panel members spoke personally of their racial experiences and feelings of hopelessness living in Cabrini-Green. Questions and dialogue took place following our presentations. Both white and black members of Holy Family's congregation collaborated in the dialogue. There are many stories I could tell relative to this program, but none more significant than the one I participated in at a Sioux Falls, South Dakota, church. This was not only my first participation in a forum, but it was also my first airplane trip. Our forum presentation was followed by a potluck luncheon where we could sit and interact with anyone who might want to discuss something said in the forum or raise unanswered questions. During lunch I had a conversation with an elderly white woman who wanted to talk about the problems of interracial marriage. I don't ever remember talking about my family's background, but for some reason I spoke of my biological father as, using the words of my grandmother, an "old white Dutchman" whom I had never known. Hearing this, the elderly lady, without thinking, blurted out, "I knew there was something good about you!" Immediately, I responded, "This says a whole lot about my black mother, doesn't it?" The elderly lady apologized, saying her response revealed something about herself that she had never realized.

My Aunt Rebecca was in her mid-eighties when her sister Ursula Fleming-Bently died in 1966. Shortly after her death, Rebecca was terrorized and robbed during a home invasion.

CHAPTER 7

Theological Education

1967–1969

After living in the Cabrini-Green projects for four years we moved back to the West Side into our former apartment at 3617 West Grenshaw Street. The apartment had been restored to its original size. We lived there for the next two years, retaining our membership in Holy Family Church and attending weekly worship services. I was working at the Hines Veteran's Administration Supply Depot when Dr. Martin Luther King Jr. was assassinated in April 1968. Numerous employee radios warned of city-wide riots, fires, and looting. The governor had given emergency orders to deploy the Illinois National Guard into various areas of the city. Our supervisors suggested that whites living in the suburbs leave for home or remain at work because of wide-spread sniper fire and city streets being shut down by police and National Guard units. Seeing dark smoke on the eastern horizon in the direction of my home, I became concerned for my family and decided to leave work. The only exit open was one hospital gate, and before I could leave a young black man approached me, asking for a ride. He explained that he was a patient who had just been discharged, and none of the buses from the hospital were running because of riots in the city. I told him to get in but that I was only driving to the West Side and would have to drop him off on Roosevelt Road. I was so preoccupied about the safety of my family that I don't remember any of our conversation. After arriving on the West Side I dropped the young man off near our home. As he left I noticed large crowds beginning to gather around the shops in the business section of our neighborhood. When I arrived home, Doris and the children were glad to see me, just as I was to see them all safe. Concerned about the possibility of fires reaching our building, I told Doris I was going back out on Roosevelt Road to see what was happening. The look in her eyes expressed her concern for my safety; she did not want me to leave. When I arrived, a large crowd of young people had gathered at the corner and was stretching and pulling a metal security gate away from the front of a liquor store. I watched as they begin looting the store. As I continued watching, three young black men left the crowd and walked toward me. When they came near, another young black man jumped out in front of them, saying, "He's alright, he's with me!" It was the same young black man to whom I had given a ride from the Veteran's Hospital!

The strange thing about the Chicago riots was that there were no emergency vehicles or police anywhere. Mayor Richard M. Daley had kept police out of our neighborhoods and stopped all traffic in our area from going into white neighborhoods. All I could hear was the deafening, frightening noise of breaking glass amid shouts and cussing from crowds of young people who completely had surrounded local businesses. Seeing huge crowds looting the stores, one of our local businessmen hired armed, black, private-security guards to protect his grocery store. There was a tension-filled stand-off between crowds of looters and the security guards who, armed with rifles and shotguns, had encircled the entire store. A number of looters were engaged in small talk with some of the guards. They never threatened the store in any way. The entire scene was surrealistic, looking more like a war zone than my neighborhood. Suddenly, realizing that I was in danger, I returned home; Doris was worried and still angry at me for leaving. She had not been able to get in touch with any family members because our telephone line was dead. After hearing that there were no fires, only looting of stores, she calmed down and decided to continue cooking the fish she was preparing for our dinner. As we ate, Doris and I saw the fear in the faces of our children. We had turned the radio off, but hearing the shrill sounds of sirens we turned it back on to get updates. We heard that the rioting was increasing throughout the city. The wails of sirens were now closer to our home, and we soon discovered that they came from fire trucks. We continued eating our dinner but heard the sound of gunfire and saw smoke coming from the direction of Roosevelt Road. Realizing that the riots were escalating, I Ignored Doris's pleas to stay home and went back to Roosevelt Road to see if we were threatened by the fire. The crowds were larger, and the noise was deafening with sort of a buzzing sound. I heard sporadic gunfire and saw smoke coming from several businesses, including our local pharmacy. Hurrying back home, I told Doris that it was time to pack a few things, put them in our car, and leave. Seeing the urgency on my face and hearing the tone of my voice, our children became visibly shaken and began crying. Keith was so frightened, his little body began shaking like a leaf. A number of young people living next door came running from the direction of Roosevelt Road carrying television sets and other looted items into their homes. This became a teachable moment for our children; we told them that this was not the right thing to do and that the parents of those young people should not have allowed them to loot and bring stolen property into their home.

The only barrier separating us from the fires was an alley in the back of our home. Wind-blown, glowing red embers and sparks began to land on our roof, back porch, and garage. We were all frightened, but Doris and I went out and helped our landlady, Clementine Irwin, soak her garage roof and back porch with water from a garden hose to keep her home from catching fire. As the glowing embers grew thicker, we tried to talk her into coming with us or go elsewhere. She had no way of communicating with her family or the fire department because of dead telephone lines, and she refused to leave home. We had no choice so we left, worried about having to leave her alone. I drove off toward the home of my sister Lenora, who was still living in the North Side Cabrini-Green apartments. My decision to go to Cabrini-Green was based on the assumption we would be safer there because it is more difficult to burn down concrete buildings. However, we found the highway entrance leading to the North Side blocked off with armored vehicles by the Illinois National Guard. So with the smell of thick smoke hanging in the air, hearing gunshots and shrill sirens, we headed toward the home of Doris's family's on Monroe Street. We arrived to discover fires in their neighborhood were the same as ours. It seemed as though the rioting, fires, and looting were aimed at neighborhood businesses and not residential areas.

This sounds crazy, but I wasn't afraid, so once again I did something not too smart. I walked over to Madison Street to see what was happening.

But this time my brother-in-law, Ernest McShan, went with me. When we arrived on Madison Avenue we saw block after block of business buildings in flames. Standing and sometimes sitting on the sidewalk watching, Ernest and I saw black firemen spraying water everywhere in an attempt to put out the fires. There were no white firemen because the fires were only in black neighborhoods, and white firemen would have been in danger of being shot by snipers. As I looked at a black fireman, a loud gas line exploded in a building he had just left, causing it to go up in flames. I spoke to him, "You haven't finished putting out the fire in that building." If it hadn't been so sad, his response would have been almost comical: "There's no way we can put out all these fires. We just go from fire to fire spraying a little water here and a little water there, trying to keep the fire from spreading."

Satisfied, for the moment, that we were safe and none of the fires were threatening our families, Ernest and I left. Upon returning home we found the lights out and no electricity. Later, my sister Lenora told us that we would not have been any safer on the North Side because there were more random sniper shootings than on the West Side. In fact, she said they had to lie down on the floor because shots from an automatic weapon had been fired in the direction of her tenth-floor apartment.

Following the Chicago riots and with civil rights marches taking place in the South, the national office of the American Lutheran Church made a decision to become more involved in what was happening in our society. In fact, they initiated a national program, without any black or other minority input, called "Project Summer Hope." This program was designed to last for only one year, with hopes of eliminating white institutional racism. The church's well-intentioned but lamentable response to the criticism of having no black input in the program was that they were unable to find "qualified black professionals." But we've been professional blacks all our lives! The church was simply echoing the mantra of a racist society that "We can't find any qualified blacks." Dr. Martin Luther King Jr. was a qualified foot soldier of God, obeying his Commander-in-Chief to march to a different drum beat—non-violence. His weapon was the Word of God, not guns. Dr. King reflected the light of Jesus Christ by confronting America with its racial sin. The truth of his words quenched the fiery darts of despair giving hope to a weary people—blacks and whites! The truth of his words deeply affected my life in the decision I made to enroll in seminary. My desire to become a Lutheran pastor was clearly defined as I recalled Jesus' vision, beckoning me to "follow him." I knew it would be as a pastor that I would also become a foot soldier for the Lord, God.

One day while having a conversation with Pastor Downing, I casually spoke of being interested in becoming a minister but had family responsibilities and was too old to enroll in a seminary. I never mentioned anything about the vision I had of Jesus, but I told him: "I can't afford the cost of a seminary education, and I have to take care of my family responsibilities. I tried working two jobs while in college and that was too much."

Pastor Downing quickly responded saying, "I don't think you're too old. When I enrolled in seminary I was older than most of the other students." Further conversations helped me to clarify what was needed for me to become a Lutheran minister. Seminary requirements and tuition were discussed, but my first priority was family stability. Pastor Downing began helping me navigate the American Lutheran Church system and partner with suburban white congregations for financial support. I shared my plans with the church council seeking their feedback, approval and support. Their major concerns were transparency and the national church's commitment to structure a realistic financial package for my family expenses and seminary tuition. After prayerful consideration Holy Family congregation approved my seminary enrollment. Continuing financial arrangements and seminary degree requirements would be worked out in partnerships with other congregations, the national American Lutheran Church organization, the Lutheran School of Theology at Chicago, and eventually Wartburg Theological Seminary in Dubuque, Iowa.

We assured Holy Family's church council that they would receive continuous updates on our progress. Following a series of congregational meetings and conversations with partnership churches, our church council gave its unanimous approval for me to move ahead with plans to enroll in the seminary. However, we realized a pressing need and important key to our plan was to be consistent in our rhetoric of black empowerment and responsibility for everything affecting our lives.

Therefore we invited other black, ordained Lutheran clergy, regardless of their synod affiliation, to meet with us so we could seek their wisdom and gain their approval and support. Perhaps this was the most significant move we could have made to unite in black solidarity as well as learn from their experiences as ordained Lutheran clergy in a predominantly white church. While it is true there is only one church, neither white nor black, at that time it was necessary for us to make this distinction.

Sister Kathleen Ehlert, a Lutheran Church–Missouri Synod deaconess who was serving on the church staff at Holy Family, was so excited and exuberant over the council's approval of my decision to enter the seminary that she spilled the beans to Doris, telling her the news before I could. It was devastating news for Doris to hear that I had made a decision without her that would cause dramatic changes in our family. It was normal for us to discuss and share family concerns. I felt terribly guilty and did not intentionally betray her, but in my own excitement I strayed from the model of respect and sharing that had always been in our marriage.

Doris immediately asked to meet alone with Pastor Downing. This is when I discovered that she was feeling more than anger at being left out of my decision to enroll in seminary. She had a lot of unanswered questions about how the children would be affected and her new role as a pastor's wife. She had not been given an opportunity to share her concerns, fears and misgivings as a young black mother and wife. In retrospect, without Doris's questions we would not have made it to where we are today. Indeed, this was a *kairos* moment for us as a family. As the female head of our family, she challenged my unilateral decision, and her concerns are best articulated in a college class paper she wrote:

> ME—A MINISTER'S WIFE? After fifteen years of marriage and six children, my husband decided to return to school and become a minister. This meant giving up his good paying job as a computer programmer. He had worked hard and taken a cut in salary to get into this particular field of work. The idea of returning to school full time was absurd. Where would we get the money to pay the bills and tuition for school? There was no way I wanted to be a minister's wife! I was quite content with my life as a housewife and mother.

I didn't want to become involved in the church; I preferred my privacy. I couldn't imagine being the wife of a minister, especially in the white Lutheran Church. It seemed as though all ministers' wives had a college education and either played the piano and organ or directed the choir. I had none of these qualifications and no desire to acquire them. These negative emotions began while living in Chicago, Illinois. My family and I were members of Holy Family Lutheran Church, where my husband served as Vicar-Intern. The treasurer of the church once said, "Now that you are going to be a minister's wife we should send you to music school." Another member stated, "Since Lonnie is going to be a minister, you'll have to share him with others. You've had him all to yourself for sixteen years." Opinions such as these made me feel insecure and I hated the idea more; I even disliked the people who made such statements.

In 1967, my husband enrolled in the Lutheran School of Theology at Chicago. Arrangements had been made through the American Lutheran Church for seminary tuition, and a "Black Clergy" fund was set up, which was used for household finances and was equivalent to his normal salary. This was one worry off my mind; however, there was still the fight within myself of not wanting to be a minister's wife. The devil was really working on me! I even contemplated divorce. When Lonnie wasn't around, I would often cry myself to sleep. I prayed and even cursed about putting up such a strong defense over something I seemed to have no control over. I was a frightened and miserable woman. I talked to family and friends about my situation. All of them expressed the same feelings: "Support your husband and don't be so selfish." As Lonnie became more involved in his seminary studies, I felt lonely and threatened, unimportant and less needed in his life. I was more disenchanted with the idea of being a minister's wife than ever. If I had not been employed in a part-time job, I think I would've had a nervous breakdown. My husband didn't realize I was so much against his decision until I became ill with a stomach ulcer. It was at this point that I was able to convey my true feelings. He assured me everything would be alright and to have a little faith. I apologized to him for not being open and said he should continue his studies because not only did I believe he had a "true calling" from God to become a minister, but there were so many other people from different congregations supporting him. Now that my feelings were out in the open, I could try harder to cope with my feelings of inadequacy and insecurity. My next alternative was to talk to our pastor, Rev. Fred J. Downing. He gave me some sound advice when he said, "Doris, you are the mother of six beautiful children; and they are your first priority. Take care of them. Get involved only where you want to be. Don't try to be someone you're not; just be Doris." This was music to my ears! At times I would feel okay, but then the feelings of insecurity and inadequacy would emerge once again. I felt like Dr. Jekyll and Mr. Hyde. Living in housing at the Lutheran School of Theology didn't help matters. We were a full-fledged family of eight, and in our immediate surroundings were families of husband and wife with one or two children, and of course, these were college graduates. Whenever seminary students and spouses met socially or politically all I would hear about was "at Dana College we did this or at Augsburg College this happened." Because I had no college education, I was really uncomfortable. I participated in these meetings only once in awhile; other times I would use my children as excuses for not attending.

It wasn't until August of 1970, when we moved to Dubuque, Iowa, and my husband matriculated into Wartburg Theological Seminary for his final year of study, did I begin to feel better about becoming a minister's wife. There we lived in an atmosphere of older couples like ourselves, who had children closer to the ages of our children. This made the move more acceptable by all. There were about nine older couples, and sometimes we had family get-togethers. These students talked more about their families and what they did for a living before coming to the seminary. I felt more at ease with this group of students.

May 17, 1971, was a very special day for my husband and me. He graduated from Wartburg Theological Seminary, qualified to be called and ordained as a minister in the American Lutheran Church, and I graduated from being a selfish, private, insecure person to an outgoing, understanding, and patient minister's wife. I learned to accept myself as I and as God wanted me to be! Our first parish was in Houston, Texas. This was a testing ground for Lonnie as a minister and me as a minister's wife. It wasn't as bad as I had imagined. I did what I enjoyed doing; I taught Sunday school. No one expected more. My husband currently serves as co-pastor at Prince of Glory Lutheran Church on the near-north side of Minneapolis. After ten years of being a minister's wife, I still cannot play the piano or organ nor do I direct a choir, but I continue to teach Sunday school. I am very comfortable with my involvement at Prince of Glory because I do the things I desire to do, not necessarily the things a minister's wife should do.

Since these early questions and struggles, Doris has realized that God's plans for her life were as unique and valued as those of any other pastor's wife. She did not have to fit in; she was already in! Our family was in God's loving hands, and all our needs were met.

In 1967, a pre-seminary strategy planning committee convened at Holy Family Lutheran Church. Black ordained Lutheran clergymen met with us to share their wisdom, and approval for my enrollment in seminary at the Lutheran School of Theology at Chicago. Pastor Downing had contacted these ministers and initiated conversations with the Lutheran School of Theology about my desire to attend seminary. Pastor Downing did not participate in my meeting with the black pastors. I was really nervous, even a little afraid, of what might happen at this meeting because I needed their acceptance and support to enroll in seminary. I saw myself as a rank-and-file servant of the Lord in the presence of men who outranked me in status, education, and pastoral experience. Although black, they were strangers I had never met, with no idea of what questions might be raised. However, I knew God was with us because I was firm about my calling and determined not to have any extraneous preconditions or arrangements detrimental to our family structure. Those attending the meeting were the Rev. Dr. Nelson Trout, dean of the Black Pastors Consortium of the American Lutheran Church (ALC), who later became the first ALC/ELCA black bishop of the Southern California Synod, and the Rev. Robbin W. Skyles, dean of the South Chicago Land District of the Lutheran Church in America (LCA). Our discussions targeted potential roadblocks to my ordination and specific academic degree support for ordination by the American Lutheran Church and the Lutheran School of Theology at Chicago (LSTC). We attempted to address as best we could the socio-economic, political, and ecclesiastical dynamics involved in our new approach to a degree and ordination.

The first priority was to discuss financial security for my family until my seminary education was complete. There was also concern about me not having a college degree and the suggestion that I enroll in college for two years to get a B.A. degree before enrolling in seminary. This was a legitimate concern because of how a theological degree may be viewed by some, limiting my opportunities and effectiveness in ministry. We expected my lack of a college degree would severely limit my calls to white Lutheran churches. It was also felt that not having a college degree would be even less acceptable to some blacks, "who sometimes overly valued educational degrees." My response was, "I'm not so naïve as to not expect this kind of rejection in choosing to enter the seminary without a college degree, but I trust God's love, wisdom, guidance, and strength to complete whatever mission He has given me." I explained, "At my age, the time is now for me to be ordained as a Lutheran pastor, which precludes completing two more years of college before enrolling in seminary."

In retrospect, my decision had been made prior to our meeting because God had given me the confidence and self-esteem to pursue my call to ministry. These black pastors were determined that under no circumstances should I allow myself to be enrolled as a special student. Their experiences as black pastors of congregations in the Lutheran church validated their concerns. Approving my decision to enroll in seminary without a college degree, these pastors insisted that my seminary classes/studies should be the same as those of any white student seeking a Master of Divinity degree. For clarity of purpose and agreement, the black pastors met with LSTC seminary administrators and faculty, and they were assured that "when Lonnie successfully completes curriculum requirements of a Master of Divinity program, he will receive the degree as any other seminary student."

Finally, our discussion turned to answering the question of how to acquire adequate financial commitments from the ALC Illinois District and the national American Lutheran Church. I had resigned my job as a GS-9 IBM 360 computer programmer at the Hines V.A. Hospital and enrolled as a full-time seminary student. The black Lutheran clergy were unanimous in their support of maintaining the same level of income for my family while in the seminary as when working at the Veterans Administration. The following resolution was unanimously approved: "As the American Lutheran Church has expressed a sincere desire and need for more Black Lutheran Clergy in the American Lutheran Church, both the Illinois District and the National American Lutheran Church should establish a designated financial support package for the theological education of any Black candidate desiring to become a Lutheran Pastor- —and that we coordinate our support through the Division for Service and Mission in America (DSMA)."

Some white Lutheran congregations had already pledged financial support, and in the spirit of good stewardship and ecclesiastical decorum it was incumbent upon us to seek approval by the national American Lutheran Church. The resolution was amended stipulating: "All initiatives for raising funds should be a cooperative effort coordinated by the Division for Service and Mission in America of the National Church and the ALC Illinois District to invest in theological education and training for all black Lutheran seminary students." To maintain momentum, give direction, and nail down specifics, the black pastors strongly suggested we present their resolution at the Illinois District convention, which if approved would establish a black Lutheran student seminary scholarship and grant fund to support black students enrolled in Lutheran seminaries. The black clergy further stated that there should be a continuing resolution amendment requesting endorsement and financial support by the national American Lutheran Church in Minneapolis.

Later, when presented at the Illinois District convention, an attempt was made to add another amendment to our resolution restricting its financial support as "one time only" and renaming it the "Lonnie Branch Seminary Education Fund." I immediately opposed the amendment requesting that my name be removed as it would only provide financial assistance for one black seminary student, thereby defeating the original intent of the resolution to address the need for more black pastors in the church. After a lively and heated debate, our original resolution was approved without being amended. It was entitled the "ALC, Illinois District Black Students' Seminary Scholarship and Grant Fund." Another separate resolution was approved directing the ALC Illinois District Metropolitan Ministries Committee to restructure its existing membership to include black members of congregations to formulate recruitment guidelines, solicit financial contributions, and disburse monies for black student seminary scholarships and grants. Contributions sent to Holy Family Lutheran Church by other congregations for my personal seminary education would now be sent to the Illinois District Metropolitan Ministry Committee. This committee was responsible for securing funds to assist and support black Lutheran seminary students in their theological education. The committee would provide financial support for my seminary education and all black students enrolling in a Lutheran seminary. The ALC Illinois District and national American Lutheran Church had now become partners in mission for my theological education and that of all potential black seminary students. Holy Family Church had successfully pioneered a financial structure to assist black seminarians, approved and memorialized by the ALC Illinois District convention. Additionally, I also received a small stipend from the Division for Service and Mission in America to work as vicar-intern at Holy Family Lutheran Church. Aware of my own fears, weaknesses, and short-comings, I thanked God for preparing the way for me to enroll in seminary.

While living on the West Side at 3617 West Grenshaw Street I resigned my job at the Veteran's Administration and enrolled in the Lutheran School of Theology in the spring of 1967. Prior to enrollment, like all students seeking degrees, I was required to take several preliminary entrance examinations and complete Greek and Hebrew classes. Most of the white students completed their Greek requirement in college and only needed to take a Hebrew class while in the seminary. I had completed neither language requirement and so I enrolled in both Greek and Hebrew classes in the spring and summer semesters of 1967-1968. I successfully completed both before regular classes began in the fall. I was blessed to have an unusual opportunity to be tutored in Greek by the Rev. Charles J. Christensen, an ordained ALC minister who was also a member of Holy Family Lutheran Church. During one of my tutoring sessions, he was so tough on me that I wept. He apologized, explaining, "I yelled at you because I want you to meet the language qualification for seminary enrollment and know Greek as well as any white student." Although he had completed his own class requirement of Hebrew in seminary, Pastor Christensen did not think he was knowledgeable enough to tutor me. So I had to learn Hebrew on my own. I have no idea why, but it was easier than Greek, and, surprisingly, I received a higher grade.

During the spring of 1967 I decided it would be a smart move to complete one of my degree requirements by enrolling for three months of clinical pastoral education at Lutheran General Hospital in Park Ridge. Being out of college for fifteen years, the C.P.E. program provided me an opportunity to reorient myself into an educational environment. With approval by the Lutheran School of Theology, I enrolled as a clinical pastoral education student at the Lutheran General hospital. Because of its suburban location, the only black or other racial minority patients in the hospital were construction workers living outside the community or automobile accident victims brought in from nearby highways. These three months were difficult because of daily roundtrip commutes to the hospital and night emergency calls, when I had to return to the hospital. Nevertheless, it was a new opportunity to learn about hospital care from staff, patients, and families and complete one of my seminary requirements. There were six students or chaplains in our group—four Lutherans and two young Catholic novice priests. Rev. Arthur Ree, an ordained Lutheran minister, was our clinical pastoral education supervisor. He paired us into groups of two and assigned us to different floors, sections, or units of the hospital. The "on call" chaplain covered the evening and night emergency room (trauma center). I was paired with one of the Catholic chaplains and assigned to the hospital's oncology unit, occupied by patients with cancer or other tumors. We had the privilege of looking at patient medical charts, giving us background information as how to best provide pastoral care. Being the only black student in our class did not give me many choices in patient selection by race or religious denomination—everyone was white. However, I was really happy to find that I was not the oldest student. Rev. Paul Yjelle, an ordained Lutheran pastor, was older than I was, and during our three months together we became close friends.

I had two very significant experiences at Lutheran General Hospital. The first involved discussion of a written verbatim by two of our student Catholic chaplains; they had collaborated in writing a single verbatim on one of their patients. Verbatims are written reports of patient visits, required for critical analysis and group discussion. All visits were written from memory. The student priests may have received a request from the female patient because she was Catholic. After sharing their verbatim with us, we were asked to respond to a question asked by the patient: "Why has God allowed my breast cancer to return? Why, why me? The cancer wasn't supposed to return after five years. It's been over five years, and now it's back!" The novice priests said they had been unable to give her a satisfactory answer, and after some discussion, none of us seemed to have an answer. As the woman had already been visited by both priests, I asked if they thought another visit might help and, if so, could I visit with her? Even now, as I remember this incident, I have no idea why I wanted to make that visit. *I had no answer to her question.* As every chaplaincy visit required a written verbatim, I promised to bring a verbatim to our next meeting.

During my visit, the patient asked me the same question, and I haven't the slightest idea why I responded the way I did. I simply said, "Why not you? Are you implying that there's someone else who deserves to have this cancer more than you do? Should a member of your family have it, or some other person?" She began to cry, and I felt sorry for my remarks. I felt sure this was the end of my seminary career. After asking permission to make the visit, I had screwed up and not handled it in a professional manner, and may have worsened the healing process for the patient. Now I was afraid to keep my promise to write a verbatim and even less desirous of sharing it in a discussion with my classmates. The visit ended with a reading from the Lutheran *Occasional Services* book and prayer. Before leaving, she thanked me and asked if I would visit her again. Gathering enough courage I wrote a verbatim of the visit and shared it with the other chaplains. Both priests said that on a follow-up visit the woman told them about my visit and had a more positive attitude about the return of her cancer. God is good all the time—even when you feel that you have fumbled the ball and see yourself as a professional failure.

Before completing my final quarter of clinical pastoral education there was another extraordinary spiritual occurrence. A distraught and angry doctor in our oncology unit attended one of our weekly nurses' information and support group meetings. He requested our assistance in helping one of his patients, a middle-aged woman. He just had informed her that her cancer had metastasized (spread) to other parts of her body and that she was dying. After being told about her condition, she had become withdrawn with severe depression and was possibly suicidal. She and her husband were members of an Assemblies of God church. Earlier they decided to go without medical treatment and pursue a discipline of healing prayer. Because there had been no medical treatment, the cancer had metastasized. The doctor was angry at her church's approach to medical care. I did not know anything about the Assemblies of God. After venting his frustrations and anger, he asked for help from both of us chaplains assigned to the unit. Perhaps out of respect for me as a Protestant, the Catholic chaplain asked if I would make the visit. Immediately following our nurses' support group meeting, I visited the patient.

The patient's name was Shirley, and her husband was Geoffrey. Although Geoffrey had been there when the doctor gave his hopeless prognosis, by the time I reached Shirley's room he had gone and the door was closed. I lightly tapped on the door until I finally heard a soft voice asking me to come in. Upon entering, I was surprised to see the window blinds closed and the room in semi-darkness. I was really scared. Actually, I felt like leaving the room and returning to my office because

I had never conversed with anyone about their impending death. I really wanted to help Shirley, but I did not know if I had anything new to offer. The doctor had mentioned that he had prayed with her and, perhaps, this was where I could begin. Even though I had experienced the healing power of prayer in my own life, I had no idea of Shirley's religious beliefs or if she had been visited by her own pastor. I almost panicked while struggling for answers as to how I might best show God's love in this particular situation. I vaguely remember leaving the door ajar in the semi-dark room and moving quietly along the wall to meet Shirley as she slowly moved towards me. She had been crying and apparently was just closing the window blinds when I came in. I introduced myself and apologized for not getting there in time to meet her husband.

I let her know of my conversation with the doctor. Shirley said that she understood his anger at being limited by their religious beliefs in providing medical care. I responded, "I'm certain that he felt helpless and so do I. I have no idea of who the Assemblies of God are or if your pastor would want me to be here. I understand your doctor had prayers with you and your family. We all deeply care about what you're going through." Shirley assured me that I wasn't intruding and she wasn't suicidal. It seemed as though all my unspoken questions were answered by the prayers in my heart. In fact Shirley calmed down and, in her soft voice, began sharing her feelings with me, including personal beliefs about her family and church. Somehow we connected and for the remaining three months of my clinical pastoral classes I made regular visitations. My supervisor was aware of these visits with Shirley and consistently asked for a verbatim to discuss in our group sessions. I was just as consistent in making excuses, promising to present this particular verbatim before the end of the quarter. However, I did continue writing and presenting class verbatims of other patient visits. Realizing that I had deeply connected with Shirley, the nurses on our oncology unit encouraged me to continue visiting. Shirley rarely talked about her illness only her family life. Actually we became friends, and I didn't try to analyze or evaluate how she was handling her impending death. Our friendship became more important than her illness, and we learned more about our commonality in the importance of family life. With a big smile, she fondly spoke of her Scottish background and how she had left Canada to live in the United States. She and her husband had one married son, in the U.S. Air Force, stationed at a base in Germany.

One day, as I was about to visit Shirley, I heard loud incoherent sounds coming from Shirley's room. I stopped at her door before entering her room. Noticing the door was slightly ajar I slowly pushed it open while softly tapping on it. Shirley was sitting on the edge of her bed and her husband was kneeling on the floor. This was the third time in my life that I had heard similar sounds and as he profusely wept he spoke in words that I could not understand. I knew he was praying in tongues. Feeling that I was intruding, I closed the door as quietly as I could and remained in the hospital hallway until the door to Shirley's room slowly opened. Shirley's husband, Geoffrey, explained that Shirley had told him about our visits and that he hoped I would continue them. He told me that he was praying and hoped I did not think he was crazy. I told him that I had been with others who prayed in tongues and did not think he was crazy. I let him know that I hadn't understood his prayers but assured him that God did, and that was more important.

Although Shirley's condition appeared to remain constant, her doctor said that the time of her death was drawing near. Geoffrey's visits became more frequent. I always gave them their private space but had noticed Geoffrey's lack of touching or embracing Shirley. I believe his grief was so painful that all he could do was pray and leave after briefly visiting her. One day after hearing Geoffrey pray in tongues I asked to speak with him alone. Standing outside in the hallway I said, "Geoffrey, I've never seen you embrace Shirley or heard you tell her how much you love her but maybe I haven't been present when you did. Shirley knows that you and God love her, but praying in tongues is only one part of her need. She's still alive and needs your love expressed in hugs and kisses now! God is with you both, and I believe the beginning of an answer to your prayers is to physically show your love to one another." Geoffrey seemed startled and was visibly shaken by my remarks. He gathered himself, thanked me for sharing my observations, and said he would give a lot of thought and prayer to what I said.

Evidently he did, because the next visit I made to see Shirley, Geoffrey was already in the room hugging, kissing, and crying with Shirley in his arms. She definitely heard, understood, and felt his love for her. I immediately left before they could see me. When I saw Geoffrey again, he thanked me, saying, "I hadn't realized that hugging as well as touching was such a powerful part of healing, not only for Shirley but for me as well. Now I know that when I pray in tongues I can also embrace my wife and tell her how much I love her." Once again I had taken a risk of caring for another human being with the possibility of adverse repercussions, but God was there to help us all. I decided there was no further need for regular visits with Shirley or Geoffrey because they had their own pastor. However, I did ask the nurses in my unit to keep me informed of her progress and when I might be of help.

One morning at 2:00 a.m. I received a call from the hospital informing me that Shirley was dying and that Geoffrey, their son and daughter-in-law were there from Germany. Geoffrey had asked for me to come, and I was told that I needed to arrive in the next hour or so. I hastily dressed and drove to the hospital. Geoffrey greeted me as I entered the room and thanked me for coming, then introduced me to his son and daughter-in-law. Their pastor was not there, so I invited them to join me in prayer. After prayer, I glanced toward Shirley and saw the nurse who had escorted me into the room was now placing a cool, wet cloth on her head. She held Shirley's hand, speaking slowly and softly, informing her who was there with her. Shirley was breathing slowly, not struggling; in fact, she appeared to be rather comfortable. Other than a blood pressure monitor on her arm, there was no other medical apparatus or IVs attached to Shirley's body. Six of us were in the room, and I was the only clergy present. This was my first experience at the death of someone other than in my own family. Waiting for Shirley to die was an eerie and scary experience, and I felt totally unprepared and helpless. I didn't want Shirley to die, but I couldn't keep her from dying. I had prayed; what else could I do? As her condition deteriorated, Shirley's breathing became harder. When she gasped for breath, I panicked and slowly retreated, finding a little comfort by leaning against a wall on the other side of the room. I was embarrassed and had hoped that no one saw me retreat to the other side of the room. But as God would have it, when I left Shirley's bedside her family and the nurses moved closer, speaking softly to Shirley, assuring her of their presence. Every eye was filled with tears and I began weeping. I was shocked when she suddenly looked directly at me, asking, "What are you looking at?"

Of all people, I thought she would have been the least likely person to see me leave her bedside. But I didn't have a chance to answer her because the others asked me to return to her bedside and do something—that's all they said: "Do something!" Although crying profusely I read the Twenty-third Psalm. As I ended the reading, Shirley died. God is good. I prayed again, and, with tears flowing from all our eyes, we hugged and said our goodbyes.

Later the nursing staff support group met for a debriefing session. I didn't want to attend the meeting because I was embarrassed about what happened in Shirley's room. All I could think about was my weaknesses. However, I received warm accolades and the sweet music of thanks from the nurses. They said: "We've never seen a chaplain crying at the death of patient, with the patient requesting he return to her bedside." The head nurse of the unit said, "From time to time we are assigned to less stressful units because of the constant pressure and the toll it takes on all of us. It's been good to work with you." God is good, all the time! Yes, I truly needed encouragement and was strengthened to continue my seminary odyssey.

Shortly after Shirley's death I met with her husband, who began crying as he hugged and thanked me again for being there for him and the family. He gave me a small plaque that had hung on the wall of Shirley's room, saying: "She really loved this plaque and I know she would want you to have it." I was also given a personal gift, a large Jerusalem Bible. Later Geoffrey sent me a truly inspirational letter expressing the thanks of his son and wife, hoping to somehow stay in touch. I wrote my last class verbatim on one of my many visits with Shirley, but I never wrote about my last visit with her.

In the fall of 1967, following completion of clinical pastoral education, our family moved into seminary student housing at 5436 South Woodlawn Avenue. My brothers and members of Holy Family Church helped with the move. Doris continued to work as a part-time sales clerk at the Sears store on the West Side until the lengthy roundtrip commute became too much for us. Doris was a busy little bee, the "Energizer bunny," and soon began another part-time job near our home at a Par-Rexall Drugstore in the 53rd and Kimbark strip mall. All our children were in school except our youngest child, David. Both our mothers shared babysitting chores for David. The seminary was near my mother's home where I could go and share seminary experiences with her over coffee. Working as vicar-intern at Holy Family and seminary classes prevented me from having time to visit others in the family.

LSTC's recently constructed building was shared with a small number of white Roman Catholic students. We had around 250 students, including a few post-graduate students. When I enrolled there were five other American black students and a couple of African students. I was the oldest American black student in the seminary. Larry Stephen Emery and Thomas Minor were two of my closest black friends. Tom Minor, like me, had only two years of college credits but would later earn enough credits to receive his B.A. degree. Larry Emery was closer to my age and had graduated with a degree from the Chicago Teacher's College. One day after we both preached a videotaped sermon in our homiletics class and reviewed it, Larry said: "I didn't like my delivery as much as yours, Lonnie. You were much more sincere while I was acting and trying hard to impress our professor." I thought Larry's sermon delivery was much better than mine, and I particularly admired its biblical connections.

Another black student was a young ordained Baptist minister. He made it clear that his only reason for enrolling at the seminary was to earn his Master of Divinity degree. Another of the black students, Michael, was married to a young white woman named Sharon. Although we had a biracial couple at Holy Family Lutheran Church, experiencing another marriage in this context was an affirmation for me of human life moving forward in spite of racism. Seminary students seemed to accept and respect their relationship.

Soon after enrolling in the seminary, a white student shared with me his thoughts of committing suicide. I have no idea of why he chose me, other than that I was an older black student and a stranger whom he would probably never see again. He told me that he was depressed and could not sleep because he was not able to maintain a straight "A" grade. His parents had expected him to excel in his seminary education with an "A" in every class. For him, not measuring up to their expectations meant he was a failure that would bring shame on his family. I responded as a friend, trying to encourage him to see that life was far more important than measuring up to the standards and expectations of others, even if they happened to be family members. I was an average "C" student and told him that my age and family responsibilities made it extremely hard to get a higher grade. I shared my difficulty in studying after being out of college for fifteen years. Finally, I said, "For me, grades are not as important as learning," and I urged him to share our conversation with his counselor. This was a surprising, new experience because a white person never before had come to me for any kind of help. The more I thought about our conversation, the more I empathized with Doris who had to adapt to new environments, family relocations, and coping with what she thought a minister's wife should be.

My seminary counselor, Professor Robert Granskou, an ex-army paratrooper with a degree in social work, was an excellent advisor who guided me through curriculum requirements in the Master of Divinity program. He encouraged me in so many ways, especially in helping me see what I would be up against as a black Lutheran pastor. Professor Granskou may not have been black, but he knew a lot about what it was to be white and saw many difficulties confronting me as a black pastor. He had his own personal concerns about the enrollment of black seminary students and felt there were many unanswered questions which had not been adequately addressed. As he put it, "The Lutheran church is setting you black students up as martyrs!" It sounded as if he was saying that we were being set up as sacrificial lambs or perhaps even more demeaning, as failures and "token blacks"—nothing more than an experiment by the Lutheran church. Nevertheless, I stood by my decision to enroll in a white seminary, saying, "No one can set me up as a martyr. If I ever become a martyr, God will help me do whatever He has given me to do." Professor Granskou meant well and perhaps his comments were some kind of a test, but it was his use of the term "set up" that triggered my angry response.

Another significant experience occurred during my middler year when worshipping in the chapel. The 60s were a time of dissent and nonviolent civil rights protests. During a non-violent campus protest against the war in Vietnam at Kent State, thirteen students had been killed by the Ohio State National Guard. Immediately after the morning worship, brief prayers were offered memorializing the students who were killed. Within two weeks of the Ohio State killings, two students at Jackson State University, an all-black university in Mississippi, were killed by the Mississippi State National Guard while protesting racial segregation. During the service there was no mention of the two slain black students nor were any prayers and memorials said for them. When the benediction was said every black student stood, each of us addressing the lack of concern for the black students killed in Mississippi. We black students knew that we were free to initiate prayers or memorials, but we wanted to see the same initiative, concern, and sensitivity expressed for the victims at Jackson State as had been for those at Kent State. Some of the white students offered apologies, but it was a lack of apology from our chapel worship leader that led us black students to call for an immediate boycott of classes by the entire seminary student body. As these events were occurring two weeks prior to the end of our semester break, the entire student body had to vote to cancel classes and accept a "pass-fail" grade. The primarily white student body voted to boycott classes but stated that participation was voluntary and classes would not be continued as usual.

Following our vote, it was decided that we black students should be responsible for structuring a special two-week program focusing on changing the seminary curriculum to reflect a sensitivity and response to the civil rights of blacks. We were challenged to teach and sensitize white seminary students and faculty about the importance of black history and our continuous struggle for civil rights and racial equality. To accomplish these objectives we committed ourselves to planning meetings at least three times in one of our homes. Our first meeting was in the home of the biracial couple, Michael and his wife, Sharon. During our final strategy meeting, the only African student in the seminary, who had quietly participated with us, asked to pray about what we had planned. But someone shouted: "This isn't a time for prayer. It's a time for action!" I immediately responded, saying, "Prayer is action, and there's always need for prayer! We're seminary students and therefore role models, and we should never engage in any of God's business without prayer." Our African brother prayed, and we were truly blessed. In his quietness he had become the epitome of what a good listener should be. He understood and summarized our needs, included our white seminary brothers in the petition, and placed all our plans in God's hands. The prayer resulted in a willing, energetic, and cooperative spirit of mutual respect for the boycott leaders.

We used every available resource to accomplish our goals, soliciting volunteers and others from the surrounding black academic community and churches. Honoraria were provided by the seminary for most of the speakers; that helped us secure religious educators from the University of Chicago Theological School and indigenous organizations. Our goal was to develop a theological rationale in support of the civil rights movement reflected in our seminary community and curriculum. As part of our strategic planning, for maximum exposure and visibility, we notified the *Chicago Defender,* a black-owned newspaper as well as other black radio and television media to cover our two-week boycott. We used the seminary cafeteria as a place to make picket signs which drew the attention of white students who were eating their lunch. A number of them asked to help us make and carry picket signs, but their lack of sensitivity had hurt us so much that we denied their request. Everything we did was focused on racial sensitivity and promoting a black theological agenda for curriculum change. We thought our denial to the white seminarians request to help in our protest would be the end of the matter. But God is indeed good all the time! After we had walked around the seminary's perimeter several times with picket signs, some of the white students who were in the cafeteria came out, insisting we let them carry some of the protest signs. After being refused again, a number of white students began making their own signs, while others actually took the signs out of our hands and began walking with us. For me, this was truly a *kairos* moment. The white students began admitting their ignorance of civil rights issues, lack of concern, and insensitivity for racial justice. Indeed, confession is good for the soul, and we were glad to see their determination to walk with us in a racially inclusive seminary learning environment.

Our strategy to secure black professors and create seminary classes with historical black church theological contributions was successful. Structural change in seminary education became a reality in the final week when our protest ended with a worship service. The service was designed by our strategy group and filled with traditional black religious music with subliminal theological messages. We needed assistance from seminary faculty with Holy Communion, but our reconciliation strategy was in washing the feet of the faculty but not allowing them to wash our feet. What a surprise for our seminary professors! They pleaded with us to let them wash our feet. I could not bear listening to their pleas, and as I looked into the tear-filled eyes of one of my professors—a man I truly respected—I began weeping and was the first black student to break ranks, allowing him to wash my feet. There appeared to be no disunity as all the other black students quickly followed my example. The Lutheran School of Theology had never seen so many black faces inside its building. This was the only contact most black community leaders and residents had with the seminary. The minds, hearts, and doors of the seminary were opened, and more people of diverse racial and cultural backgrounds would be welcomed.

Prior to our final day of protest and concluding worship service, I invited Pastor Fred Downing from Holy Family Church to give his perspective on our congregation's theological application of Christ's missional mandate and its effect in Cabrini-Green. He connected our solidarity with the black civil rights protest as a prophetic call to the church and gave a condensed overview of Holy Family's ministry. He gave examples of how its mission approach had impacted evangelism in the Lutheran church. White seminary students were exuberant as they listened and surrounded him with applause. But when he began challenging them about the legitimacy of their call into ministry, the room suddenly became quiet. What angered them was when he said, "If you're only in seminary to avoid being drafted as soldiers for the Vietnam War, you should rethink whether you've truly been called by God." The silence was deafening, and you could hear the proverbial pin drop in the room. Finally a lot of angry responses spewed out of the mouths of many white students. No doubt there were some draft-dodgers in the crowd, and he had touched their last nerve by challenging their reason for enrolling in the seminary. They wanted to know what authority he had to confront and admonish them about their reasons for being in seminary. The students did not know that during the Korean War Pastor Downing had served as a sailor on one of the largest U.S. Navy aircraft carriers. In response to their angry questions he spoke softly, but in a distinct compelling voice, asking only that they take another look at why they were in seminary.

The events of these two weeks sparked my desire to write a paper for my Church and Society class focusing on the involvement, or lack thereof, of America's white Christian churches in the civil rights movement and their theological stance on slavery. My family experience in the black church was one of a biblical understanding of God's opposition to slavery and the oppression of others. Seeking information in the seminary library, I discovered that the Quakers were not only antislavery but had aided Harriet Tubman in using the Underground Freedom Railroad to help escaped slaves. I wondered why God had guided me into becoming a Lutheran instead of a Quaker, because during the abolitionist movement in America many white southern Lutheran masters owned slaves. Initially, *they opposed slavery but began to quietly adapt to it as the norm instead of the gospel of Jesus Christ.* I was deeply disappointed and disturbed to find little or no historical challenge to slavery and racism by the institutional Lutheran church. In fact, I almost gave up writing my class paper until I stumbled across an old worn and tattered document about the Frankean Synod Lutheran Church convention. It stated that in 1837 a group of Lutheran pastors in New York formed this new synod because of dissatisfaction with their church's position on the institution of slavery. They named their new synod in memory of August Hermann Francke and became known for their socially progressive views. *The Frankean synod was strongly abolitionist, pro-temperance, and pacifist.* In fact, this was the first synod to ordain a black Lutheran pastor, Daniel Payne, who later became a bishop of the African Methodist Episcopal Church (AME). Rev. Payne was born a free man in Charleston, South Carolina, of African, European, and Native American descent. He studied at the Lutheran Theological Seminary at Gettysburg in Pennsylvania but dropped out of school because of problems with his eyesight. Later, Rev. Payne became one of the founders and the first African-American president of a college in the United States, Wilberforce University in Ohio.

The African Methodist Episcopal (AME) Church was born when Negro church members protested the practice of segregated communion in their local congregations. Negroes and whites were not allowed to commune together. Whites came to the altar rail first to receive Holy Communion. Then Negroes, who because of segregation had to sit in the balcony, were served last. In protest against these racist rules, Negroes left the balcony and knelt beside their white brothers and sisters to receive Holy Communion. This resulted in white ushers yanking them up from their knees at the communion railing. Following this incident they left the Methodist Church and formed the AME Church. Rev. Payne's accomplishments had not come without protest and a determination to resist racism. Now my own determination had paid dividends because I had found a reason to remain in the Lutheran church. I presented my research paper, thinking that there probably were other students who may never have heard of the Frankean Lutheran Synod and its antislavery stand.

Holy Family's church council approved space in the church for the Black Panthers' breakfast program for children. This was another program of the congregation to support the children of our neighborhood. The first such program began as "The Free Breakfast for Children," which spread from a small Catholic church in the Fillmore District of San Francisco to many major cities in America. The impact of the breakfast program shamed the federal government into adopting similar programs for public schools across the country, even while the FBI assailed them as nothing more than a propaganda tool by the party to carry out its "Communist" agenda. There were all kinds of assaults against the party's social programs, from police raids who smashed eggs on the floors of churches they invaded, to free clinic supplies crushed underfoot and party newspapers destroyed. The party was denounced by the FBI as a group of Communist outlaws bent on overthrowing the U.S. government. Armed with that definition and the machinery of the federal government, J. Edgar Hoover director of the FBI, waged a campaign to eliminate the Black Panther Party. All of this culminated in the killing of Chicago party leader Fred Hampton. Allowing the Black Panthers to use our church for their breakfast program to feed children in Cabrini-Green had threatening repercussions. Pastor Downing and I had to physically block the church's front entrance doors to keep the Chicago police from disrupting the Black Panther's breakfast program.

The police made various attempts to get inside our church, using ploys like, "We heard that there's some kind of trouble here, and we'd like to come inside and see if everything is alright." They were denied permission to enter without a search warrant. We assured them that everything was fine and invited them to come back and worship with us on Sunday morning. Historically, the church has been honored as a place of asylum or "sanctuary," where immunity from secular law is provided as long as the person seeking asylum remained inside the church building and grounds. Our congregational council understood the risks involved in our use of "sanctuary" but had decided to support its intent as essential to our ministry.

As you can imagine, our little congregation was walking on shaky ground, not on good terms with the ALC Illinois District. Nevertheless, we were determined to put flesh on our understanding of a Christian mandated mission in our neighborhood. We were branded guilty by association and in collusion with the "communist" Black Panther party, plotting to overthrow our government. But it was going to take more than intimidation and withdrawal of financial support by Illinois District leaders to keep us from serving breakfast to hungry black children. Our support of the breakfast program in our church building was seen as a viable Christian sign of love in Cabrini-Green. However, other black churches were afraid of negative labels and had decided to distance themselves from the Panthers' breakfast program. Although approved by our church council, Pastor Downing and I were maligned by the Illinois District of providing church property for membership recruitment, Communist indoctrination, and the violent overthrow of the government by the Black Panthers. Of course these accusations were false and were created out of fear and the media's biased interpretation of the Black Panthers Breakfast Program.

Another aspect of our partnerships deeply troubling the Illinois District was Holy Family's relationship to the Conference of Inner City Ministries (CICM). This social arm of the American Lutheran Church was born in the early 1960s in Columbus, Ohio, and Minneapolis, Minnesota, through the creativity of four white Lutheran ministers—Revs. Robert Graetz, Robert Hanson, Robert Hoyt, and Paul Boe. The ALC Division for Service and Mission in America gave its financial support for a short time, and the organization became powerful in developing sensitivity, changing church agendas, and modifying policies to reflect the true nature of Christ Jesus' missional mandate.

Because of the district's concern, we raised a number of questions relevant to the goal of our ministry: What were the immediate issues and/or future needs for missional effectiveness by the church in our neighborhood? How could we, as Christians create positive change in the lives of the oppressed people of Cabrini-Green? And what should we do to further enhance congregational growth-—and what would it look like in terms of leadership? Should we continue going forward or look backward and return to the status quo? Our only hope was to reflect Jesus' commission to baptize people, and confront and condemn all dehumanizing systemic racial institutions oppressing the people of Cabrini-Green. Following in the footsteps of Dr. Martin Luther King Jr. we urged the Lutheran church to be true to its Christian social mission, denounce politics of the status quo, and advocate for equal partnerships with black people. Holy Family's commitment to the organization reinforced our sense of purpose, empowerment, and church partnership. The organization briefly influenced decision-making in the American Lutheran Church, creating structural changes to realistically reflect the love of Christ in partnership with racially diverse groups. Although the organization was short-lived, without its new missional approach for racial equality and economic parity there would have been little meaningful social change in the American Lutheran Church.

Following the riots of 1968, while still enrolled at the Lutheran School of Theology, I received an emergency call from Pastor Downing's wife, Janelle, to come to the church. She said that Pastor Downing and a young girl, Carmella Boyd, a member of our congregation were standing outside the church talking with a couple of gang members, and she was afraid that her husband and Carmella were in danger. When I arrived, Janelle was standing inside the church looking out at us and crying. I remained outside with the pastor and Carmella. One of the young men had a long knife inside his belt which resembled a large machete. Carmella was the oldest daughter of Leonard and Evelyn Boyd, who lived in the same public housing building as we did. As it turned out, these two men were not threatening the pastor, only having a conversation with him and Carmella. However, this was a sign that family life for the pastor and his wife was becoming increasingly stressful. After eight years, Pastor Downing was suffering from ministry burn out. and we all were keenly aware of the painful impact it was having on his family life. In 1969 he resigned without a call because the Illinois District said they "couldn't find a congregation suitable to his qualifications." Finally, in 1970, he received and accepted a call as pastor to St. Paul's Lutheran Church in Tescott, Kansas.

During my middler year at the Lutheran School of Theology, I was called, with seminary approval, to serve as vicar-intern at Holy Family. I was placed under the supervision of Rev. Ned Elasass, chaplain at Lutheran Social Service of Illinois. This call as vicar-intern included a small stipend and also completed my seminary internship requirement. As vicar-intern, my duties consisted of those similar to an ordained pastor but without any authorization to consecrate Holy Communion. I completed my internship in the summer of 1970 before enrolling in Wartburg Theological Seminary in Dubuque, Iowa, for my senior year of studies.

Following Pastor Downing's resignation I received numerous phone calls at night and early morning hours from police and church members notifying me of break-ins at our church. We no longer had a resident pastor and had become a victim of break-ins. As vicar-intern I often drove to the church to provide police with security checks and to lock the building. Members of the congregation would always be there waiting for me to arrive, providing whatever support I needed. I sometimes suspected that these break-ins were in some way connected to or condoned by the Chicago police looking for evidence of our connection and involvement with the Black Panthers. My suspicions were heightened when nothing was ever stolen from the church during the break-ins.

Pastoral care and weekly worship services at Holy Family were provided by Rev. Ned Elsass. Deacon Roy Hampton and I served as his assistants. Whenever Pastor Elsass was unavailable, the deacon and I conducted worship services. During one of those times I experienced a deeply moving *kairos* moment. It happened when Rev. Elsass informed me that he was unavailable, and I would have to do the service without him. It was a congregational traditional to have Holy Communion every Sunday and, in preparation for the service, I met with worship leaders to inform them that we would have Holy Communion as usual. Gloria Jarhman, our choir director, cautioned me not to consecrate Holy Communion because as a vicar-intern I was not yet qualified or authorized by the Illinois District to consecrate the bread and wine. She was correct, but I ignored her suggestion, saying that even though I was not ordained our circumstances should not deny us from having Holy Communion. Gloria said that if I consecrated the elements she would refuse Holy Communion and others would as well. Of course I understood and respected the personal choice of each communicant. When Doris heard what had happened at the worship committee meeting she advised me not to consecrate Holy Communion. Deeply concerned myself, I said that I would think about it and make my final decision on Sunday morning. I prayed throughout the night and began the worship service the following morning without telling anyone about my decision.

When the time came to consecrate the bread and wine, I reminded the congregation that I was a seminary student serving as vicar-intern and was not ordained or authorized by the American Lutheran Church to consecrate the communion elements. I continued, "However, I now ask for your prayers and support. As baptized, confirmed members of this congregation, I ask you to please take the *Lutheran Book of Worship* from your hymn racks and let us together read the words of consecration for our communion elements of bread and wine." When I began to speak the words of consecration from our altar book, the congregation followed in unison, speaking the words with me. When the congregation had consecrated the bread and wine they came forward as usual, kneeling at the altar rail to receive Holy Communion. The first person coming to the altar rail, with tears in her eyes, was Gloria Jarhman. This was not a personal victory for me but a witness to our faith in Christ Jesus. What a grace-filled *kairos* blessing! Jacques Ellul, a French lay theologian, says, "If you start taking everything into account, you will do nothing and arrive nowhere! Exploring new possibilities always involves risk-taking; life isn't built on absolute certainties but on the power of our faith in Jesus Christ." I believe this and the congregational council decided that Holy Family Lutheran Church was going to continue its ministry of reconciliation with or without an ordained pastor. Our leadership team remained intact and as strong as ever!

These were extremely busy and scary times for me, and I imagine this was no less true for our congregation. We were all afraid of what the future held for our congregation. The leaders of the Illinois District, Metropolitan Ministries Committee, had the same fears but for what I believe were different reasons. My leadership role suddenly grew as the congregation looked to me to hold us together. The church council was standing firm on its constitutional right to call its own pastor and elect congregational leaders. Eventually, my increasing responsibilities as vicar-intern, congregational president, and in particular my networking with the Conference of Inner City Ministries became critical issues within the Illinois District. I received several intimidating letters from the district threatening to remove our congregation's financial support, including my seminary educational scholarship. I was told to back off, drastically limit my leadership responsibilities, and allow the Illinois District to handle the entire ministry transition.

The Holy Family Church Council met several times with the district president, Dr. Elmer Nelson, and representatives of the Metropolitan Ministries Committee trying to resolve the issues of congregational autonomy to call our own pastor as well as continue my leadership. Although our congregation never said it, the Illinois District believed that attempts were being made to have me qualified and called as the pastor of Holy Family. I had never given any thought to that possibility. At one of the Illinois District meetings I was told to vacate my position as congregational vicar and council president. Because I held both those positions of leadership, the procedures of the American Lutheran Church, Illinois District, was being impeded in the calling of a new pastor to our congregation. I was also told to stop my participation in the Conference of Inner City Ministries. The congregation unequivocally said they were not going to ask for my resignation from any of my positions.

All subsequent meetings with the district president and leaders of the Metropolitan Ministries Committee to resolve our differences ended abruptly and in anger. This happened whenever members of our congregation challenged the district's rationale for violating the national church constitution with regard to our right to call another qualified pastor and their proposition that it was necessary for me to resign as church council president. Because of this impasse, the District Metropolitan Ministries Committee violated our congregational representative structure by meeting with a couple of disgruntled inactive members of the congregation of the church to create division. To alleviate tensions between the Illinois District and our congregation, I resigned as president of Holy Family's congregational council. However, I retained my position as vicar-intern because it was a seminary degree requirement. Upon accepting my resignation, our congregational church council reaffirmed, with a letter sent to the district, the importance of retaining my vicar-internship as a seminary degree requirement. The congregation encouraged me to maintain my contact with the ALC Conference of Inner City Ministries. Charles Jackson replaced me as president of the church council, followed later by James Harris.

Shortly after resigning, we learned "the deck had been stacked" in terms of how inactive members of our congregation had been illegally selected for membership on the Metropolitan Ministry Committee to manage the Black Students Seminary Education Fund. This committee was now responsible for disbursement of funds for my seminary education. The Illinois District Metropolitan Ministries Committee found at least one, if not two, dissidents from Holy Family whom they manipulated and placed on the committee. Later one of them apologized, saying, "I was confused in how I was selected to the committee without the approval of the church council." He said he felt that he was tricked by what was said to him, telling me what we already knew that "they were trying to get rid of you." I forgave him, saying that, "I completely understand and have made my own share of mistakes."

We continued to receive letters from the Metropolitan Ministries Committee, threatening to withdraw financial funds unless we refocused our ministry and terminated my leadership. During Advent/Christmas 1969, following a failure to reach an agreement with the Illinois District regarding termination of my leadership, the Metropolitan Ministries Committee informed us that our financial support, including my seminary tuition and vicar-internship had been withdrawn. The letter was completely devoid of Christian love or the ALC, constitutional rights of our congregation. The letter ended saying, "We wish you and yours a blessed Advent and joyful Christmas season." These Christian people were "rubbing salt" into my already wounded spirit. I felt guilty and assumed responsibility for placing my family and our congregation's ministry in jeopardy. The pain I felt was magnified because I would not be able to financially provide for my family. The letter indicated further sanctions if we did not allow another pastor, of their choosing, to be immediately installed in our church. The letter was a clear violation of the American Lutheran Church's constitution, because all funding for mission congregations came directly from the national church, not the Illinois District.

Our congregational autonomy was violated insofar as individual congregations always have the final word in the calling of their pastor and election of leaders. It was even more apparent that Pastor Downing's ministry of social justice was perceived as a threat and a thorn in the side of the Illinois District. And, now that he was gone, I was perceived in the same light. A letter received by a member of our congregation indicated as much: "Lonnie is a cancer that needs to be surgically removed from the church." I was no longer perceived as a child of God but a malignant disease! How had I become a disease in the body of Christ, the church? It makes me wonder what the letter writer thought of Christ Jesus' confrontation with societal evils of his time.

Although deeply hurt, Doris and I realized that the letter had demonic implications. Our congregation's relationship with the Illinois District had been grounded in condescension and paternalism. We worked hard to avoid having a black pastor, *not of our choosing,* foisted on us. We knew the Illinois District wanted someone who was malleable and could be controlled. My own knowledge of the church's ecclesiastical structure was limited. I was sailing in uncharted waters and, looking at our family's future, was filled with doubt and trepidation. I had no idea how this changing situation would effect Holy Family's missional mandate or our family. But in retrospect, our faith in God's grace was sufficient, and all the pain inflicted on us would have no destructive effect. "Whether you turn to the right or to the left, your ears will hear a voice behind you saying, this is the way; walk in it!" (Isaiah 30:21, NIV).

CHAPTER 8

Resolving Conflicts

1969-1970

Receiving no encouragement from the Illinois District and having little hope of appeal to improve the situation at Holy Family, we met to develop a plan to deal with church finances and continue the support for my seminary education. Christian friends began mobilizing resources and demanding respect for our congregational autonomy to call a pastor and continue our ministry in Cabrini-Green. Charles and Jean Sweet, white members of the Midvale Lutheran Church in Madison, Wisconsin, sent a letter to the president of the American Lutheran Church, Dr. Frederick Schiotz, protesting arbitrary and unconstitutional actions by the Illinois District in withdrawing funding already secured and designated by the Illinois District Convention and pledged as financial support for black seminary students. (Our friendship with Charles and Jean began with their church's involvement in Holy Family's Friendly Town program.) Some ALC national church leaders also gave their support, and the Lutheran School of Theology at Chicago lobbied the American Lutheran Church to not allow recent events to disrupt my seminary education. These were angels sent by God to provide support, guidance, and protection for our family and congregation.

"A great cloud of witnesses" had surrounded us—the people of Holy Family and our white brothers and sisters from suburban and out-of-town Lutheran congregations. All were united in their fervent prayers and faith in Christ Jesus that I would be strengthened to continue "running with perseverance the race" of becoming an ordained black pastor in the American Lutheran Church. Ida Lockett, our congregational treasurer, assured Doris and me that "no matter what happens the church council will see to it that I receive my salary before any other bills are paid."

However, the congregation could make no such guarantee for my seminary tuition, financial resources that had to be restored by the Illinois District. Our church council called a special congregational meeting shortly before Christmas. There a resolution was approved for members of the congregation and neighborhood people to go with us to Minneapolis to present our grievances to the national American Lutheran Church president, the Rev. Dr. Schoitz. We phoned Dr. Schoitz to schedule our meeting, and the following night a number of cars drove to Minneapolis in the midst of a blustery winter snowstorm. Twelve confirmed members of Holy Family and two people from a neighborhood organization traveled in our motorcade. Our congregational president, James Harris, and his wife, Ruth, who was white, drove all night to attend the meeting. Another white woman, Pat Noble, a lawyer in our congregation, rode with them. On the way to Minneapolis James was stopped for speeding by a Minnesota state trooper. After pulling him over to the side of the road, the trooper shined a flashlight in his face, then on his wife and their friend Pat Noble, who was sitting in the back of the car. He asked both women if they were okay and if everything was alright. As a black man, James, fully aware of the racial turmoil happening in our country, admitted that he was a little scared. These were dangerous times, no matter where one lived, when a black man was at risk driving in a car with two white women. After talking with them the trooper gave James a warning and allowed him to continue on to Minneapolis. Being a congregation with minimal finances, we could not afford motel accommodations, so a former member of our congregation, Leatrice Jones, who had moved to Minneapolis, took most of us into her home. With only one available bed we slept "ready-rolled" on a sofa or in living room chairs. Using blankets as pallets, some slept on the floor.

Our meeting with Dr. Schiotz began at 9:00 a.m. that morning. He immediately informed us that he only could give us an hour to present our grievances because he had other appointments. Although he had information on the extent of our grievances, he was adamant in not giving us more time to discuss the issues. I almost responded to his seeming lack of empathy but was told by our delegation not to speak unless I was asked. The president of our congregation, James Harris, spoke to our grievances. Two black members from Prince of Glory Lutheran Church and the Conference of Inner Cities Ministries (CICM), T. Williams and

Mel Brown, also attended the meeting. I was surprised to see them, but later learned that our networks within the ALC Conference of Inner City Ministries had informed them of our arrival. Without them we would have been isolated and ineffective in addressing our grievances. Mr. Brown was chosen by our delegation to respond to Dr. Schiotz's time constraints on the meeting, saying,

> You ought to be glad so many black Lutherans came this far to see you today. They drove all the way from Chicago in a snowstorm—and you're only going to give them an hour to present and discuss their grievances? You're the president of this national Lutheran church, and they're looking to you for help. We know that you're aware of what's been going on in the Illinois District and can do something to help us. Their congregational autonomy has been violated by the ALC Illinois District, and Vicar Branch's leadership should be vindicated and his seminary education funding should be restored. He's a senior at the seminary, and his classes are close to completion. The church says that it wants more black clergy and now this happens! We're very concerned that procedures used by the Illinois District have been un-Christian, insensitive, and unconstitutional. The Illinois District appears intent on ruining his career to prevent him from becoming a candidate for ordination in the American Lutheran Church. This blatant attack against Vicar Branch is also aimed at the missional-mandated ministry of Holy Family Lutheran Church. In fact, it's a total contradiction of the expressed acknowledgement by the American Lutheran Church in its need of more black Lutheran pastors. You can't tell me that as the national president of this church you can't do something about what the Illinois District president has perpetrated against this young man, his family, and their congregation. Your power as president of the national Lutheran Church is greater than that of the Illinois District president!

What a powerful opening statement—not only addressing time limitations imposed on our meeting but speaking to the complex nature of our grievances requiring additional time. There were approximately 5000 American Lutheran Church clergy in the United States and only eight were black. Following Mr. Brown's opening remarks, James Harris spoke softly, echoing the words of Mel Brown:, "Dr. Schiotz, we need more than one hour to discuss our grievances. If not given more time we're prepared to stay here all day. You'll have to call the police to have us forcibly removed and arrested for trespassing. The Lutheran church doesn't need this kind of publicity." We were determined to remain until given adequate time to discuss our grievances.

Dr. Schiotz quickly left the room saying he would try to cancel his appointments and just as quickly returned saying he had taken care of the matter. Our little motley delegation must have seemed a bit odd because, after checking our credentials, Dr. Schiotz briefly dialogued with the two residents (non-church members) about their presence at the meeting. However, James Harris answered Dr. Schiotz's queries, informing him that they were invited as witnesses to what decision will be made and its effect on the ministry at Holy Family Lutheran Church. One of them was dressed in a brilliant multicolored (red, green, and black) African dashiki and carried a tall, beautifully hand-crafted African shepherd's walking cane. We spent the day discussing whether the Illinois District had the authority to choose our pastor and elected congregational leaders, reschedule Sunday worship, and impose their vision of mission on us. This meant challenging the unilateral action of the Illinois District to withhold funds from us designated by the ALC Division for Service and Mission in America for our congregational ministry.

If we had acquiesced in any way regarding our congregational autonomy to call of our own pastor, elect council leaders, schedule worship services, and apply our understanding of mission, we would have been nothing more than pawns, another enslaved Negro American Lutheran Church congregation aiding and abetting paternalism. Dr. Schiotz had lunch served in our meeting room, and we spent the entire day discussing the congregation's grievances. Finally acknowledging our grievances warranted his attention, he stated that "tensions between Holy Family and the district have gone on far too long." He promised to meet with the Illinois District president, with a follow-up meeting at Holy Family.

After returning to Chicago, we received a letter confirming the meeting, stating that he wasn't "afraid to come to Holy Family Church at anytime and would come in the name of the Lord." I don't know why this was in the letter, because we had assured him it was safe to meet at Holy Family. However, we were surprised to receive another letter rescheduling the meeting place to Mayfair Lutheran Church, 4533 West Lawrence Avenue, on the northwest side of Chicago. The letter stated that the location was changed because of rumors and anonymous phone calls saying the Black Panthers had threatened to disrupt the meeting. District officials demanded that Dr. Schiotz change the meeting place.

When our delegation of twenty-eight confirmed members arrived at Mayfair Lutheran Church we saw several police cars. I can only assume they were there because of the fear that the Black Panthers might come to Mayfair Lutheran Church. Our presenters and speakers were William Clover Jr., James Harris, and Patricia Noble. We were all asked to identify ourselves as confirmed members of Holy Family Lutheran Church. When asked about the presence of police, Dr. Schiotz said that he had denied an earlier request for plainclothes police to be present at our meeting. Nevertheless, when our meeting was called to order there were two unidentified white people present whom, at our request, Dr. Schiotz asked to leave because they had not been invited. One man explained, "I heard there was going to be a meeting here and decided to attend." Believing the two white men to be plainclothes policemen, we asked that the credentials of all unidentified persons be challenged. After purging the meeting of those uninvited persons, the meeting began.

An agreement was reached to have a six-month moratorium, during which Holy Family Lutheran Church would be removed from the jurisdiction of the Illinois District and placed under that of the ALC Division for Service and Mission in America (DSMA). During this time, Holy Family Church would choose six interim pastors, and DSMA, under the direction of Pastor H. Manford Knutzwig, would choose six more. Each pastor would serve on two non-consecutive Sundays. In addition, Holy Family would again receive its subsidy funds, which had technically been withdrawn by the Illinois District and replaced by a voucher system, allowing the Illinois District to completely take over the congregation. I was reinstated as seminary vicar-intern under the supervision of Rev.

Ned Elsass of Lutheran Social Services of Illinois. Dr. Schiotz personally promised to restore funding for completion of my final year at seminary, with the understanding that our congregation and Vicar Lonnie speak well of the ALC, Illinois District, and that we cease looking to our former pastor, Fred J. Downing, or to the Conference on Inner Cities Ministries for counsel, which would be provided through Pastor Knutzwig's office during the interim six-month period. The congregation was further asked to "assure itself that any groups using the premises of the church be groups that project a Christian attitude." This meant that we should have no further relationship with the Black Panthers' breakfast program in the church building or with neighborhood gangs.

After a brief discussion clarifying issues and in the interest of the congregation, the proposal was accepted which effectively placed limitations on our work with neighborhood organizations. It also placed constraints on our relationship with the Conference on Inner Cities Ministries. As to communication with Pastor Downing, to the best of my knowledge, no one in the congregation had any contact with him following his resignation. There were other crucial points eliminating my leadership role with the intent to weaken, control, or stifle the congregation's ministry in Cabrini-Green. Approval of the proposal effectively cancelled my work in the congregation as I agreed to complete my final year of seminary study at Wartburg Theological Seminary in Dubuque, Iowa. I thought the proposal was best for my family and our congregation. My priority was to complete my seminary studies. Later, I was interviewed by *Incite,* a church news publication of the Lutheran Human Relations Association of America, Chicago Area Chapter. I was asked the following question: "Why does Holy Family continue to remain in the American Lutheran Church despite constant harassment from Illinois District officials?" My reply was, "Members of the congregation prefer the biblically mandated focus of the Lutheran liturgy (the work of the people)."

This was true, but I should have said more. First, the Illinois District's harassment was localized and did not represent all regions of the American Lutheran Church. Moreover, we believed that our work at Holy Family opened the door for continued, meaningful partnerships in a missional model for other black congregations.

Finally, our congregation had experienced eight years of love by a white man, Pastor Fred Downing, whose pastoral career was jeopardized because of his witness to the transformational power of Christ's love for those living in Cabrini-Green. His obedience to God's call for a Christian ministry of reconciliation caused his pastoral calls to other churches to be drastically restricted and limited. It seemed that no church wanted a pastor with such a radical approach to the gospel of Christ Jesus. Members of our congregation empathized with what happened to our former pastor; they believed that he and his wife came very close to experiencing limitations similar to those that have always been placed on black people. You might say that they were being "black-balled." Nevertheless, I continually thank God that Holy Family Lutheran Church still stands as a beacon of hope in the midst of the rubble of the now-demolished Cabrini-Green public housing projects. With the land now vacant and available, gentrification is rapidly taking place. New apartments and amenities are being built for white people without any consideration of providing affordable housing for impoverished blacks.

CHAPTER 9

Wartburg Theological Seminary
1970-1971

In earlier conversations with the late Rev. John Houk, director of the ALC Division for American Missions, I was informed that it was "the American Lutheran Church's strong desire for me to complete my theological studies at Wartburg Seminary in Dubuque, Iowa." He said that this move was necessary to facilitate my ordination as a pastor in the American Lutheran Church. What Rev. Houk didn't say, but quickly became apparent to me, was that by moving to Dubuque I would be effectively removed from the Illinois District for at least one year with only limited contact at Holy Family Lutheran Church. Our family was completely exhausted from the continuous stress of moving from place to place, and we resisted being pressured to leave Chicago. However, we were caught between a rock and a hard place, and staying would cause a lot of pain to the people of Holy Family Lutheran Church as well as my own family. In the midst of all the uncertainty, I had not given myself much credit for what I was bringing into the Lutheran church as an ordained black pastor. I also felt obligated to honor the Lutheran church's financial investment in my theological education, as well as support from other congregations.

To help me matriculate at Wartburg Theological Seminary, Rev. Houk sent an airline ticket, asking me to come and discuss the pros and cons of making the move. When I arrived in Minneapolis, he explained that I should not feel obligated because of the financial assistance given me for my seminary education, but that the American Lutheran Church truly needed me to complete my studies and become one of its ordained black pastors. He added that it would be to my advantage to complete my studies at Wartburg as a way of building collegial relationships with

American Lutheran Church seminary professors and the senior students in my graduating class.

After reassurance of continuing financial support from the American Lutheran Church's Division for Service and Mission in America, I returned to Chicago and shared what we had discussed with Doris, asking her thoughts about moving to Dubuque. She said, "You have to do what you have to do to complete your seminary education. That was your goal. But you should know there are a lot of people at Holy Family who want you to graduate from the Lutheran School of Theology here in Chicago and become their pastor at Holy Family." I acknowledged her insights, but we moved to Dubuque so I could complete my Master of Divinity degree studies at Wartburg Theological Seminary. Making this move satisfied the requirements for my being called as an ordained pastor to any congregation or specialized ministry in the American Lutheran Church.

As Doris had warned me, my decision to enter the Wartburg Theological Seminary caused deep pain among members of Holy Family Lutheran Church. In fact, a special meeting was held to discuss what I considered legitimate concerns relevant to our moving to Iowa and the ramifications it would have on continuing the ministry of our congregation. Losing a second leader since the resignation of Pastor Downing, the congregation of Holy Family was rightly concerned about its future. My feelings were intense and complex, because I deeply cared about all the people—and would continue needing them as much as they needed me. Whatever decision I made, there were no guarantees for a painless separation. I decided to accept some responsibility for the congregation's pain, but I reminded them of our shared responsibility to move forward on our journey and live with the pain of separation. I was leaving a congregation I loved—the people who had traveled to Minneapolis to support me in the crises surrounding my theological education. They too had invested in my future and had become extended members of my family. Seeing tears trickling down the cheeks of some and hearing angry words from others, I felt deeply hurt and even guilty, as though I had let them down and maybe betrayed them in some way. However, I believe that at that moment there was so much pain that it was difficult for us to see the fruits of God's blessings in our lives. After all, our dedication to a ministry of reconciliation was experienced in a deeply intimate way that might be severely restricted in higher levels of the institutional church.

At our meeting, I heard for the first time from some members of the congregation of their hope that I complete my seminary education and become pastor of Holy Family. I am sure this had been one of the fears of the Illinois District which did not want me becoming pastor of the congregation following Pastor Downing's resignation. I was reminded of the words Doris had spoken to me sometime earlier. Perhaps I had been unable to see their hopes of my becoming their pastor because of a preoccupation with my seminary studies. As far as I can recall, the idea of my becoming their pastor had never been raised in prior meetings of the church council. I felt deeply honored and humbled. As a black man, I had never been given this kind of respect, encouragement, and support, especially in the context of such a diverse racial group. Some of our members saw Wartburg Seminary as a bastion of white conservatism, and they feared that I would in some way be changed into someone with a different approach. They were wrong in their assumption because I found many professors at Wartburg Seminary to be very open-minded and as theologically progressive as those at the Lutheran School of Theology in Chicago. The members of Holy Family were also wrong in fearing that I would be influenced in ways that would change the direction of my call to a ministry of reconciliation. However, they were correct in expressing their concerns. Many of us blacks, after receiving higher educational opportunities leading to upward mobility, tend to forget those problems inherent in our socio-economic political system that can have a negative impact on our ethnic heritage. Speaking slowly and softly, actually not knowing how to respond, I wiped away tears and said, "Even though Pastor Downing and I were as close as two people could possibly be in working together in our ministry, it wouldn't be a good idea for me to become your pastor. I'm truly honored, but I sincerely believe there are well-meaning members of our congregation who would expect me to become a carbon copy of Pastor Downing. This wouldn't work for me, and therefore it wouldn't be a good congregational match. I have to be my own person! I love all of you and am deeply sorry, but in my heart of hearts I believe your pastoral call should be to another man, preferably another black Lutheran pastor. Please continue supporting me and my family with your prayers and memories, thanking God for what we have accomplished together. Dubuque isn't that far from Chicago. Both Doris and I have family members here, and whenever we return to visit them we'll also get together with you."

Shortly after this meeting, one of our white members came to me apologizing for how she had misspoken in anger and disappointment at my decision to complete my final year of seminary studies in Dubuque. I told her there was no need to apologize as I clearly understood her concern and the loving, racially diverse Christian relationship we have at our church. I reminded her of the limited options I had in accomplishing my goal to become a pastor in the Lutheran church. Finally, I acknowledged my difficulty in leaving Chicago but reiterated the necessity of the move for completion of my educational goals and for the well-being of Holy Family Lutheran Church.

In the fall of 1970, we moved to 333 West Wartburg Place, directly across the street from the seminary, where a bronze statue of Martin Luther, a founding father of the Reformation, stood. Dubuque is located in southeastern Iowa along the beautiful picturesque bluffs of the Mississippi River. Also located in this city of arts and learning were the Presbyterian University of Dubuque as well as Saint Thomas Aquinas Catholic Seminary. Other than three Africans from Tanzania, I was the only black enrolled in the seminary. The move was of course traumatic for everyone, but most of all for our six children, who once again had to leave the safe environment of cultural and family surroundings. It seemed as though we were a family of black pioneers, always moving ahead, in the midst of changes, to improve our lives. When we arrived at Wartburg Seminary, a group of smiling, very friendly white students met us, eager to help move us into our new residence. It seemed as though they had been starving to have a relationship with us.

In anticipation of our arrival, arrangements had been made between Wartburg's seminary administration and the seminary librarian, Rev. John Burritt, to vacate his first-floor seminary apartment to accommodate our family. I will always have fond and delightful memories of Rev. Burritt, who was especially attracted to Doris and immediately became our friend, providing valuable orientation to our new seminary life and encouraging us whenever or however he could. The move was good for everyone because Rev. Burritt was not married and had lived alone for some time in his large apartment, with room to spare. One of the older white seminary students, Leslie Simonson, and his wife, Sharon, had four children and were already living in the second-floor apartment above us. Sharon and Doris quickly became friends. I think mutual concerns about raising young children as well as about the future of their husbands' careers made their conversations relevant and informative. Leslie Simonson, who was rather quiet and reserved, and I busied ourselves with seminary studies. As seniors, I'm certain that we too were preoccupied with concerns about our lives following graduation. Later we learned that a number of student homes were reserved for older married seminary students who did not have as many children. The Branch and Simonson families had little choice in becoming friends.

Living in the same two-story apartment building with six of our children and four of theirs, all we had to do was follow the lead of our children. I'll never forget the time when two children from each family who had been playing together in the front yard ran into the house extremely agitated and crying. A car filled with a bunch of white teenage boys had driven by, yelling at the Simonson children and calling them "nigger lovers." One of the Simonson boys was so angry he actually ran down the street after these racist antagonists, throwing rocks at their car and wanting to fight with them. Doris and I assured the children that everything was going to be just fine and that we would all be safe. I am certain that both Doris and the children informed Sharon and Leslie of what had happened. Obviously, people outside the seminary community had taken notice of our moving into the apartment. Equally obvious was that the Simonson children seemingly had never been predisposed to racial prejudice and they knew it was wrong. For our children, the incident was nothing new. They had already learned what it means to live in the midst of racism, but for the Simonson children the experience was devastatingly unsettling.

Another memorable experience occurred when both families huddled together in the basement of our seminary apartment when a severe rain storm with tornadic winds had suddenly appeared out of nowhere. The Simonson family alerted us to the dangerous nature of the storm and immediately took their children into the basement. I hesitated because I assumed that if necessary we could quickly go downstairs. As the wind grew stronger and the house began to creak, the pressure in my ears became intense. By this time the full fury of the storm was upon us. Doris and I struggled to close the front door, but no such luck—the wind had torn the latch completely off the door. Alarmed and frightened, I took a quick look out the front door and saw what appeared to be a swirling cloud of dust heading in our direction across the low-lying. I yelled as loud as I could to Doris to quickly get everyone downstairs in the basement with the Simonson family. We didn't keep track of the time, but it seemed that the storm lasted only about ten minutes. When we finally emerged from the basement, rain had poured through the open front door, debris was scattered everywhere, and the mulberry tree in front of our house had fallen on the ground, barely missing the cars parked in our driveway. The only other damage was several cracked windows in the kitchen and dining room. Seminary student work crews immediately began cleanup, assessing property damage and possible injuries on the campus. Weather reports indicated that the storm damage was due to "straight line" winds, but I will always believe we were hit by a small tornado.

It's important that I name the following professors because of the significant impact they had on my life and that of my family as loving, liberal, progressive thinkers: Seminary President Dr. Kent Knutson and his wife, Norma; Dr. William H. Wieblen and his wife, Ilah; Dr. William Streng; and especially Dr. Peter Kjeseth, who shortly before my graduation approached me with the possibility of my being called as a chaplain to a correctional facility in Iowa. Norma Knutson, wife of our seminary president, filled an especially important role in helping our family integrate our new seminary environment as well as the city of Dubuque, its schools, churches, shopping malls, transportation, and business center. Three of the Knutson children, close to the age of our oldest children, Patricia, Terrance, and Michael became close friends. Our younger school-age children Cheryl and Keith, were enrolled in Bryant Elementary School. Michael was enrolled in Washington Junior High. Patricia and Terrance enrolled in Dubuque Senior High School, where Patricia graduated in 1971. I gave the welcoming address and prayer for her graduating class. Shortly before I graduated from Wartburg

Theological Seminary in 1971, President Kent S. Knutson was elected bishop of the American Lutheran Church.

While in class one day my professor made a remark relative to my being the only American black student at Wartburg Seminary, saying, "Lonnie, you must feel like a prima donna!"

I quickly responded, "No, I don't think so. Being here among whites is nothing new to me. I've been around white people all my life. But I can imagine how my being a black student here is something special and radically new for all of you!" My response caused a lot of laughter among the white students in my class.

After this incident there were no further comments or innuendos by any seminary faculty as to how my being black might become problematic in my learning. However, following this incident, a couple of white students approached me asking for help to understand what it was like being a black man in our racist society and in particular what was meant in our usage of the terms "soul" and "soul food." I responded, "I came to this seminary to concentrate on completing my final year of studies, not to teach anyone about my cultural traditions or life as a black man. Why don't you phone my wife to find if she has time or is willing to try and answer some of your questions? I'm sure she can explain better than I can the meaning and use of the words 'soul' and 'soul food.'" Doris did accept the challenge, inviting both students into our home, giving them an insight into our rich cultural background, and of course including a nutritious soul food dinner.

A few weeks later, four other older seminary students in my senior class asked me to join them in creating a survey document to use in writing a research paper on the pros and cons, benefits and drawbacks, of pastors working in an "ordained multiple-staff ministry." Our project began by formulating questions focusing on concerns and problems in relationships and expectations for both clergy and laity at churches where several pastors were responsible for the church's ministry. Considering our time limitations and regional demographics, we selected fifteen to twenty multiple-staff Lutheran congregations to whom to send our questionnaires, one for each member of the pastoral staff as well as for the congregational president. Enclosed with each letter was an explanation of what we were trying to accomplish, with self-addressed, stamped return envelopes enclosed. Information found in our survey would be mailed to each respondent upon request. The next step in gathering information for our research paper was to schedule a personal interview with at least one of the multiple-staff congregations. Because Bethlehem Lutheran Church in Madison, Wisconsin, was the nearest Lutheran church with a staff of five pastors, we decided to schedule an interview with the senior pastor. I cannot remember the number of members in this congregation, but there were job descriptions for five pastors, defining responsibilities of each in a variety of congregational ministry needs.

After arriving at the church we had a long wait before finally seeing the senior pastor. Taking advantage of our unexpected wait, we decided to explore the church and observe whatever we could. We noticed a rather anxious and highly agitated middle-aged white woman who seemed to be in some kind of pain and never sat down during the entire time of our wait. She continued pacing back and forth, pausing only to speak with the church's receptionist, asking how long before the pastor would be in his office. Occasionally stopping at the closed office door, as though anticipating its opening, she seemed totally unaware of our presence. Attached to the closed door was a small brown plastic sign engraved with the words Pastoral Counselor. When the door finally opened, she was greeted by a pastor whom we assumed was her counselor, who apologized for being late for her appointment. Observations like these became essential information for our research paper, and each of us gave special attention to this particular incident. Prior to the pastor's arrival, the woman appeared very close to a state of panic, causing us to wonder why someone else was not available to help her.

The senior pastor finally arrived and ushered us into his office. He gave us an excellent presentation and overview of his experience in an ordained multiple-staff ministry, making us aware of problems that can arise whenever there are personality differences among the pastoral staff or a lack of clarity in congregational expectations. In other words, clearly defined job descriptions were essential and had to be constructed so they could be easily understood by pastors, leaders, and members of the congregation. Although we had only a couple of short interviews with the other pastors, the information they provided was very helpful to our research paper. My experience in working with my white classmates was really enjoyable. Another group of students had come up with a similar project, and we wanted to excel in our written report. We each received an A for our grade on the report.

Shortly before graduation, senior seminary students were assigned to various districts or regions as candidates for ministry calls by American Lutheran Church district presidents. Ordination required a candidate to receive as well as accept a letter of call from either an organized American Lutheran Church congregation or the national church council. These regional district assignments were made available as job opportunities in various Christian ministries for every graduating senior student. Because Dr. Vernon Mohr, president of the Southern District, had selected and assigned me to work in his district, we invited him to our home for dinner.

During his visit, Dr. Mohr told me that he selected me because of my having come from a congregation active in neighborhood ministry. This, he said, made me the best qualified seminary graduate to begin a new mission start in Houston, Texas. I would be working with an established Lutheran church as a mission developer in a new mission start. I was glad to learn of Dr. Mohr's confidence in my abilities, but told him I was certain that being black gave me an advantage over my classmates. He informed me that the new ministry was located in a black middle class neighborhood, including a large apartment complex named South Park Village. Many of the apartment residents were twenty- to thirty-year-old unchurched but articulate black college students and graduates. Hope Lutheran Church, the institution with which I would be working, was located approximately six miles from the proposed new mission start. The congregation was very active in neighborhood evangelism and was experiencing significant loss of its white membership because of a considerable influx of non-Lutheran black people moving into the neighborhood. Of course, for realtors, home builders, and business developers this changing neighborhood had become a virtual gold mine. The national church believed that Hope Lutheran Church would provide a substantial congregational base of support to help me establish the new ministry, which we would name South Park Mission, American Lutheran Church.

Later, we met as a family to discuss our move to Houston. Knowing that I needed a job, we tentatively resigned ourselves to another changing situation, and I accepted my first pastoral call. I am certain that as much as I prayed about the call and the move to Houston, Doris must have prayed harder. Although the civil rights movement had made a significant impact on segregation, we knew that racism was still alive and well, and this became a significant safety concern as we contemplated moving south. We had no income or savings whatsoever, so my being employed was our highest priority, especially since there was no time available for me to look elsewhere for employment. So in May 1971 I accepted my first pastoral call to begin a new American Lutheran Church congregation in Houston. I was the first black American Lutheran Church student to graduate from Wartburg, in a class of forty-four seniors. Unlike most of my older white counterparts, I received a Certificate of Graduation and a Master of Divinity degree. Following my acceptance of the degree, one of the white graduates commented that he and some others had "hoped I wouldn't accept the Master of Divinity degree and stand with the older group of students who had only received a Certificate of Graduation." I explained to my colleague, "I earned the degree with passing grades in the Master of Divinity degree curriculum as prior agreements between the Lutheran School of Theology in Chicago and Wartburg Theological Seminary." In fact, at the end of my final year in seminary I had earned a B grade average. What was even more interesting and significant was that earlier I had received an encouraging comment from one of my younger white seminary colleagues. Relative to my having only two years of college and no bachelor of arts degree, he said, "You're probably not aware of it, but you're more theologically qualified with knowledge of how to apply what you've learned in relationships than most of the graduating white students in your age group. Seminary accreditation rules allow institutions of higher education to enroll a limited number of students without college degrees, and there are a couple of students enrolled here who have no college education whatsoever." I wasn't aware of being less qualified or more knowledgeable of ministry applications than my white seminary colleagues, but I was never ashamed of not having a college degree. My only interest in seminary was to get a theological education degree and go to work. Thank God for having addressed my seminary education plans with those black Lutheran pastors in Chicago!

Following my graduation from Wartburg Seminary I lost contact with Larry Stephen Emery, one of my closest friends at LSTC. However,

I kept in touch with Tom Minor who attended my graduation from Wartburg. I will always remember both of my black seminary colleagues and their roles in our protest and boycott of classes at LSTC. After Tom's ordination he became pastor of Holy Spirit Lutheran Church in Chicago. Later he accepted a call to serve as a military chaplain in the U.S. Navy.

Doris and I sent graduation and ordination invitations to our families, members of Holy Family Lutheran Church, and to suburban white Lutheran churches that supported us on our journey. A large number of people, black and white, responded and came to Dubuque to celebrate my graduation. Our home was filled with groups of people, keeping Doris quite busy as a welcoming committee of one.

Among those attending my ordination service at Holy Family Lutheran Church in Chicago was my former Boy Scout master, Charles Tousaint, and my close boyhood friend, Jimmie King, who had been released from prison. While walking to the church on the day of my ordination, I spotted a young man leaning on a Yellow Cab. He looked familiar, but I didn't recognize him until he spoke to me. It was my friend, Jimmie, who was now married to a woman who had three children and was employed as a Yellow Cab driver. Although I knew he was out of prison, I didn't know his address, so I couldn't send him an invitation. But Jimmie told me that he had seen my picture in local Chicago newspapers, the *Tribune* and the *SunTimes*, both announcing the date and time of my ordination at Holy Family Lutheran Church. These newspapers indicated that I was being ordained as the ninth black pastor in the American Lutheran Church, and he wanted to be at the church service. Jimmie said "nothing of much importance happens here," and that he was really proud of me because I had done something positive with my life. Tears came to my eyes as he gave me some disturbing news about our old childhood friends, the guys with whom both of us used to hang out. He told me that most of them were now either dead or in prison, and that a mutual friend, Fat Sonny, had been beaten to death underneath the elevated train tracks. I told him that I was more proud of him than whatever I had accomplished because he had made it out of prison, got a job, and took responsibility for a new "ready-made" family. I also said that I didn't think I would have had strength to overcome low self-esteem and drug addictions to make it out of prison alive. As I talked with my dear friend, I also learned that his mother, Willa King, had died sometime during his imprisonment.

On July 11, 1971, I was officially ordained by Rev. Kent Knutson, president of the American Lutheran Church, at the Lutheran Church of the Holy Family in Chicago. I became the ninth black pastor ordained in the American Lutheran Church. Those participating in the Rite of Ordination were Rev. Howard Kreiselmeyer, pastor of Holy Family Lutheran Church; and two of my mentors, the Rev. Fred J. Downing and the Rev. Larry Hunt (president of the ALC Black Clergy Association). Pastor Hunt had been the eighth ordained American Lutheran Church black pastor. Roy Hampton, the first black deacon of Holy Family Lutheran Church, also participated in the service. And I will never forget the presence of three other pastors whose confidence in my abilities and commitment to the church were demonstrated in manifold ways. They were all white pastors—the Rev. Ned Elsass from the Lutheran Social Services of Illinois; Rev. Karl Brevik, pastor of Trinity Lutheran Church in Evanston; and Rev. Nolan Watson of St. Mark Lutheran Church in Mount Prospect, Illinois. Following Pastor Downing's resignation, these ministers continued to provide counsel and assistance to Holy Family. The sight of a full sanctuary of racially diverse people sitting in the pews in front of me was awesome. I became tongue-tied and did not know how to clearly express everything that was in my heart. However, I began by acknowledging and giving thanks to all the people of our congregation and neighborhood supporters from Cabrini-Green. I deeply loved and honored them as vitally important in my life. Without their trust, confidence, and support I would have never made it to this point in my odyssey to become a pastor. I wanted so much for them to realize that it was God's love that made them worthy to be counted as important,

ALC President Kent Knutson officiated at my ordination.

and we should never forget this was the day that the "Lord had made . . . for us all!" (Psalm 118:24). I thanked everyone, including members and representatives of all the white suburban Lutheran churches who had partnered with us. We were God's chosen people, together, realizing how we had been transformed into members of one holy family, the Body of Christ! In ending I said that, "Without love there can be no mutual respect and even less faith in God—and we wouldn't be this racially diverse 'family.' This glorious miracle belongs to God!" The unbroken tie binding us together that day was a complete package tied together by the grace of God in Christ Jesus.

CHAPTER 10

South Park Mission

1971–1973

Following my ordination in August 1971, our family began a two-week automobile trip to Houston, Texas. Our travel arrangements was planned to coincide with our first vacation together as a family. Before we left Chicago, the Rev. Karl Brevik, a white pastor at Trinity Lutheran Church in Evanston, expressed his concerns about the safety of our family of eight driving to Houston in our 1967 six-cylinder Chevrolet. To assist in our safe arrival in Houston, members of Trinity Lutheran Church gave us a large down payment on a new 1971 Chevrolet nine-passenger station wagon. Perhaps my odyssey on the train to the Land of Promise was moving us into other Lands of Promise. When we arrived in Houston, the only available housing was temporary lodging with Rev. Donald Flachmeir, pastor of Hope Lutheran Church, and his family. Pastor Flachmeir and his wife, Belva, graciously opened their home to our family of eight. We would have a longer wait for our new parsonage to be built in Crestmont Park, less than a mile from the South Park Village Apartments.

The new parsonage would give me easy access to people living in the apartment complex as well as to local homeowners. My letter of call was to work closely with Rev. Flachmeir and the ALC Regional Mission director, Richard Fenske, to develop the foundation for a new mission church ministry in Houston. Hope Lutheran was an old, well-known neighborhood church that had recently added a basketball gymnasium to its structure. The gymnasium attracted large numbers of black teenagers, but few seemed interested in attending worship services or becoming members of the congregation. They didn't know who Lutherans were, and Hope Lutheran Church didn't have the staff needed to connect with these families. Because of a rapid influx of blacks into the neighborhood and a new direction in the church's mission, the congregation had experienced a steady decline in its mostly white membership. However, a small group of black and white members remained at Hope Lutheran Church, supporting the congregation's new direction in mission outreach. They embraced racial change and opened the church to new mission programs. Members from both racial groups continued their participation in the American Lutheran Church's Conference of Inner City Ministries. It was at a CICM conference when Pastor Flachmeir and members of Hope Lutheran Church first became aware of my presence.

It was with "fear and trembling," that I embraced my opportunity to work with black residents to build another Lutheran congregation called South Park Mission. The South Park Village apartment complex, with its large number of black college graduates, was invited to assist in planning the ministry of South Park Mission. The area was highly competitive, because other primarily black churches were also interested in these new residents. Area demographics were available from research conducted by Hope Lutheran Church and the ALC Division for Service and Mission in America. Hope Lutheran Church members had met for some time with a number of local non-Lutheran black churches and organizations with mutual neighborhood concerns. I was grateful to become part of these strategy meetings with neighborhood leaders identifying and responding to local needs and concerns. Hope Lutheran Church provided temporary office space, equipment, and secretarial services for my work in the South Park area. Our family was pleasantly surprised by the "southern hospitality" of the church's remaining white members and I'm especially reminded of Tom and Mary O'Banion, who were also members of the Conference of Inner City Ministries. The O'Banion family gave us a very warm and hearty welcome to Houston and Hope Lutheran Church became the place for our family's Sunday morning worship. Weekly mission strategy meetings continued at the church, attended by neighborhood non-Lutheran black churches, mostly African Methodist Episcopal (AME), United Methodist, and Disciples of Christ. This experience "opened the eyes of my heart" to see how well blacks and whites worked together in a common Christian bond of justice and respect for the oppressed poor.

My initial work began with the boycott of a local bank, South Park National Bank of Houston. The boycott was triggered by the bank's refusal to accept the deposit of my first, rather large mission check from the American Lutheran Church in Minneapolis. I have no idea what the problem was, but it seemed that I did not have the right kind of identification or credentials to make a deposit. However, Hope Lutheran Church, whose financial account was at this bank, had provided substantial identification for me, so I really have no idea what more was needed in order to deposit my check. As racial transition continued in the neighborhood surrounding Hope Lutheran Church, the congregation served as a central hub for community action meetings. I immediately became part of an ecumenical organization of ministers called the Southeast Inter-faith Council, organizers of the South Park National

Picketing South Park National Bank.

Bank boycott. These black Christian congregations had experienced numerous racial affronts while making transactions at the bank. During the boycott, police and news media helicopters hovered above the crowds of people representing various church and neighborhood organizations boycotting the bank. Many in our group were arrested, but perhaps because I was such a recent arrival I was protected by the organizers, who told me to not put myself in a position of being arrested. In fact, the boycott organizers had already decided who should have the honors. Eventually I was cleared by the bank officers to have my check from the ALC Division for Service and Mission in America deposited in South Park National Bank. However, I decided to make the deposit in another branch of the bank located in a different neighborhood. The manager of this bank, who was white, remarked, "I don't understand what the problem was; the check is good. I'll open an account for you right away."

After living with the Flachmeirs for a week, a rental house was located on Doulton Street, near Hope Lutheran Church, and the congregation secured and rented it in our name. We were shocked to find the house infested with giant cockroaches. Of course, we had seen roaches before, but never the size of these. We had been told that "everything in Texas is bigger," and these cockroaches quickly made us believers. Exterminators were hired to fumigate the entire house. We cleaned the house of dead, nasty, crunchy cockroaches. One of our next-door neighbors came over, introduced himself, saying he was going to have to call exterminators to his home because of the wave of roaches he had seen coming from our house heading in his direction. The following week the moving van arrived with our furniture and other household goods. With the help of members of Hope Lutheran Church, we moved in. Living in this house provided us many new experiences. A concrete bayou partially filled with water was located close to our house. Most bayous in the southern United States are used as drainage ditches for heavy rains and flooding, so we immediately warned our children not to play near or in the bayou. We experienced our first hurricane while living on Doulton Street. The psychological effect of hearing the eerily howling winds and seeing the large amount of rainfall was quite profound. Fearing the worst, we huddled together in the hallway of our home in semi-darkness with a few candles for light as the winds blew through the house. The nearby bayou quickly filled with water and was soon rushing over the surface of its bridge. We were really scared and wished we were back in Chicago. Our neighbors smiled, saying that there was no reason to be overly concerned. They reassured us that all our homes were located miles from the Gulf of Mexico coastal area and we were only experiencing the residual effects of the hurricane.

Following these teachable moments of home relocation, we breathed a sigh of relief and thought the pace of settling in would begin to slow down. However, we soon found ourselves saying goodbye to our oldest daughter, Patricia, who left for Wartburg College in Waverly, Iowa, to enroll as a college freshman. While still unpacking our household belongings I received a letter from my regional mission director, Rev. Richard Fenske, informing me that he had enrolled me in the Division for Service and Mission in America (DSMA) National Pastor's Training Laboratory, in Columbus, Ohio. He said my attendance at the training laboratory was required because of my status as a mission pastor. This meant leaving Doris and the remaining children alone to continue unpacking our belongings and getting acquainted with our new church and neighborhood.

The training lab was located at the Trinity Lutheran Seminary and Capital University complex in Columbus. There were about eight new mission pastors attending the lab, including one student who had graduated with me from Wartburg Seminary. We slept in one large dormitory room on beds separated by night tables with lamps. We were given meal tickets allowing us to eat our meals in Capital University's cafeteria. The Rev. Bob Hoyt was our director and facilitator. The lab's programmatic content was excellent insofar as it helped identify some vulnerabilities that might limit our effectiveness in ministry. During one of our class assignments a particular incident was etched in my memory that stood out above all others. It strengthened my resolve to always be vigilant in affirming the God-given goodness of my created ethno-racial background. My heritage, slavery included, is grounded in my being created in God's image.

This is what happened. As a lab assignment, Rev. Hoyt had arranged for us to visit a local tavern to experience the German festival of Oktoberfest. The night out together was well planned. We had designated drivers and were expected to share our experiences following breakfast the next morning during our daily check-in time. The tavern was crowded with people. I was the only black person, but I had been in this kind of situation before and was rather comfortable. Although this was to be a learning experience, we were there to also relax and enjoy ourselves. Beer was the festival's "drink of the day," and as night wore on some of us, including myself, began feeling the effects of the alcohol. However, I was sober enough to notice that Rev. Hoyt hadn't been drinking as much as the rest of us and was in touch with everything that happened. When it was time to leave, he told us "to pack it in" and return to the seminary. We left in separate cars and once there I immediately went to bed. I believe my friend Bill, who had graduated with me from Wartburg Seminary, decided to go to another tavern and did not get back until later.

Very early that morning I was awakened by the loud sounds of someone weeping and vomiting in the bathroom. I do not know if anyone else was awakened, but I was the only one to get out of bed. It was Bill. His bed was located directly across from mine, and when he finished vomiting he came in and sat at the side of his bed. Weeping louder, he began pounding very hard on his chest. I sat up in my bed, asking him what was wrong. I smelled alcohol and immediately realized that he was stinking drunk. He continued to weep and with slurred speech tried to explain that "we were both cursed." I noticed that it was four o'clock in the morning but after this remark I woke up fast, listening to why Bill thought we were both cursed. As though trying to make up his mind whether to continue talking to me, he suddenly ripped his shirt open causing buttons to fly everywhere. I saw a large beautiful tattoo on his chest of an old "man of war" sailing ship. And there were other tattoos on the upper parts of his arms. Still weeping and pounding his chest, Bill explained that he had these tattoos put on while serving in the Navy and now they had become a curse to him, "reminding him of those times when he was a really bad person doing bad things." He asked, "What would members of my congregation think of me if they saw all these tattoos? How would I be able to preach and be a minister to them?" He continued crying and explained, "That's why I always wear long-sleeved shirts during worship services, even when it is hot. I don't want them to see my tattoos. I'm afraid they'll reject me as their pastor!"

At this point I couldn't help but express my anxiety by asking Bill, "Why am I cursed? I don't have any tattoos." He tried to explain some kind of distorted white, ethnocentric biblical perspective based on a racist interpretation of Genesis 9:20-27, the story of Noah's drunkenness following the flood and how his three sons responded to their father's nakedness. Bill obviously believed whatever he had heard about the story because he said that I was cursed in being born with a black skin. He said that as a descendant of Ham I could not do anything to remove the curse, "but I can have my tattoos removed," he said. I wasn't angry at Bill but I didn't know what to say to someone, in so much agony, living under his own self-imposed curse.

Finally I said, "Then why don't I feel cursed, like you? And why haven't you had your tattoos removed? That should relieve you of the burden of being cursed?" He never responded, but hastily retreated to the bathroom where I heard him gagging and vomiting again. In seminary I never thought of Bill as being cursed with so much pain and guilt over something as simple as tattoos. However, I believe he needed not only to share his feelings, perhaps even confess his thoughts of what the tattoos reminded him, but also it was his way of having a deeper conversation with me about the lives of black people. Feeling sorry for Bill and very tired and sleepy, I ended our conversation and went back to bed.

That morning I shared what had happened with Rev. Hoyt. He asked me if I thought what had happened was important and, if so, to share everything at our group meeting following breakfast. As you might guess, Bill arrived late for breakfast, and our group discussion began late. However, his lateness allowed us time for briefing everyone about what had happened last night and setting some guidelines to support both of us. After opening our group session with a prayer, we used Scripture as a way to open a dialogue and help Bill deal with his inner conflict concerning distorted ethnocentric theological interpretations of blacks being cursed by God. Before the session ended, Bill opened his shirt and allowed everyone to see the beautiful sailing ship tattooed on his chest. From his facial expression, it seemed he had somehow received the courage to let us look on his nakedness and found that we would not laugh or turn our backs on him. We saw Bill's tattoos and drunken nakedness and, as his brothers, we covered him with a security blanket of understanding, acceptance and love, freeing him of his self-imposed curse. As for me, I was never threatened or in doubt about my identity. In fact, I felt strengthened because I had been tested and sealed as a child of God, freed of any curse because of Christ Jesus.

When I returned to Houston, Hope Lutheran Church continued sharing office space, secretarial service, office equipment, and supplies. However, I began to sense a need to more clearly define my pastoral boundaries as they had become skewed and confused because of my frequent presence at the church. This was contrary to the goal of my pastoral letter of call to develop a new congregational ministry in the South Park/Crestmont Park area. Instinctively I knew that the growth of a culturally new Christian denomination among black people would be slow and had to be grounded in active neighborhood growth, with variations on traditional Lutheran worship, especially the music. I had no plan or direction when once again God "opened the eyes of my heart." I felt like I was drowning in a deep sea of failure and hopelessness when God spoke to me saying, "Calm down. Be attentive! Don't be so fixated on yourself—success or failure. Look around and see what's happening!" Blinded by a fear of failure primarily based on the expectations of others, I hadn't seen what was happening around me. After getting my attention I could confidently say God had indeed spoken to me! I became more acutely aware of my surroundings.

I had been standing behind the backstop screen of a baseball diamond but not paying much attention to the Little League baseball game. Suddenly I became more alert as I listened to the incessant cussing and heckling directed toward the black players every time one of them made an error. The heckling was coming from a group of older black teenagers who were watching the ball game. A number of male black adults also watching the game said nothing to the hecklers. Without thinking, I reacted to the heckling with an outburst, angrily yelled out at the teenage hecklers, "What the hell do you know about playing baseball? These little guys are better ballplayers than you'll ever be and wouldn't even break a sweat in beating you in a baseball game!" Being an ordained minister was entirely new to me, and I had forgotten that I was now wearing a black clerical shirt with a white collar. For me, the black shirt and white collar meant measuring up to whatever "wearing the collar" should mean for pastors. However, I remembered the time when my dear friend and mentor, Rev. Fred Downing, emphatically said, "None of us is worthy to wear the shirt and collar. Obey God and do the best you can to become what He has called you to be!"

Two of the hecklers responded, asking me, "Aren't you supposed to be a preacher? You shouldn't be talking to us like this!" Although they were cussing and ridiculing the young players, they thought nothing of correcting me.

I immediately apologized for my angry outburst, explaining to them, "You guys are older and should know better! Instead of putting the Little Leaguers down, you should be encouraging them. Suppose one of them was your little brother. Would you want someone making fun of him?" I repeated my earlier challenge, saying, "You probably don't know how to play baseball and couldn't even beat these little guys in a baseball game!" They didn't live in the South Park Village apartments but in the newly built Crestmont Park Homes surrounding the apartments. These homes as well as the Village apartments provided vital contacts for the new South Park mission outreach.

Feeling guilty about my inability to control my temper and the effect it might have on these boys, I invited a black member of Hope Lutheran Church, Oliver Custard, to help me organize a baseball team with him as coach and manager. Earlier, he had said he was interested in working with me to organize the South Park Mission congregation. I needed his help to show these teenagers how two black men could demonstrate mutual respect in teaching them to play winning baseball. I told Oliver that this was my first step in connecting with both neighborhoods in forming a new congregation. At our first team organizational meeting, the boys elected leaders and chose a name for the team—the Benguas, which is Swahili for "Black Warriors." Later, a well-known furniture company donated a television set, a pair of large living-room lamps, and a living room chair to be raffled off as prizes, with the money being used to purchase baseball uniforms. Selling raffle tickets became one of many teachable moments for these youngsters in learning to work together for what they needed in order to succeed. Those who were able to buy their own uniforms helped sell tickets for those who were unable to do so. We held a baseball team party and invited parents as well as others to participate in the drawing of tickets for the donated prizes. With the proceeds we were able to purchase tailor-made fitted baseball uniforms with the official name of our team sewn on them. You should have seen the boys' faces and heard all the positive chatter as they put on their new baseball uniforms! Mr. Custard and I caught their excitement and felt that something good was happening in their lives. Additional baseball equipment, including gloves, bases, and catcher's equipment, was donated by the Harris County Community Action (HCCA) Program, which sponsored our neighborhood athletic programs.

These teenagers were really good baseball players had the skills but did not know how to play together as a team, and no one had ever challenged them to do better. It was really difficult for these boys to learn that winning was the result of playing together as a team and not as individuals who happened to look good in new baseball uniforms. Nevertheless, we kept the pressure on for them to cooperate and respect one another. In their first year they not only learned to play together as a team but won a first place tournament trophy given by the Harris County Community Action Program. Many local fans as well as occasional onlookers slowly began recognizing South Park Mission Church's connection with the Benguas and developed a relationship with me in my pastoral involvement with the boys. I continued to wear my clerical collar but acted with a little more awareness of the context and improved my self-control. When the baseball season ended, most members of the team registered to play basketball in the HCCA athletic program. The Benguas' baseball team name was now adopted by a basketball team. The young athletes of our new basketball team continued their momentum in becoming winners by earning another first-place trophy as well as tournament honors.

I worked hard at building relationships not based on my pastoral status but as a friend. This was the first of many struggles to follow God's will in various ministry contexts, and it would continue throughout my missional odyssey. What at first glance seemed to be a bunch of rag-tag, rowdy black teenage nobodies became the Benguas, HCCA neighborhood champions in both baseball and basketball. No matter where these young men were living, their lives now included hope. They had become winners! The small membership of South Park Mission provided some additional trophies to be awarded to individual team members who exhibited exceptional cooperation and leadership in areas of personal respect and teamwork whether playing in a game or sitting on the bench. The South Park Mission Benguas baseball and basketball teams became well known in the South Park Village Apartments and gained a reputation for being winners.

Our young mission congregation continued to grow and held meetings in my new office, which was now located in the large, two-car garage attached to our new parsonage. After moving into the parsonage on Canterway Drive, I joined the Crestmont Park Homeowners Civic Club and was immediately appointed block captain of our subdivision to solicit membership into the Civic Club. Although Mr. Custard and I were always encouraging baseball team members to think about the importance of the church in their lives, we were both surprised when a few of them began attending worship services. All we needed was time and patience to build relationships. Some who had initially worshipped at Hope Lutheran Church and had Bible studies in my home were now coming to worship with us at Rev. Albert T. Allen's congregation, the Sunnyside Christian Center, Disciples of Christ. Their parents began to attend meetings at the church concerning neighborhood needs or special events highlighting the achievements of our teenage athletic programs. Although some boys said their parents belonged to a church, I discovered they were all un-churched. This became most apparent when a member of the baseball team asked me to visit his home. His parents were threatening to throw his younger sister out of their home because she was pregnant. He said the family was falling apart, and he did not want to go home. He said I was the only person he could think of who might be able to help. The visit with his parents went well, and I really felt good that I could be there for them.

Trying to avoid the risk of these teenagers feeling uncomfortable in expressing themselves, I had become lax in not asking them to use so many cuss words. One day when the garage was left ajar, Doris overheard some of the boys cussing and opened the garage door. She angrily shouted at them, "There'll be no cussing in this house. You can express yourselves better than that! Do you talk like this around your parents?" Wow, it was so quiet you could hear the proverbial pin drop! They did not know how to respond, so they asked me what to do. I told them the only thing needed was an apology. Immediately, one of the young men went in and apologized to Mrs. Branch. Earlier, Mr. Custard, who knew most of them, said the boys needed the confrontation I had given them. He assured me that they had already forgiven me, but now they would not only remember that I was tough on them but so was my wife. In fact, Oliver made a number of visits with me to the boys' homes to introduce me to their parents. These visits gave me an opportunity to have conversations assuring them that their sons were in good company and medical insurance coverage was provided for all the ball players. I used the opportunity to give their parents a brief description of the Lutheran church's Christian beliefs and invited them to help me begin a new church in our neighborhood.

With one exception, I visited the home of every team member. One of the ball players, whom I will call Henry, was rather quiet and withdrawn.

Previously, without giving his reason, Henry had told me he did not want me to visit his home. Round-trip transportation to games was always provided, either using my station wagon or occasionally both my car and Mr. Custard's car. Neither of us had ever gone inside his home. One day after returning the boys to their homes, Henry told me that he would like me to drop him off last and meet his mother. What a pleasant surprise! When we arrived at his home, he asked me to wait in the car while he went inside to get his mother. After a few minutes Henry came outside, followed by his mother. As they approached my car, I got out and walked toward Henry and his mother. Before reaching them, I noticed that Henry was facing his mother and motioning with his hands. I immediately recognized that he was using sign language to communicate with her. When I finally walked up to them, Henry's mother folded her hands together as if in prayer and bowed her head down in front of me. I almost cried; I know my eyes were teary. Now I understood one of the reasons why Henry had not wanted me to visit his mother. Later, Mr. Custard, who personally knew Henry and his mother, gave me some additional information about the family. Henry was an only child, and his father had left his mother and was no longer living with them. With his father's absence, Henry's mother had been abused several times by men who had taken advantage of her, causing him to become very protective of his mother and suspicious of all men. I will never forget when the three of us were together and how Henry, using sign language, communicated with his mother about our baseball program and my vision to build a new neighborhood church.

Mr. Custard eventually had a bad automobile accident with another car, resulting in the death of two people. Following the accident, he lived in the parsonage with us for three months, continuing to assist me in my outreach mission at the South Park Village Apartments.

It had now become necessary to move my office at Hope Lutheran Church into our newly-completed parsonage located very close to the South Park Village Apartments. I left because my letter of call was to South Park Mission and not Hope Lutheran. Initially my leaving was a little scary but necessary because of normal transitional problems in meeting new people and leaders—some looking for power and recognition while others were seeking direction complicated by an influx of new ideas. It was a strategic move made to lessen turf conflicts encountered in attempting to organize a new Lutheran church mission. At this point, Albert Pero (Pete) and Fred Wimberly, Lutheran pastors provided me substantial guidance and much needed support.

After settling into my new office in the parsonage garage, I began having small group Bible studies, confirmation classes, and worship services in my home with a small number of new people and a few white members from Hope Lutheran Church interested in building a new ministry in the South Park Village Apartments. Most of the new people were those who had participated in the South Park National Bank boycott.

I continued to participate in the American Lutheran Church's Conference on Inner City Ministries, attending a conference in Denver with Michael Sams, one of an increasing number of young South Park Village Apartments residents interested in what I was doing. My relationships with apartment residents had grown because of continuing visits with them and supporting them at various neighborhood meetings. Soon I was able to build a close relationship with the black manager of the apartment complex. The Lutheran denomination was new to him, so I began to build our relationship by giving him a vision of my mission and ministry as supported by the national American Lutheran Church in Minneapolis. I explained how my biblical understanding and vision for evangelism would initially be directed at but not limited to the apartment residents. I explained that future ministry objectives would include nearby homeowners, which was essential to fostering a sense of neighborhood partnership. Pastoral care—such as baptism, premarital and family counseling, weddings, and funerals—was an important component. The apartment manager approved of these objectives and gave me a small rent-free office with use of equipment in the apartment complex. I also received rent-free space for conducting weekly Sunday worship services. These ministerial services were added to the South Park Village rental brochures as being available to all apartment residents. I assured the manager of continuing to nurture positive relationships and partnerships with the other neighborhood churches, because we both understood the need to guard against my presence in the apartment complex being perceived as favoritism or worst yet as a religious denominational preference. In fact, we agreed that there was no need for a written contract, because the physical location of my office and the worship space were considered temporary.

A couple of dissidents from Hope Lutheran Church, who had been leaders in the bank boycott, perceived my approach to this kind of ministry as nothing more than "apartment house chaplaincy" and remarked that I was only an itinerant preacher with no actual church building or roots in the neighborhood. Nevertheless, I saw my move as an excellent opportunity to reconcile residents of the South Park Village Apartments and Crestmont Park homeowners as one community. Yes, there was some positive management trade-offs involved in creating a visible religious presence in South Park Village. For one thing, the residents would not have to travel far or spend gas money to have a church in the apartments and the ministry of an ordained pastor. From my perspective, the apartment complex offered a number of useful amenities, among them a large gymnasium that included a full-sized basketball court for our youth. In fact, most of the South Park Mission basketball games were played in this gymnasium. Other facilities included were a daycare center and spacious community meeting rooms made available for me to hold special neighborhood meetings as well as church services. Various other athletic activities, such as karate classes, were also offered to apartment residents. I mention karate because of the pride I have in my oldest son, Terry, for enrolling in the classes and eventually becoming a close friend of the young instructor, Nat Hopkins. To this day they remain friends and frequently keep in touch. From the beginning, Mr. Hopkins was very supportive of my initiative to create a religious environment for apartment residents.

While still struggling as a fledging mission developer, I was suddenly confronted with another difficult ministry decision. I received a letter of call from the Church Council of the American Lutheran Church asking me to accept a special ministry partnership with Lutheran Social Service of Iowa. The call to become a correctional chaplain at the Iowa State Reformatory for Men in Anamosa created a real dilemma for me. Although I had taken my first call to Houston as a mission developer because I needed employment, I now felt extremely guilty about leaving, feeling less than successful in what I had accomplished at South Park

Mission. The initial research and design phase of the position for a black correctional chaplain at the Iowa State Reformatory had begun a year prior to my graduation from Wartburg Seminary. Some of the seminary professors thought I was qualified to fill this special ministry need and had specifically designed the position for me. However, at the time they were unable to develop a structural partnership and financial package for the position. The Iowa State Department of Corrections had agreed that a black presence was needed on the treatment staff at the reformatory and were especially open to the proposal because there would be no financial expenses incurred by the State of Iowa. In other words, the American Lutheran Church would donate my services as a black chaplain to the Iowa State Department of Corrections. I thank God for the church's confidence in my abilities to become a correctional chaplain. However, I felt additional guilt because my decision to accept the call would force us to move again, causing pain for the entire family. Although no one in the family had ever expressed it openly, I always felt that I was creating instability in our family by moving from one place to another.

Enclosed in the letter from Lutheran Social Service were the following instructions:, "If interested in the position of Correctional Staff Chaplain, you should respond by letter, making immediate travel arrangements to come for an interview at the Iowa State Men's Reformatory." Looking at the position description and taking everything into consideration, I felt ambivalent. I had fallen in love with so many people in Houston, especially those young black athletes who were involved in a mission that would now seem incomplete if I left. And although there was only a verbal agreement with the manager of the South Park Village Apartments, my departure also meant leaving the ministry I had begun with the young residents. On the other hand, I knew that I had only come to Houston because of a need for immediate employment. My family still felt homesickness and isolation in being so far south, away from family members and friends in Chicago. Most of all, I had a deep need to trust God insofar as seeing this particular call as God's way of guiding me into a more specialized phase of ministry that would also bring us geographically closer to family in Chicago. As I visited families of the South Park Mission athletic program and South Park Village Apartments, I told them about the call I had received. It was heart-wrenching to hear their comments and observe their faces when listening to my explanations for leaving.

In hearing of my dilemma and concerns for those I would be leaving behind, my close friend Rev. Albert T. Allen, a Disciples of Christ pastor, invited me to combine our two small congregations on Sunday mornings with worship at his church, Sunnyside Christian Center. I had come to know and respect Pastor Allen from his participation in the boycott of the Bank of North America. Our proposal to members of South Park Mission and Sunnyside Christian Center was to mutually covenant as one congregation with frequent meetings to strengthen relationships and develop a structure providing guidance for joint worship services. We decided to use the names of both congregations, Sunnyside Christian Center and South Park Mission. There was no competition between our denominations, and we began celebrating joint Sunday worship services and continuing to support the South Park Mission Youth Athletic Program, residents of the South Park Village Apartments, and Crestmont Park homeowners. However, our first priority was to create community awareness by inviting the residents of all three neighborhoods to work in a garden project growing fresh vegetables on a plot of land belonging to Sunny Christian Center. Rev. Allen must have been a farmer before his call as the pastor of Sunnyside Christian Center. What a wonderful experience! We all became co-workers in the neighborhood vegetable garden project.

My final step in considering the call to a chaplaincy position at the Iowa state reformatory was to drive to Anamosa for the interview. In his letter, Chaplain Ramon Runkel of Lutheran Social Service in Iowa indicated that he would also be there. I knew that if I accepted the position at the reformatory, I would be the first black chaplain. Only later did I learn there were no black staff members, including guards, at the prison. Most of the prison employees lived in the all-white city of Anamosa. It seemed as though every ministry call presented me with not only new challenges but learning opportunities! I asked a member of our South Park Mission Group, Nathaniel Smith (Nate), who lived in the village apartments, to help me drive to the prison in Anamosa. Nathaniel was a real blessing because he strongly encouraged me to go and took personal time off from his job to help with the drive. Doris, too, went along.

Entering the prison was a new experience for all three of us. Even though I understood the concept of "specialized ministry," its expectations and desired results, the prison looked especially foreboding, seemingly a place where there would be little or no opportunity to provide religious needs for the inmates. The outside walls were constructed of weather-worn, graying white limestone, covered in places with mildew. The limestone had been excavated from the rock quarries of nearby Stone City. The prison looked like an old castle with gun towers that could be seen at the corners of each. As I entered the prison, I had all kinds of fears of failing if I took a ministry position of this nature. But who can measure or define success whenever we obediently respond to God's call? Doris, Nate, and I entered the prison through a wide arched front entrance leading to a rather large open atrium. The warden's office and other offices providing supportive services for inmates and families were located in the atrium. Also inside this atrium area was the prison's central command control center where correctional officers operated two large barred gates. On the other side there was a huge corridor lined with cells on both sides. Most inmates referred to the cells as their "house."

Rev. Ramon Runkel, staff chaplain at Lutheran Social Service in Des Moines, greeted us in the atrium area. He told us that the prison director of treatment, Jack Baughman, would arrive soon and would be doing the interview for my position at the prison. The interview was much shorter than I expected, but it was very informative. Following the interview, Doris and I spoke with Chaplain Runkel about other concerns, especially as to who at Lutheran Social Service of Iowa would be providing us with ministry information and support. Doris and Nathaniel were allowed to listen and observe the interview. Mr. Baughman informed me that the reformatory was a medium-security prison and that all social workers, counselors, and correctional chaplains were under his supervision. When Lutheran Social Service wrote the position description, they developed the proposal specifically to provide a black chaplain for the Iowa State Men's Reformatory, and it was this title that became a specific concern for the director of treatment. He wanted everyone to understand that my position as a staff chaplain would in no way exclude my providing a ministry for both white and black inmates. His concern was a legitimate one. However, I wondered if Mr. Baughman had expressed the same concern for black inmates when he interviewed the two white chaplains. I assured him that although I was solidly grounded in my own racial heritage, I had no problem with having the word *black* removed from the title of the chaplaincy position description. I explained the nature of my call as first coming from God, not the seminary, and God has placed no limitations on to whom I should minister; rather, it included everyone in the prison. I continued to explain: "I would never have received a theological degree from Wartburg Seminary if not qualified to provide religious needs to all those incarcerated here in this prison." Mr. Baughman made it clear that the first priority of the prison was security and not rehabilitation. I told him that I understood and accepted the necessity for security and the safety of prison staff and the citizens of Iowa.

With this additional information and the valuable feedback given me by Doris and Nathaniel, I decided to accept this new call in specialized ministry as a correctional chaplain at the Iowa State Reformatory for Men. Before returning to Houston, Doris and I decided it would be best for our family to move to Cedar Rapids instead of Anamosa. We tentatively scheduled our arrival for sometime in August or September, with hopes that I would begin my work at the reformatory soon afterward.

Returning to Houston was extremely difficult. Once again Nathaniel was extremely supportive and encouraging, saying that he thought I was needed at the prison and should continue to move ahead in my career. Saying goodbye to those who had worked with me in ministry at the South Park Mission was extremely hard, but it was not nearly as hard as the deep sorrow I felt in having to uproot our family and make another move. Aside from expressions of "Oh, no, not again," I have no idea what others in the family thought, but I felt as though we were a family of modern-day nomads. However, I firmly believed our journey together as a family was by God's design and guidance. Our children had matured enough to realize that with each move we were getting closer to the family members we had left behind in Chicago. With each move we had also grown into a more socially and racially acculturated family without losing our own racial identity and heritage. Yes, God is good all the time!

After returning to Houston, farewell meetings were held with members of the South Park Mission, our youth athletic teams, and their families. Although many had already heard of my pending departure, meetings were held to provide more accurate information and respond to questions that only I could answer. Many of these people had been with me from the beginning, helping to structure and develop this ministry. I was astonished at the expressions of deep sadness and weeping at our meetings. For me, this was another one of God's *kairos* moments in realizing how God had touched the hearts of our youth as they shared their personal lives with me. One of them began his goodbye conversation by describing what had happened the night before our meeting. He said three members of the baseball team had "stayed up all night smoking pot, wondering why I had to leave and thinking about all the things we had done together and how much they really loved me." Apologetically, he assured me that it was not the pot talking or causing them to feel the way they did. They were truly grieving and asked again if there was anything they could do to keep me in Houston. At this point, tears came into my eyes to try once more time to explain, perhaps even justify, my leaving. I told them I was convinced that God would heal the pain we all felt whenever we remembered our relationship and what we had come to mean to each other.

Following this meeting with the teenagers, Doris and the women of our small congregation planned farewell parties at the Sunnyside Christian Center and the South Park Village Apartments. Although these goodbye gatherings were more joyous than my earlier meeting with our youth group I saw a lot of sad faces and subdued tears. I was the saddest of all because this was my first ministry after graduating from seminary, and I felt like a complete failure and guilty for leaving before officially establishing a congregation. Everyone wanted to know who would continue the South Park Mission ministry and how what we had begun could be retained. This was *déjà-vu* all over again for me, because I had experienced similar feelings before leaving Holy Family Lutheran Church in Chicago. I was completely at a loss in trying to address all of their concerns, but I assured them that Rev. Richard Fenske, the mission director in Dallas, and Pastors Albert Allen at Sunnyside Christian Center and Don Flachmeir at Hope Lutheran Church would provide those answers that I could not.

CHAPTER 11

Iowa State Men's Reformatory

1973–1976

After three years of ministry at South Park Mission, our family—now only six—traveled by car to Cedar Rapids. Our oldest daughter, Patricia, had already enrolled at Wartburg College in Waverly, Iowa, and our oldest son, Terrance, had decided to join the U.S. Air Force. Cedar Rapids is located twenty-five miles southeast of the Anamosa reformatory, and my commute to work would be fifty miles round-trip, five days a week. Cedar Rapids is the second largest city in Iowa and is the county seat of Linn County. City Hall and the Linn County Courthouse are located on Mays Island in the Cedar River; the city is one of few in the world with governmental offices on a municipal island. The city lies on both banks of the Cedar River, twenty miles north of Iowa City, the location of the University of Iowa, and a hundred miles east of Des Moines, the state's capital and largest city. As of the 1970 census, Cedar Rapid's population was 163,213. St. Luke's and Mercy Hospitals are the two largest hospitals. Notable colleges and universities include Kirkwood Community College, Coe Presbyterian College, and Mount Mercy Catholic University.

Lutheran Social Service of Iowa included a housing allowance in my salary package for rental housing or to purchase a home. We were blessed to receive an interest-free loan from one of our family members for a down payment on a home which allowed us to become first-time home buyers. Our new home was located in southwest Cedar Rapids near Bever Park City Zoo. The zoo was close enough that on any windy day we could hear the roar of lions. We had chosen to live in Cedar Rapids because more schools were available for our children and there was more potential for partnering with Lutheran churches in support of my chaplaincy at the reformatory. Michael and Cheryl enrolled at

Washington Senior High School, where he met and became friends with the twin sons of a local black physician, Dr. Percy Harris. Cheryl excelled not only academically but also in a variety of sports including basketball, baseball, and track. Keith enrolled at McKinley Junior High, eventually entering Washington Senior High, and David enrolled in Johnson Elementary School. As always Doris did a tremendous job in getting our children enrolled in these three different schools. She was always busy organizing and skillfully managing household affairs and caring for our children while working as a part-time sales associate at Killian's Department Store in the Lindale Shopping Mall. Doris also found time to get involved in various programs at Our Savior's Lutheran Church. In retrospect, I feel that my loving wife provided more for our family needs than I did because of her availability for our children. Indeed, every day, in so many ways, God reminded me that our togetherness as a family was God's will!

The selection of a church was easy because Our Savior's Lutheran Church was near our home. Rev. William (Bill) Hilker and Rev. Marvin Ehnen were pastors of the church and had learned that we were in town. It was not long before Pastor Hilker visited our home, informing us about the congregation and inviting us into membership. After learning that I had to be at the prison every Sunday, he graciously offered to provide transportation to church every Sunday for Doris and the children. He also promised congregational support for my ministry at the prison. Eventually, our membership at Holy Family Lutheran Church in Chicago was transferred to Our Savior's in Cedar Rapids.

Our Savior's was a very friendly church, making it easy for our family to adjust in our new environment. There was virtually no evangelical outreach to blacks and other minorities by the congregation, but I am convinced there were many tangible benefits from our presence in the congregation's life and ministry that would facilitate future efforts in outreach. Doris, with her personality and ready smile, made a lot of friends and introduced me to all of them. Eventually she became a Sunday school teacher at the church. One day while she was teaching Vacation Bible School, a young boy, six or seven years old, begin having convulsive epileptic seizures and fell from a church pew onto the floor. Everyone kept their distance from the child until his mother, who was in another part of the church, could come and care for her son. Being afraid and perhaps not knowing what to do, no one approached the child to help him. But Doris, seeing that it was taking a long time for the mother to arrive, sat down next to the child. Cradling his head in her lap she began caressing his hair and forehead while whispering to him. When the boy's mother finally arrived, he had begun to calm down. She thanked Doris and said, "You did the right thing. He's fully aware of what was happening to him and really scared because he couldn't do anything about it. When you put his head in your lap and rubbed his head he knew he wasn't alone!"

Although I maintained a presence in the congregation, my direct participation in its ministry activities was limited. Even so, I was able to recruit several members of Our Savior's Lutheran Church congregation for the volunteer "man to man" prison mentoring program. All volunteers were required to pass criminal background checks and trained to work with the inmates. The program consisted of my pairing inmates with male volunteers (no females) from our congregation to provide support to inmates and their families even after the men were released and transitioned back into the community. I had oversight and responsibility for the program, training and receiving reports from the volunteers. A monthly average of twenty people from local church communities worshipped with the inmates every Sunday morning. Inmates were not allowed to sit with their families and other worshippers during the service. Doris and our children also had an opportunity to worship with inmates at the prison during one special Christmas Eve service.

When Michael was sixteen years old he became ill with what we at first thought was a common cold. A local doctor said he had nothing more than a cold, so we tried everything we could think of to treat it, but nothing worked. Seeing no improvement in Michael's condition, we made an appointment to have him examined by Dr. Percy Harris, one of two local black physicians living in Cedar Rapids, who was on the staff at St. Luke's Hospital. Eventually Dr. Harris became our primary family physician. Following chest X-rays, Dr. Harris diagnosed our son's illness as "walking pneumonia," meaning that he was able to function from day to day but was in danger of becoming seriously ill. He expressed a mild criticism of the first doctor for not taking chest X-rays before dismissing

Michael's illness as simply a common cold. Michael was immediately hospitalized at St. Luke's for a number of days and treated for pneumonia with antibiotics and other medications. Before leaving the hospital, Michael was given another chest X-ray, which revealed a large dark spot in the lower left lobe of his lung. Concerned about the spot, Dr. Harris recommended that we allow him to schedule a consultation for Michael with his colleague, Dr. Montague Lawrence, Cedar Rapid's other black doctor, a thoracic pulmonary surgeon who was not only a consulting surgeon for hospitals in the Cedar Rapids area but also instructed medical students in heart and lung surgical procedures at the University Hospital in Iowa City. Dr. Lawrence was widely recognized for having operated for lung cancer on the well-known radio talk show host, Arthur Godfrey. Following Michael's examination we were informed that the dark spot on his left lung was necrotic tissue—dead tissue resulting from his bout with pneumonia. Dr. Lawrence said that unless it was removed there would always be a threat for any number of lung infections and even a place where cancer might begin. He recommended removal of the lower left lobe of Michael's lung where the dead tissue was located. He assured us that Michael's lung would eventually heal, expanding close to its normal size in the process of his regular breathing. After consulting again with Dr. Harris, Doris and I decided it would be best for Michael to have the surgery. Pastor Marvin Enhen from our church remained with us through four hours of surgery. Marvin provided us with good conversation which helped the time go by quickly. The surgery was successful, and our family was still together and growing in many ways! After his graduation from Washington Senior High School, Michael enrolled as a freshman at the University of Iowa in Iowa City, where he attended classes for two years. He commuted to the university, forty miles round trip, driving from Cedar Rapids and back home in his little orange Volkswagen that we called the "Bug." I was really proud of Michael because he purchased his car with money earned from working at a neighborhood Hy-Vee Supermarket.

    The Iowa State Reformatory was a medium/maximum security prison but now is the largest penitentiary in Iowa, housing over 1,200 male inmates. The prison was established in 1872 and constructed from locally quarried white limestone built in the style of a castle. The Boy's Training School was located in Eldora, near the capital city of Des Moines.

During my three-year tenure as chaplain at the reformatory, the state's maximum-security prison was located in Fort Madison, on the banks of the Mississippi River. I mention these three Iowa prison facilities because of the interconnectedness of my ministry in the Iowa State Correctional system and how I would eventually connect with each of these facilities. During the time I worked as a chaplain at the reformatory, America was rebounding from widespread massive nonviolent civil rights confrontations against institutional racism. The job description written by Lutheran Social Service focused on a "ministry of reconciliation." Its intent was reconciliation with God, self, family, and community in both black and white racial groups. If recidivism rates were to be effectively lowered, it was essential that reconciliation begin with pastoral care in counseling inmates and their families while focusing on the community context in which their crimes were committed. Relative and essential to the process of inmate rehabilitation and reconciliation was the white prison staff, which was seen as the system's symbol of repression.

Eventually, the scope of my ministry necessitated revisions to my job description to include working one day a week contacting inmate families in communities and those released to half-way houses, jails, and other correctional institutions connected with the prison inmates' rehabilitation. Community visitations were determined by the cities with the largest black population. Those cities were Cedar Rapids, Iowa City, Davenport, Waterloo, Des Moines, and the maximum security prison at Fort Madison. Occasionally, I made visits to inmates attending my counseling groups who were sent to the Oakdale Mental Health Correctional facility for psychiatric evaluation. These visits were designed to maintain an awareness of counseling and continuity in support services for inmates going through psychological evaluation for rape and other violent crimes. My job clearly focused on a reconciliation with God, family, racial relationships, and restoration back into the community. An integral but vital dimension of my job was teaching new ways of thought and behavior in racial reconciliation between white prison staff, black and white inmates, families, and communities—a diverse and complex group of human beings. The definition and standards of rehabilitation and reconciliation were desperately in need of change. Most of the methods used at that time overlooked the glaring differences in the traditions, needs, and societal opportunities for the rehabilitation of black inmates. As you might imagine, I was overwhelmed physically and mentally in thinking about the expectations of all who had passively defined and structured their concept of reconciliation. I found myself often praying for God's wisdom and guidance: "And those from among you will rebuild the ancient ruins; you will raise up the age old foundations; and you will be called the repairer of the breach, the restorer of the streets in which to dwell" (Isaiah 58:12, NAS). I believe God gave me the wisdom, love, and resolve to be one of those "called to be a repairer of the breach and restorer of the streets in which to dwell." Therefore, with the power of God's love and grace, I did the best I could to faithfully follow God's expectations, not mine or those of a correctional system in need of new life.

When I arrived at the Iowa State Reformatory for Men, there were two white chaplains on the treatment staff. Father John Barnes, a Catholic priest, had worked at the prison for ten years and was considered by the treatment department as its senior chaplain. Rev. Robert Allen, an Assemblies of God minister, had been hired only a few months prior to my coming to work at the prison and was the only one of us chaplains who was salaried by the Iowa State Reformatory. However, this was also true of the white Baptist chaplain at the maximum-security prison in Fort Madison. It was clear that church, state, and federal agencies had structured their training and qualifications for chaplaincy ministry positions, so that this profession effectively had functioned as a whites-only, closed shop. Witnessing to our Christian reconciliation with God and others must begin in the household of Faith! Socio-economic, political, and ethnic racial traditions for the most part prevented partnership with churches in the black community. My comments are not made to excuse the lack of personal responsibility in the black community, but this era was in the 60s, and the civil rights movement had just begun.

Father Barnes and I had been called or, in his case, appointed to specialized pastoral ministry positions with salaries and benefits provided by our white church denominational judicatories. Following a research study initiated by Wartburg Theological Seminary indicating the need for a black chaplain at the prison, the American Lutheran Church Council in partnership with Lutheran Social Service of Iowa, Lutheran Church—Missouri Synod, the Wheat Ridge Foundation developed a structure for soliciting funding for a black chaplaincy position at the Iowa State Reformatory. This avant garde ministry model resulted in a church-state partnership that successfully financed the position and called me to serve as the first black correctional chaplain on the treatment staff. Lutheran Social Service of Iowa routinely kept me informed of various prison statistics, including an update of the inmate population. At the beginning of my work that consisted of three or four hundred young men, mostly white. Shortly before my arrival, state and other social institutions had become increasingly alarmed at the rising population of black inmates. The population of minority inmates had grown to twenty-two percent, with eighteen percent being black. The remaining four percent were American Indians or Hispanics. An important question for Lutheran Social Service of Iowa was from where had all the black inmates come, when only two percent of the population in Iowa was black.

Because it was unclear what a prison-focused ministry of reconciliation should be or how it would evolve, and my own concerns whether I had the ability and strength to accomplish everyone's expectations, I always found myself in prayer. I cannot overemphasize the power of prayer for guidance, peace, and empowerment! Eventually, I realized that in order to understand what it meant to work on reconciliation I would have to define its meaning day by day. Moreover, I was concerned about being able to handle my family responsibilities, which required an endless balancing act. And of course I had to consider what God expected of me amid all the complex expectations of the Lutheran Social Service of Iowa, prison administrators, and inmates. A double whammy compounded my feelings of inadequacy because I was a pioneer as the first black Lutheran chaplain in the Iowa State penal system. Perhaps those who had prayed and envisioned my call to this special ministry had more faith in my strength and abilities than I did. Nevertheless, in wrestling with all my doubts and unanswered questions, I requested a meeting with my white colleagues to seek their thoughts and discuss expectations of their working with a black chaplain. After all, to have any measure of success in our ministry we needed a clear understanding of our call and how to best communicate our purpose and witness inside the prison. Following our initial staff meeting, a decision was made to leave existing Sunday worship schedules as they were, with separate Catholic and Protestant services. However, Rev. Allen, the Assemblies of God minister, raised some concerns about our working together in Sunday morning worship. Although Rev. Allen and I were both Protestants, he was concerned that my being Lutheran would inhibit our working together in worship. Earlier he had expressed theological differences that made it impossible for him to work with Father Barnes in a worship service. I assured him that there were no glaring theological issues for me that would prevent me from working with him or the Catholic priest in worship services. I viewed this as a special opportunity for me to learn and do a few things differently while sharing my own religious odyssey with others. I shared my black family religious orientation with both men, ending my remarks by saying, "Our celebration of worship together has great potential to give a strong witness of Christian unity to all the inmates, a witness that, regrettably, most of them have never experienced in the churches of their own community. In fact, God is giving us this opportunity to dialogue with the inmates about what we're trying to accomplish and why." Following my comments, I asked Rev. Allen whether as Protestant Christians we could hold worship services together, and he agreed to give it a try. He gave it more than a try, because he was able to "hang in there" with some of my unorthodox language, especially the examples and stories I used to highlight my sermons.

I remember sharing this personal story with the inmates during one of my Sunday morning sermons. I began with the experiences of two young married men with families:

> Both men were experiencing money problems, and for the first time in their lives they decided to sell drugs to get them out of their financial woes. Both were amateurs at selling drugs and didn't know what they were doing. The first young man spent $500 to buy something he thought was marijuana from an experienced drug dealer. After returning home he discovered he had been scammed. He had nothing but a bag of sage tea leaves and a lot of other brownish-green leafy junk. Trying to recoup his loss, he took a friend with him who knew the drug trade and spent $500 more to buy some hashish or concentrated marijuana. He mixed the hashish with the bag of junk he had bought earlier and sold it. He made up for his losses but decided against selling more drugs. The second young man was also new at selling drugs and bought a bag of pills containing uppers and downers and probably some

other pills. He drove to a school in the neighborhood and parked his car in a place where other drug dealers waited for the school kids to come to their cars and buy drugs on their way home. As he waited, he noticed the kids were flocking to the other drug dealers like they were the Good Humor Ice Cream Man. Waiting for someone to come to him, he suddenly imagined seeing his own kids running up to the car of a drug dealer at their school. Feeling guilty and with a bad conscience, he threw the pills away. Both these young men were my brothers. The moral of this story is that you guys don't know what kind of shit you're putting inside your bodies. But you already know this and you still place your faith and trust in the hands of drug dealers!

There was some negative fallout from one of the inmates about my use of profanity in the sermon, but I was able to turn our conversation into a teaching opportunity about life with God.

Conversation with an inmate at the reformatory.

Rev. Allen and I continued working together throughout my tenure at the reformatory, not only in worship but in teaching Bible classes and occasionally as a team in group counseling. Our agreement effectively decreased our work load, and as time passed it became much easier to communicate with inmates in our separate groups. Although we continued working together, individual counseling remained separate for all three of us. Having two chaplains on Sunday mornings enabled us to alternate preaching assignments and consecration of Holy Communion. In fact, working the Protestant Sunday services together eventually made it possible for each of us to have an occasional Sunday off. This gave me an opportunity to worship with my family at Our Savior's Lutheran Church in Cedar Rapids. It was truly exhilarating to experience these opportunities given us in a ministry of reconciliation rarely seen in local Christian churches. Because I was a new face and the first black chaplain, coupled with our decision to conduct a single unified Protestant worship service, had an initial negative effect on the Catholic Sunday worship attendance, which would to some extent be a challenge for Father Barnes throughout my tenure at the reformatory. Monthly statistical reports that I sent to Lutheran Social Service were shared with Jack Baughman, the prison director of treatment, which caused some revisions to the job descriptions of my white chaplaincy colleagues. Soon an issue arose at one of our staff meetings as to who was the supervisor of our chaplaincy team and how information was to be communicated from our unit to the director of treatment. Father Barnes informed me and Rev. Allen that the director of treatment had appointed him supervisor over the chaplaincy unit. As we had not received a memo from Mr. Baughman informing us of this decision, I responded in no uncertain words, "You're not going to be my supervisor. Rev. Allen can speak for himself, but according to my job description I'm under the direct supervision of the director of treatment, which I need to fulfill certain expectations in my job description of developing a ministry of reconciliation. You're my colleague and I'll work with you in every way possible, but you will not be my supervisor! Because Mr. Baughman hasn't contacted me about this matter it's your responsibility to inform him of my response." Rev. Allen listened intently but did not speak, and I never heard anything from the director of treatment. However, Mr. Baughman did issue a memo indicating he would use Father Barnes as a liaison to share information about our weekly staff meetings and chaplaincy programs. I continued giving copies of my monthly Lutheran Social Service chaplaincy reports to Mr. Baughman, along with other conversations. My monthly statistical reports eventually gave him insight into possible new chaplaincy programs and my personal ministry goals.

Both chaplaincy offices were located near the chapel with a separate cubicle for chaplaincy clerks, who for the most part scheduled our appointments with inmates. One office was for the Catholic chaplain and the other was shared by me and Rev. Allen. Chaplaincy clerks were assigned to both of our offices by their counselors. The worship area was constructed much like any other church, filled with wooden pews fastened to the floor that seated about 125 worshippers. Aisles were located on both sides of the pews, and a larger center aisle with two steps led to the altar. A large brass cross sat on a wooden table in the middle of the altar. On the left side of the altar was a small pulpit with a built-in microphone. A lectern was located on the right side of the altar and was used for reading scripture lessons. We had a small organ in the chapel that was used by inmates and community volunteers for our worship services. Most of the chapel furniture had been constructed by prison inmates or donated by churches. Eventually, my work evolved into working with both white and black inmates who wanted to participate in chapel choirs and design the worship bulletins for Sunday services. Traditional Gospel music indigenous to our black religious experience was well received by white ethnic groups, especially whenever I invited black Gospel singers from the community to the worship services. Inmate choir practice was always supervised by one or more chaplains. What a wonderful revelation to see how talented some of these guys were! Even now, I wonder why they ended up in prison. I realized that the importance of their making good decisions in life was a factor, but I knew it was more than that. One or more correctional officers were always assigned near the chapel area, which was also located near the prison's visiting room. We received keys for our offices and the visiting room whenever we arrived at work and returned them when we left for the day. If for any reason we took the keys home with us, we were immediately called to return them to the prison.

Working together with Rev. Allen in worship services proved to be beneficial for both of us. On occasion, Rev. Allen and I celebrated special worship services together with Father Barnes and prison inmates. This was our attempt to give an ecumenical witness to our Christian unity. These services included Thanksgiving, Christmas Eve, Christmas Day, and Easter celebrated with the Sacrament of Holy Communion, which was always consecrated and distributed by Father Barnes; neither Rev. Allen nor I assisted in communion preparation or in its distribution. During these eucharistic celebrations, I always came up to the communion rail, knelt, and received the sacrament from Father Barnes. However, because of irreconcilable theological differences between the Assemblies of God and the Roman Catholic Church, Rev. Allen never participated in the Lord's Supper. As for me, my belief and spiritual faith in the words and promise of the resurrected Christ's body and blood being present in the bread and wine precluded our theological differences as to when precisely the transformation happened. I accepted Holy Communion from Father Barnes with faith in the love of Jesus Christ, even though I felt he never would have accepted it if I had consecrated the elements of bread and wine.

One day a worship service of Holy Communion was celebrated to recognize the prison's chaplaincy ministry. The Catholic bishop of the local diocese officiated at Holy Communion. Rev. Allen and I attended the service and read the Scriptures. The Chapel of the Good Thief was filled with over 100 inmates and other visitors from the community, affirming and supporting our chaplaincy ministry. When the bishop completed consecration of the bread and grape juice (not wine) for Holy Communion, I went to the altar and, as usual, I knelt at the railing as in the past, stretching my hands out to receive the communion wafer. But Father Barnes, who was assisting with communion, passed me and gave it to an inmate kneeling next to me. The bishop, who was closely following Father Barnes, knew I was a minister because I was wearing my clerical collar. Puzzled and thinking that perhaps Father Barnes may not have seen me, the bishop extended the chalice for me to dip a wafer into the grape juice. Then, realizing that Father Barnes had intentionally not given me a communion wafer, he also passed me and extended the chalice to the same inmate kneeling next to me. Hurt and angry, I immediately left the communion rail, returned to my office, and went home where I prayed about the incident.

Later, several inmates who were present at worship and saw the whole incident asked me why Father Barnes had refused to give me Holy Communion. Unwilling to risk the possibility of an angry answer to their question, I told them to ask him. I remembered a similar incident in the Bible when conflict had arisen between Peter and Paul. Paul's words reflect some of my own anger: "When Peter came to Antioch, I opposed him to his face, because he was clearly in the wrong. Before certain men [Jewish Apostles] came from James, Peter ate with the Gentiles. But when they arrived, he withdrew and separated himself from the Gentiles because he was afraid of those who belonged to the circumcision group. This caused other Jews to join him in his hypocrisy, so that by their [combined] hypocrisy even Barnabas was led astray. When I saw they were not acting in line with the truth of the gospel, I said to Peter in front of them all, 'You are a Jew, yet you live like a Gentile and not like a Jew. How is it, then, that you force Gentiles to follow Jewish customs?'" (Galatians 2:11-14). Although my experience with Father Barnes was not exactly the same as Paul's, I thought there was a direct correlation between the ecclesiastical hypocrisy of Father Barnes and the Apostle Peter's two-faced relationships with the Gentiles. In giving me Holy Communion when his bishop was not present, but refusing to give it when he was there, Father Barnes had effectively separated himself from me as his Christian colleague to the inmates. Those kneeling at the altar rail were not there because they were Jews, Roman Catholics, Lutherans, or Assemblies of God, but because we were all Christian brothers. I deeply felt that as representatives of Christ we had lost an opportunity of witnessing to the meaning of a ministry of reconciliation.

It took a couple of days before I calmed down and spoke to Father Barnes about the incident. I told him that some of the inmates had asked me why he refused to give me Holy Communion, and then I read the text from Galatians 2:11-14. I let him know how much he had hurt me and that we had lost an opportunity to witness to our Christian unity in the presence of his bishop. I was still angry, feeling that reconciliation was not only essential to all our job descriptions but especially in our prison mission. I criticized his actions as hypocritical, probably reinforcing negative feelings of correctional officers, inmates, and others about religion in prison rehabilitation. Angrily I said, "You're a Catholic, yet here in the prison when your bishop isn't present you live like a Protestant!" He immediately apologized, asking for forgiveness, while explaining that he had already been called on the carpet by the bishop, who wanted to know why he had refused to give me Holy Communion. I forgave him, saying that I would continue attending special Catholic worship services for the sake of the inmates but that I would no longer receive Holy Communion. When I shared our conversation with Rev. Allen, he said, "I knew he was like this and that he would never give you Holy Communion in the presence of his bishop." I responded to Rev. Allen, explaining, "I had my own misgivings but received Holy

Communion from him because it was my way of giving meaning and witness to our ministry of reconciliation in the prison. I had thought Father Barnes to be more progressive because all the inmates receiving Communion were not Catholic and I was never asked to not receive Holy Communion."

As time passed, one of the white correctional officers assigned to the Chapel of the Good Thief became a close friend. During our Sunday worship services, I noticed that he not only monitored inmate behavior during worship services but was very attentive to what was being preached in our sermons. Following many of our services he would have a lively discussion with us, questioning whether or not what we preached made a difference. One evening following dinner, I was surprised to receive a phone call at home from his wife informing me that he had suffered a stroke and wanted her to bring his gun to the hospital so he could kill himself. She said she needed help and called me because her husband often spoke about me. She wondered if I would go with her to St. Luke's Hospital to visit him. I agreed, saying I would bring my wife to keep her company.

When we arrived, Doris and I briefly talked with her in the hallway. This was the first time I had met his wife. When we entered his room Doris and I followed his wife to his bedside. The room was quiet and semi-dark. Upon reaching his bed, she leaned over and kissed him. I could see the sad, pitiful, and hopeless look on his face. He noticed us but in the darkness of the room he had not recognized me. When he did, his facial expression changed to one of complete shock. I took advantage of his surprise and—I must admit, my response was not that of a trained pastoral counselor—I angrily asked him why he had put his wife in the position of doing his dirty work by asking her to bring him his gun. I said, "If you really want to die, you don't ask someone you love to bring the instrument for your death. And while you're at it, you should have asked her to pull the trigger!" As he quickly glanced at his wife, tears came into his eyes. I couldn't tell if it was a look of anger or embarrassment. He admitted that he was scared, wasn't able to think clearly, and didn't know how to handle his illness. All he could think of was the gravity of his situation, that he was no longer a man, and would lose his job at the prison. We assured them of confidentiality and our continuing support. I encouraged him to trust his wife and family to handle everything at home while he cooperated with his doctors on getting well. We ended with prayer and a reminder of the Alcoholics Anonymous credo of taking "one step at a time" as well as "one day at a time." Our conversation revealed that they were members of a church in Anamosa, but they hadn't attended in some time. I encouraged them to reconnect with their church, informing their pastor of their need so they would receive continuing spiritual support.

After saying our goodbyes and moving toward the door to leave I noticed that my friend was still looking as hopeless as ever. Nothing seemed to have changed, and our prayers appeared meaningless. I also noticed that his wife's face reflected her husband's demeanor. Suddenly, without knowing why, I left both women at the door and walked back to his bed. I leaned over and whispered these words in my friend's ear: "If our prayers don't help, I'm going to come back and give you the worst cussing out you've ever had!" Startled, my correctional officer friend looked up in disbelief but had the biggest smile on his face I have ever seen. I left his bedside and returned to the women, who had been waiting for me and saw everything. Although they asked me what I had said to make him smile, this was strictly between the correctional officer, me, and God! It seemed as though I was never completely able to maintain appropriate boundaries when it came to challenging traditionally established religious norms and structures that restricted growth in reconciling human relationships. But regardless of the unorthodox manner in which I initiated caring relationships, spiritual healing and reconciliation had taken root.

Ten or twelve weeks later during a Sunday morning worship service, my correctional officer friend walked into the Chapel of the Good Thief with a cane in his hand. He was greeted by the inmates with cheers and applause! The prison administrators had not forced him into early disability retirement as he had feared, but instead assigned him light duty in and around the chapel area. He informed me that he and his wife had begun attending their church again. Eventually he was able to walk without a cane, and I was reminded of a time long ago when God was with me in my recovery from polio. I, too, had walked again without crutches or a cane.

We chaplains had separate orientation sessions with all new inmates entering the prison system. These sessions provided information about Catholic and Protestant chaplaincy programs, including worship services in the Chapel of the Good Thief. Inmates were invited to enroll in individual and/or family counseling and Bible study. These orientation sessions provided me with most of the "kites" (request slips) from inmates wanting to enroll in one or more chaplaincy activities. Kites were nothing more than permission slips allowing inmates to move from one place to another to attend various counseling groups, jobs, and other rehabilitation activities in the prison. It was during one of these orientation sessions when I become aware that there were some Black Muslims in the prison. My chaplaincy colleagues felt the presence of these men in their Bible study groups was threatening because they perceived the Muslims as disruptive and therefore undesirable. However, I embraced the presence of Black Muslims in my groups as an opportunity for all of us to learn more about both our religious beliefs. I also took advantage of every opportunity to include them in my counseling groups. My success in communicating with inmates from diverse religious backgrounds, including Muslims, opened the door for the other two chaplains to slowly begin having Bible studies with non-Christians. Perhaps in some way my openness to include and respect racial and religious diversity in all my groups was the beginning of a true ministry of reconciliation.

The inmate population reflected the diverse racial ethnic, cultural, and religious groups of our society. In one of my groups, a white inmate ventured his opinion that "We don't have any racism inside the prison because we're all prisoners!" Of course none of the black inmates agreed with him, but most of the other white inmates also disagreed. Perhaps this was a test for me, and everyone was waiting for my response. And I did respond, saying, "Then all of the white people in America who are not in prison should be put in prison so they can be cured of their racism. The truth is that when you were imprisoned, racism was imprisoned with you. Just ask those here in this group; they'll tell you it can be seen everywhere in the prison!" My response was followed by laughter from both black and white inmates. I cautioned them not to direct their laughter at the white inmate who had made the statement because, although mistaken, he did have the courage to speak what he thought.

In one way or another, these experiences always gave me an opportunity to strengthen my relationships with the inmates. I found one of the best resources for counseling was in my willingness to share the stories in my own life's journey. I opened my religious background, traditions, and beliefs for discussion and evaluation by the inmates. This approach made me vulnerable—and they put me to the test many times, but somehow I found the wisdom and strength to continue building relationships. At times it seemed as though I was totally one with those inmates who participated in my groups. Through God's grace I had earned their trust and respect as a loving advocate who fostered their self-esteem in giving them hope and a new direction in their lives. During one of my inmate group counseling sessions a young white inmate complained over and over about how hard it was for him to serve his time. As he continued complaining, a young black man, who had earlier identified himself as a Black Muslim, interrupted him, saying, "I don't know why you're complaining so much. Your time is shorter than mine, and besides your daddy's going to take care of you!" No one said anything because we were unsure what he meant. Finally, I asked him to explain. Directing his words at the white inmate, he said, "The warden is your daddy. The assistant warden is your daddy. The prison guards and social worker/counselors are all your daddies. And with all these daddies, you at least have some hope of getting out of prison sooner than me. The only 'daddy' I have is seeing Chaplain Branch here in the prison." At that time, I was the only black staff member in the prison. We're all familiar with the phrase "being in the right place at the right time." If only for this young black inmate, I was in the right place at the right time, and my presence had become a visible, tangible ray of hope for him. As a Vietnam War veteran, he continued telling us about the negative impact racism had on his discharge from the army. He and a white friend were discharged on the same day. They had gone through basic training together as well as all the dangers of combat that had put them in harm's way. This experience had solidified their friendship. But as they prepared to be discharged and return home, the white soldier told the Black Muslim inmate that they could no longer be friends. "We were friends in the army, but things are different now," he said. "We're going back to the States, so you'll have to go your way and I'll go my way!" The Black Muslim inmate shared his feelings of anger in telling his story of how they both had partied together, drank, smoked weed, and had sex with women, and how hurt he had been by his white friend's rejection of a continuing friendship.

Immediately following this particular group session I began receiving more kites from black and white inmates requesting Bible study or individual and/or group counseling. I believe this incident had helped most of them decide to trust me in handling personal criticisms and conflicts while maintaining an openness to discuss the community realities awaiting them after their release from prison. In fact, I received a kite from a white inmate who was unable to attend my Bible study group because he was locked in "the hole," isolated from the general prison population because he had kicked a correctional officer. The kite he sent me requested that I visit him and bring him a Bible, which I did. During my visit with him I noticed several copies of *Reader's Digest* lying on his bed and scattered on the floor of his cell.

Following my visit with this inmate I received a call from the director of treatment asking me to come to his office. He told me not to give any more Bibles to inmates confined in an isolation cell. He stated, "They're there for punishment and shouldn't receive any source of spiritual comfort." I tried to be as respectful as I could with my response, saying, "When you have all those copies of the *Reader's Digest* removed from his cell, which in some way give him spiritual comfort, then I'll personally ask him to return the Bible I gave him!" It seemed that there was always some kind of power struggle going on in the prison. I was not questioning the director's authority, only trying to give him a clearer insight into that inmate's needs. The Bible I had given him remained with the inmate in his isolation cell, and I was never called into the director's office again about the distribution of Bibles.

Any success in developing a ministry of reconciliation was soon short-circuited. One of the white inmates, who regularly attended my Bible study sessions, told me he was dropping out of the group because his social worker/counselor said he was not giving credits to anyone attending my Bible study group because he did not consider it to be counseling. Other inmates in my group began describing their experiences with this particular social worker/counselor. However, some committed to remaining in my group without receiving credits because, as they said,

"I'm learning a lot about the Bible as well as things I didn't know about myself." I asked the inmates to continue attending my Bible study group until I could talk with the counselor.

It took a few days of prayer to consider the possible reasons behind this counselor's decision and the effect it might have on other chaplaincy programs because of his not-so-subtle references to our counseling abilities. I went to Father Barnes and Rev. Allen for help, asking if their Bible study groups had been declared "off limits" in terms of being granted counseling credits by social worker/counselors. They informed me that the same social worker/counselor had refused to grant inmates credits for their Bible study groups, but that they had never said anything to him about it. Their thinking was aligned with those of the social worker/counselor—that is, if an inmate was truly interested in Bible study he would attend classes without receiving credit from his counselor. There is some validity to this line of thinking, but I was beginning to feel alone in trying to defend what I thought were essential ingredients for a Christian ministry of reconciliation and rehabilitation. I strongly sensed that there were moral issues involved that had become a roadblock to reconciliation and were much broader and more complex than racism alone. I had felt for some time that we chaplains were more or less tolerated and not respected for our expertise and ability to effectively counsel inmates towards rehabilitation. Religion is essential to our societal moral traditions and yet it wasn't a priority for most social worker/counselors, other prison staff and administrators. My guess is that these counselors had their own personal problems with Christianity effecting positive change, so as chaplains it was our job to defend our counseling, defining our ministry as essential to the rehabilitation of inmates. I suspected that the director of the treatment department who hired me reflected a similar attitude toward us as did the social worker/counselors. Christian religious counseling was not perceived as being very effective in the inmates' rehabilitation and therefore dismissed by many of the social worker/counselors and correctional officers. Many of them were outspoken about their opinions and often said, "The inmates are just giving you guys a good snow job!" I believe some of these negative feelings were due to the social worker/counselors' lack of knowledge concerning our educational background, training, and competency in pastoral care counseling. However, I also believe that this negative perception was as much our fault as that of the social worker/counselors.

Finally I decided to make a phone call to the inmate's counselor about his refusal to give counseling credits for attending Bible study and the negative impact that his decision was having on attendance in my group. Also, I expressed my concern that what he was doing might influence other counselors to follow his lead. He adamantly defended his position, but my Bible study group was my largest and most consistent activity, and I wasn't about to give up so easily in losing any of them. However, prayer had already provided me with a solution to the problem. First, I reminded the young counselor that he had not yet found the time to accept my invitation to attend one of my Bible study sessions to observe my counseling techniques and teaching methods and how they contributed to inmate rehabilitation. Then I said, "It's a fact that there's no better book for counseling and encouraging responsible ethical behavior than the Bible." I informed him that I would continue using the Bible in these sessions but was changing the title of my group from Bible study to religious counseling. I asked for his approval and assurance that he would give counseling credits to all the inmates attending my renamed "religious counseling group." My discussion with the counselor was personal, because I thought my white chaplaincy colleagues should speak for themselves. The social worker/counselor agreed to my proposal! God is good all the time, and my family of white and black inmates in my renamed "religious counseling group" was still together!

When I reported my conversation with this counselor at our weekly chaplaincy staff meeting, one of my colleagues responded, "There may be a perception gap between what we do and what the social work/counselors believe we're doing that effectively impacts the inmates' rehabilitation." Problems of this nature were never on the agenda of our weekly chaplaincy staff meetings, nor did we at this time discuss what we should do about lessening the counselors' perception gap relative to the effectiveness of our work at the prison. It appeared as though we went along with whatever the administration deemed necessary for rehabilitation. However, I discovered that there was at one time a prison newsletter available that could be used to communicate chaplaincy programs, but we had never used it. I suggested that we begin writing articles in the newsletter clarifying our unique partnership with social worker/counselors and others involved in the rehabilitation process. As chaplains, it was incumbent upon us to make sure that our prison colleagues understood the powerful potential of our witnessing ministry to effect moral change and social rehabilitation in the prison milieu.

While pondering ministry opportunities and puzzled by statistics reporting an increasing percentage of blacks incarcerated in Iowa prisons, I am reminded of an incident that occurred between me and a white correctional officer. He was well known for the verbal negativity he always expressed about the ministry of us chaplains. His curt responses to the inmates also reflected his total lack of empathy for those caught up in the violence and immorality of our society and the prison environment. I'm cognizant of the dangers involved when correctional officers coddle or fraternize with inmates. Because the prison's correctional officers at that time were all white, I was the only minority racial presence available to the black inmates. They perceived me as someone in the system with the authority to help them in their personal struggles as a racial minority. On the day of this incident, I was on my way to visit with an inmate and his family. On the way to the visitors' room I had to pass a small open area where inmates were strip-searched for contraband before entering and leaving the visitors' room. As I walked past this area, I saw a young black inmate who was in one of my counseling groups. He had completed his visit and was now stooped over being examined by this white correctional officer for any contraband that might be hidden in his rectal area. Holding one of two large gate keys in my hand I continued walking toward the door of the visitors' room, then suddenly I turned around and said to the correctional officer, "I bet you never saw so many black asses in all your life!" The inmate knew who I was, but he remained in his bent-over position and did not look up. The correctional officer immediately stopped examining the young inmate and stood up. Staring at me incredulously, he said, "Chaplain Branch, you're something else!" Although I have no idea of what he meant by it, I'll never forget his response. From that day forward, this officer's personality changed. He seemed to be more relaxed and became more open, not only exchanging daily greetings but also in other conversations. This was the first and last time I used this particular approach, and I wouldn't recommend it as a model for communication in a ministry of racial reconciliation. My hope was that my remark would raise the correctional officer's awareness of his relationship to this young black man as being very limited if this was the only way he could ever see him, and that it would begin to open his eyes to our common humanity.

Following this incident, I was confronted by a crucial question of ministry: How was it possible to live for Christ without taking risks, even though taking them might have a destructive effect on my life that would affect my family? Then I remembered Luke 14:27-28, 33, where Jesus speaks of what it means to be his disciple: "No one can be my disciple who doesn't carry his own cross and follow me. And remember don't begin until you count the cost! Sit down and count your blessings, and then renounce them all for me" (*The Living Bible,* paraphrased). This scriptural reminder comforted me in taking responsibility for my actions but at the same time confronted me with a deeper question. Now I had to decide whether or not to continue following Jesus's example! I answered this concern by recommitting myself to continue my missional odyssey of faith because of what Christ had already done in my life. For me this call included ministry to the staff as well as all the inmates. I had been transformed into a strong advocate for everyone in the prison, black and white, to effectively establish a new foundation for Christian reconciliation. This spiritual experience strengthened my faith in the sustaining power of God's wisdom, love, and grace! Sooner or later I thought I would be asked to resign, but it never happened. Therefore, I faithfully embrace these healing words spoken by our Lord Jesus Christ to the apostle Paul: "My grace is sufficient for you, as my power is perfected in weakness! Therefore I will boast all the more gladly about my weaknesses, so that the power of Christ may rest upon me" (2 Corinthians 12:9, NIV).

I never truly realized the scope or intensity of my work and its effect on me and my family until I looked through copies of my monthly statistical reports. The stories have been limited to only a few. Father Barnes and Rev. Allen were loving and compassionate chaplains. However, I believe that God had given me the strength not to feel threatened when talking with inmates about institutional racism and the role it has played in the separation of white and black people. God had given me the courage to question the prison's rationale for its antiquated rehabilitation procedures. During my discussions about race I was acutely aware of how the inmates had become experts at playing us chaplains, manipulating black and white against one another to get what they wanted. However, the fact remains that most black inmates who did not participate in groups led by the white chaplains had very few opportunities for religious trips outside in the community. This was also true to some extent for white inmates, because attendance in chaplaincy religious programs or counseling was mandatory for all inmates seeking religious trips outside the reformatory.

A case in point was when I found myself the only available chaplain to take a grieving black inmate to his father's funeral in Rockford, Illinois. Although this particular inmate was not a member of any of my groups, he had been cleared and given permission by his social worker/counselor to attend the funeral if a member of the prison staff would take him. There were no correctional officers available or willing, and, although he regularly attended our Sunday worship services, Rev. Allen and Father Barnes were unavailable or didn't want to take the risk of escorting him to the funeral. There were all kinds of legalities involved, and I don't remember whether or not an Interstate Compact prison agreement existed between the states of Iowa and Illinois. The Interstate Compact was a legal agreement between two states establishing responsibility and protection for each state in case an inmate escaped or further offended while on a trip into the community. Even aware of these risks, I decided to take the grieving young black inmate to his father's funeral. I was gratified to know that up to now no inmate had escaped or attempted an escape while outside on a trip with any of us chaplains.

As the inmate and I left the reformatory we went through the control-center gates leading to the atrium outside. After going through the first gate and before opening the second gate to the outside, one of the correctional officers slid a pair of handcuffs to me through a small hole underneath the thick glass of the control-center window. He told me that it was customary to use handcuffs when taking prisoners out on trips. I was surprised because I had never been offered handcuffs in the past, although I had taken several groups of inmates out into the community on religious trips. Although I knew that the inmate and his family would be deeply disappointed if he did not attend the funeral, I responded to the correctional officer as follows: "I'm not a correctional officer, and since I've never used handcuffs on other trips into the community, I won't need them on this trip. His counselor has cleared him for this trip and never mentioned using handcuffs. If I can't take this inmate to his father's funeral without using them, I'll return him to his cell." Smiling, the correctional officer assured me that he was only kidding with me and proceeded to open the outside gate, allowing us to leave without the handcuffs on the inmate. The entire trip was made without incident, but the best part came following the funeral. With tears in her eyes, the inmate's mother came up to me and said, "God bless you! Thank you so very much for not bringing my son to his father's funeral shackled and in handcuffs." This divine *kairos* moment strengthened my faith in God, who looks at our hearts. I was encouraged by this mother because her words meant that I should "keep on keeping on" in Jesus' name. Whether or not the inmate ever told his mother about the discussion between me and the correctional officer before we left the prison is not important because I know that the moment he saw his mother's tears he would give witness to the power of Christ to change people and situations. In a similar way I helped a white inmate who faithfully participated in many of my counseling groups who was given permission to attend his father's funeral in Princeton, Missouri. His father had died while the inmate was involved in the prison's work release program. I was unable to take him to his father's funeral, but I didn't give up trying to help him. Working closely with several people, including Warden Auge, a work-release supervisor in Cedar Rapids, the director of paroles, and an Iowa state senator, I was able to help get him a furlough to attend his father's funeral. Later, the senator thanked me, acknowledging my work at the reformatory and encouraging me to let him know if he could be of help in the future. These examples of helping inmates in rehabilitation and reconciliation to return to their community came about because of relationships that I had developed while working two days each week outside the prison.

    My white chaplaincy colleagues had always been granted requests for Iowa state motor vehicles to take inmates on religious trips outside the prison. I realized that I had been refused a state motor vehicle because I was actually employed by Lutheran Social Services of Iowa, but I also knew that black inmates would perceive this as racial discrimination, making me powerlessness in their eyes to take them on trips into the community. Equal opportunity of resources added legitimacy to my ministry. Without it, black inmates would perceive my presence on the prison chaplaincy staff as tokenism and that I was therefore a "second-class" chaplain. There was also the matter of additional wear and tear on my personal car as well as the cost of gasoline that figured into these trips. I shared my concerns with Lutheran Social Service of Iowa, requesting that they provide me with an automobile to take inmates on religious trips into the community. Lutheran Social Service initially responded to my request by increasing my automobile mileage allowance. This worked rather well until they experienced a short-fall in church funding for the chaplaincy program. I also assisted in some fund-raising efforts when taking inmates on visits and participating in adult forums at Lutheran and other churches in Iowa communities. Realizing that taking inmates on religious trips was an integral component of my job description in rehabilitation and reconciliation, Lutheran Social Service suggested that I take my concerns to the reformatory's director of treatment.

Because the Iowa State Reformatory had never made any financial contribution for my position at the prison, it seemed this important issue provided an opportunity where they could help. I informed the director of treatment of my contact with Lutheran Social Service and their inability to help because of a short-fall in their budget. He told me unequivocally that there were no funds available for mileage at the prison and that he could not do anything to help me get a state vehicle. Briefly despairing, I remembered that "my help comes from the Lord, the maker of heaven and earth" (Psalm 121:1-8).

For two weeks I took my concerns to God in prayer, primarily seeking to know whether or not they were legitimate and essential to my ministry—and if so, what I should do. One night during my second week of prayer I was awakened by a voice. There was no one around but the voice continued speaking silently and forcefully in my mind, directing me to go into the room I used as an office. Powerfully, the voice directed me to something lying on my desk. As I looked more closely, I could see it was a standard form used in the reformatory to requisition an Iowa State motor vehicle. At the time, I could not remember how it had gotten there. As I continued staring at the paper, the voice spoke to me again, saying, "Pick it up and look at it. What do you see?" Still puzzling over how the paper got on my desk, and surprised by the question, I replied to the voice, "It's a form used to request an Iowa State motor vehicle." The voice spoke again, "What do you see?" I looked more intently at the vehicle request form and realized that all I needed to do was fill in the blanks, sign it, and send it to the warden for his approval. For the final time the voice spoke, "Fill it out, sign it, and send it to the warden's office." The following morning I filled out the requisition form and sent it to the warden's office. I not only received a state vehicle, I was given the warden's own private radio car! Yes, God is good all the time!

However, trouble was headed in my direction. After being given the use of an Iowa State motor vehicle for inmate religious trips, I was called into the director of treatment's office. He wanted to know why I had not gone through him to get the vehicle. I reminded him of our last meeting when he told me there was nothing he could do to help me. So, after two weeks of prayer, I made my request to someone I thought could help me. He was visibly upset but did not respond to my answer. Then he told me that in the future I would have to go through him for all requests. It was only after my conversation with Mr. Baughman that I remembered that Rev. Allen had given me the blank requisition form. In all probability Mr. Baughman informed Lutheran Social Service of our conversation because shortly thereafter I received a phone call cautioning me to be careful and communicate all special requests through the director of treatment. Rev. Ramon Runkel, staff chaplain at Lutheran Social Service, ended our conversation by commending me in doing good work at the prison and assuring me of their continuing support. I assured him that I fully understood and respected the necessity for a structured order of command, but I had done no more than the other two chaplains in using whatever help was available for the inmates' rehabilitation. However, I reassured him that in the future I would work closely with Mr. Baughman.

Through my contacts with churches and the families of inmates, my ministry quickly expanded to include as many or more whites than blacks in the surrounding community. Because of their job descriptions, my white chaplaincy colleagues rarely made community contacts.

Because of my availability in the primarily white community, I was able to officiate at the funeral in Mason City of a white inmate who was serving time for rape and died while in the reformatory. This young man's family lived in Mason City. He and his wife had faithfully participated in marriage and family counseling until the day he had a stroke and was sent to the University Hospital in Iowa City, where he was treated for several weeks. One day his wife phoned, asking me to meet her at the hospital. When I arrived at the hospital, she said, "The doctors have told me that Steve has no brain activity and I should think about removing him from artificial life support. I'm under intense pressure from Steve's family to leave him on life support. I desperately need your help." The family expressed feelings of guilt that they might be killing their loved one if they decided to have him removed from life support. I struggled to explain that it is more important for them to take ownership of the decision and not me. After listening to them and doing the best I could to address everyone's concerns, I prayed with them. Finally the family decided to remove their loved one from what they now realized was artificial life with no guarantees for a lasting quality of life. They also said they were glad it had been a family decision. After the inmate's death, I was asked if it was possible for me to come to Mason City and conduct his funeral. As I had gone this far with the family in their sad time, how could I say no? Because of the long drive, I asked Doris to go with me to Mason City. Following the funeral, the inmate's mother asked me to stay in town and officiate at the funeral of his brother, who had died in a car crash while on his way to his brother's funeral. With the death of two sons in such a short period of time, her grief was overwhelming. She did not know any other ministers to call and I was available. Because Doris and I had made the trip with limited financial resources and family obligations at home with our children, I regretfully had to refuse her request. I suggested she speak with the funeral director and see if he might help. This was one of many times when a ministry of reconciliation was clearly defined and truly effective!

I will never forget another incident in which I provided support for an American Indian inmate on work release who was living in a halfway house in Cedar Rapids. Larry Yellow Thunder was an alcoholic, more of a nuisance than a menace to the community. Because he had no transportation to get to his highway construction job, I agreed to take him to work every morning, then he would find someone at the work site to bring him back to the halfway house. Every time I arrived in the morning to take Larry to work, he was asleep. I did the best I could to encourage him to get up on time, and Doris even bought him a new alarm clock. Somehow, even though others heard the alarm clock, Larry never did. After Larry was late for work every day for a week, the supervisor of the halfway house asked me to come and talk with him, to see if we could find a way to help Larry get up in the morning and be at work on time. Following this meeting, Larry and I decided to give it another try. Before we left, Larry said he wanted to talk with me about a problem he had. As he spoke he became more and more uneasy. After I assured him that I would understand, he blurted out these words: "You're the problem! You're my problem! You're always here on time to take me to work!" Wow, what a shock! I had become a problem for Larry because I was being faithful in my promise of getting him to work. Remembering this conversation with Larry causes me to wonder whether there might be others who see Jesus's faithfulness in always being there for us as a problem instead of an opportunity for healing. My immediate response to Larry was to ask him whether he wanted me to continue taking him to work. His answer was that he would find another way of getting to work. Since it was now too late to take him to work, we returned to the halfway house. The following week, when Larry had not found another way of getting to work, he was returned to the reformatory in Anamosa.

Lutheran Social Service of Iowa, which provided financial and support staff for my chaplaincy position, had hoped that after funding my position for three years at the reformatory the Iowa State Department of Corrections would see the need for continuing my employment there. But this wasn't going to happen. During my third year at the reformatory I was informed that money wasn't available for a new chaplaincy position and that there was no justification for having three chaplains at the reformatory. This did not make sense to me because the recidivism rate had increased and the inmate population, including blacks, had grown to over 800. The State Reformatory was not built to house such a large number of inmates. There was now a new director of treatment who indicated that there was a possibility of continuing my employment in the prison but that this would involve a change in my classification, creating a new social worker/counselor position that would keep me on the staff of the treatment department. It appeared that my work was deemed valuable and had met the special needs of the prisoners, but I refused his offer, explaining that "my understanding of God's call to me is to eventually become the pastor of a church and not a social worker/counselor." My decision to resign was also influenced by an earlier conversation I had with the assistant warden in which he questioned my "institutional loyalty," but he never told me why my loyalty had come under his suspicion. I believed the question would be raised again and possibly limit the effectiveness of my work as a social worker/counselor.

In retrospect, I believe that my chaplaincy relationship with the Iowa State Reformatory suffered because of different approaches to rehabilitation. I agree completely that we must take pride in and care for the institutions in which we work, but at the same time our institutions must be held accountable to provide for the good of all. Perhaps the assistant warden felt that I lacked institutional loyalty because he knew my approach to rehabilitation held the correctional institution accountable in its lack of a holistic approach that included the reconciliation of inmate families and their communities. Christian religion is an integral part of social rehabilitation. Christ Jesus holds individuals and his Church accountable whenever we ignore his call to follow a ministry of reconciliation. Even now, I have a strong belief of knowing that it was the Holy Spirit's guidance sustaining me through my three years of working at the Iowa State Reformatory.

My Christian ministry of advocacy was firmly grounded in the context of church and community volunteers promising to faithfully care for and support inmates inside the prison as well as after their release. A personal and poignant moment occurred when "Pappy," a white Christian volunteer, gave his personal witness to the influence of my ministry on inmates at the reformatory. Pappy was a well-respected elder of an ultra-conservative branch of the Assemblies of God called the Four Square Gospel Church. Rev. Allen told me that this small group of the denomination had broken away from the Assemblies of God. In subtle and sometimes more direct ways, Pappy criticized what he felt was the inadequacy of the theology and evangelical mission that we chaplains were employing in bringing prison inmates to Jesus Christ. We tolerated him to some extent, but we also saw that he was confusing the inmates in their rehabilitation when they returned to their communities. Even so, I loved and respected Pappy. His love, sincerity, and advocacy for Christian transformation in the lives of those in prison were beyond question. Pappy always expressed his faith in tearful prayers, spoken in tongues, for God to heal the lives of prison inmates and their families. Once he asked that I pray for an inmate by "the laying on of hands." Because Pappy's request was made in the presence of the inmate, I responded, "I'll pray with you and the inmate for God's will in this matter, but only your hands are needed, not mine."

A special worship service of celebration and recognition for chaplaincy volunteers, including my farewell send-off, was held on my last Sunday at the reformatory. Over 100 inmates, black and white chaplaincy volunteers, Iowa state officials, inmates, and their families attended the service. Special recognition was given to chaplaincy volunteers, and I received several certificates in recognition of my work at the reformatory and in the community. This worship service gave me the spiritual strength I needed in moving into parish ministry. Pappy spoke tearfully of his misgivings at various times about whether or not I was a Christian but that now he knew better. I never realized he had thought this way about my Christian faith, but his open confession to all present brought tears to my eyes, and I gave him a big hug. Pappy continued, saying, "Chaplain Branch's leaving is going to be a great loss, and he will be truly missed by everyone at the reformatory." Rev. Allen and Father Barnes also made supportive comments.

In retrospect, I deeply believe my ministry at the reformatory and in that area of Iowa was given to whites so that the eyes of their hearts might be opened in our need for journeying together as equals. This is not to say that black people were not encouraged and beneficiaries of my ministry efforts. The experiences I had on my last day of worship at the reformatory can best be described in these words from 1 Corinthians 13:8 (NIV): "Love never fails! But where there are prophecies, they will cease; where there are tongues, they will be stilled; and where there is knowledge, it will pass away!" Even now, much later in my spiritual odyssey, I am continually reminded that whenever I have felt most alone and hopeless God has always been there, strengthening and guiding me and our family!

Following my meeting with Mr. Manternach, the new director of treatment, I contacted the Iowa District American Lutheran Church to have my name placed on the "Available for Call" list. After three years as a correctional chaplain involved in advocacy for rehabilitation of prison inmates, I was ready to follow God's continuing presence and guidance in Christian ministry as a parish pastor. I resigned from correctional chaplaincy at the Iowa State Men's Reformatory in 1976.

CHAPTER 12

Prince of Glory Lutheran Church

1976-1983

I received two phone calls from Prince of Glory Lutheran Church to come to Minneapolis for an interview. The pastor of the church, Rev. Mark Hanson, was the first to phone me, followed by a call from Theatrice Williams, president of the congregational council. Both men wanted to know if I was interested in coming to Minneapolis as a second pastor of the congregation. Located in the middle of the Sumner-Olson/Glenwood public housing complex in North Minneapolis, Prince of Glory was a mission congregation of the American Lutheran Church. Its location and ministry reminded me of Holy Family Lutheran Church in Chicago. The national American Lutheran Church had purchased the building, formerly St. Martin De Pores Church, from the Catholic Church and changed its name to Prince of Glory. The first pastor-developer of the new congregation was Rev. Robert (Bob) Evans. Because of his hard work, dedication, and understanding of Christian mission, Rev. Evans and the pastors who followed him maintained the same mission vision. The congregation consisted of white, black, and biracial families, as well as white seminary students and professors, some of them Lutherans and others who were not. For me, this historic ministry setting offered the potential for me to continue my work in parish ministry.

Because Prince of Glory Church was located in the middle of two large public housing complexes its first pastor, Robert Evans, recognized the need for additional space to connect with a social-ministry outreach into the public housing area. The new building was symbolically named "The Bridge." It was seen as the congregation's bridge into the community, providing leadership for social change. There were two floors that provided ample space for Sunday school classes and other church and community activities. The Bryant-Glenwood Educare Center for preschoolers, including a nursery, was located in the main church building—very similar to the Head Start program at Holy Family Lutheran Church in Chicago. The congregation included more whites than blacks, but it definitely reminded me of Holy Family with its gospel emphasis on a ministry informed by the call of Jesus Christ. Prince of Glory had great potential to effectively impact social change in the public housing complex as well as in the Minneapolis District and American Lutheran Church.

After confirming my availability for call, I was interviewed by the congregational call committee, followed by a conversation with Pastor Hanson. I asked about the history of the congregation and its ministry in the neighborhood. Further, I wanted clarification of my pastoral duties and how we should handle any misconceptions about team ministry by neighborhood residents. Although a decision had been made to use the title co-pastors for our ministry, we knew there were people who would see Pastor Hanson as the senior pastor. He had seniority as well as success in being a community activist in the Sumner Olson/Glenwood public housing complex. When he asked about my thoughts of his continuing to function as the community-activist pastor my response was, "I have no problems whatsoever with it! As a black man I've had to be a community activist all my life." My role and—more important—my hope of success were entirely different from his. As at Holy Family Lutheran Church, I was aware of the possibility of being perceived as a "nobody" or a "token nigger," as well as Mark being respected as a "white savior." I believe we both knew that our approach to missional ministry would put us between the proverbial rock and a hard place. However, the saving grace was in recognizing that Our Lord Jesus was "the Rock" of ages. I believe Mark and I embraced our mutual mission as crosses we had to carry together. Once we had defined our pastoral roles, most would be able to see our individual strengths and weaknesses but also our resolve to work as unified leaders in the congregation's commitment to actively pursue Jesus' call to be his witnesses. The interview process, which included community leaders, allowed me to raise and clarify questions concerning the risks and implications of accepting the call. Following conversations with Pastor Hanson, the congregational call committee, and community leaders, I returned to Cedar Rapids and soon received a letter of call to come to Prince of Glory Lutheran Church.

I accepted the congregation's call in 1976, becoming the second black pastor at Prince of Glory Lutheran Church. I felt this call was another opportunity given me by God to grow and share my unique abilities and gifts as a pastor in a congregational context. Pastor Hanson's knowledge of the American Lutheran Church and his experience in the public housing community in Minneapolis gave me an opportunity to learn how to effectively impact these structures to promote beneficial changes in our neighborhood and church. I am certain that God enabled Mark to learn from me as well and grow in his understanding of the needs of oppressed people everywhere, especially black people.

Doris did not mind leaving Cedar Rapids, but moving to Minneapolis became a hassle. First, we needed to prepare our house for sale in order to get a good price, combined with the hard work of once again packing household goods. Doris always arranged as smooth a transition as possible for our children. We did not realize, however, that our nomadic lifestyle was only beginning. After arriving in Minneapolis we experienced obstacles in moving into the new home we had purchased. The area in which we intended to move had been suspected of racial red-lining. Although not mandated by law in northern states, red-lining was closely related to the southern Jim Crow laws of segregation. In Minneapolis, real estate dealers, acting in collusion with property owners, placed restrictions on communities where black people could rent or own homes. Although we had been pre-approved for a loan by the Twin Cities Federal Bank, we were delayed in moving into our new home because of residual effects of this kind of real estate maneuvering to prevent blacks from living in the same communities with whites. Then, the previous owner had not moved out of our newly purchased home by the date scheduled for us to take possession. This meant that the movers had to unload all our furniture and belongings and place them in storage until she moved out of our home. We eventually had to threaten her with rental charges before she made a good attempt at moving out. In fact, Doris and Mary Lou Williams, a member of our new congregation, helped pack her belongings. Then Mary Lou and her husband, Theatrice, invited us to stay with them until we could move into our new home. Mr. Williams deeply impressed me with his social worker background and his work as ombudsman for the Minnesota State Prison System. Certainly our shared experience in prison systems was part of the relationship we established, but also I had never been in a close relationship with another black professional.

Doris and I, along with Cheryl, Keith, David, and our dog, Sheba, stayed with the Williams family for two weeks. Michael remained in Cedar Rapids attending the University of Iowa. Cheryl had not completed all her high school credits for graduation and was deeply saddened at not being able to remain in Cedar Rapids and graduate with the other students in her senior class. However, after several conversations with guidance counselors in Cedar Rapids and North Community High in Minneapolis, Cheryl was able to make an unusual arrangement for graduation. Counselors at both schools coordinated their efforts in confirming Cheryl's completion of the required credits, and she was able to graduate with familiar faces and receive a diploma with her senior class at Washington High. She later graduated from North Community High, receiving her second diploma. I am profoundly impressed with our children's abilities to express themselves while challenging anything tending to threaten their humanity or destroy our family cohesiveness. The best news in our move to Minneapolis was that our children approved of the new home at 2015 Vincent Avenue North, located just east of Theodore Wirth Park.

Michael remained in Cedar Rapids, attending the University of Iowa until the college recess when he decided to move to Minneapolis. He lived with us while attending the University of Minnesota and working at Mario's Italian restaurant. However, the University of Minnesota was not a comfortable fit and he returned to Cedar Rapids. Shortly afterwards he phoned informing us of his decision to marry Debra Robertson, a young white woman he worked with at Happy Joe's Pizza Parlor. He asked if I would be the presiding minister in his wedding at Our Savior's Lutheran Church. Before agreeing to his request I suggested that he and Debra have marriage counseling with one of Michael's pastors at Our Savior's as the wedding arrangements were being made there. Later, Pastor Ehnen phoned informing me that the premarital counseling with Debra's mother's pastor had "hit a snag." During one of the counseling sessions, Mrs. Robertson's pastor made a comment that betrayed his unresolved racial problems, but he phrased it in a way suggesting that it was expressed to him by Debra's mother, citing that "Debra came from 'good stock.'" Why had the pastor not used their Christian beliefs in being created in the image of God as a counseling tool? Being created in God's image we were all made of "good stock," regardless of ethnicity. I was more concerned about how they would handle their Christian beliefs in the midst of our racist society. An additional concern was how they could best strengthen their biracial marriage to lessen the negative impact it might have on their children. Being uncomfortable in pre-marital counseling with her mother's pastor, Debra and Michael decided to move to counseling with Pastor Ehnen at Our Savior's Lutheran Church, as I had first suggested. I was proud of them for making their own decision in changing counselors.

Michael and Debra's wedding at Our Savior's Lutheran Church was a happy occasion, highlighted by a racially diverse wedding party and a large crowd wishing them well in their marriage. However, a little sadness overshadowed the wedding because Debra's mother decided not to attend because of lingering racial problems she had about her daughter's marriage to Michael. I felt deep sadness for Debra and anger at her mother. A close friend of Debra's mother tried unsuccessfully to encourage Ms. Robertson to set her fears aside and support her daughter. In the end, it was this friend who escorted Debra to the altar and gave her to Michael. God is good, all the time! As for Ms. Robertson, I prayed that she would eventually support her daughter's choice of a husband. A new family was beginning, and it was being done the right way, God's way, as they knelt at the altar surrounded by a racially diverse group of people! Michael married Debra (Debbie) Robertson in 1981 and I served as the officiant for their wedding. Later, they moved to Minneapolis, where their first child, Nicole Marie Branch, was born. Nicole became the second grandchild I would baptize while pastor of Prince of Glory Lutheran Church.

Michael's education was put on hold as his career took a new direction in electronics and computers at the Prudential Insurance Company, where Doris also worked. Cheryl became a student at Augsburg College, completing two years of study there before transferring to the University of Texas in Austin. Shortly afterward, Keith enrolled as a student at Concordia College. Although he did well academically, making the Dean's List in his first year, he dropped out of school after two years. Our oldest daughter, Patricia, continued to live in Seattle with her husband, Pierre Humphrey, and their two children. Our oldest son, Terrance, after serving two years in the Air Force in San Antonio, Texas, remained there where he met and married Arlene Smith, the mother of two girls. I was really proud of Terry's decision to marry her because so many men shy away from marrying into "ready-made" families. In 1977 Terry and Arlene, along with one of her daughters, Emena, came to live with us in Minneapolis. Terry found a position at the Hennepin County Medical Center as a hospital supply technician. Arlene eventually found work to supplement their family income. His only child, a son, Laqueint Tyrel Branch, was born on September 9, 1978, at the same hospital. Terrance worked at the hospital until 1979, when he and Arlene moved to Austin, Texas. Tyrel was the first grandchild I baptized at Prince of Glory Lutheran Church, and if my memory serves me, I also baptized his older sister Emena Smith.

Doris's mother, Mrs. Nevada Hazel Hayes, died on February 16, 1978, at the Halsted Terrace Nursing Home in Chicago. Doris had now lost both her parents. Before Mrs. Hayes died, we were blessed in being able to make regular visits to both our families in Chicago, including visits with Doris's mother in the nursing home. Shortly after my mother-in-law's death Doris and I reaffirmed our twenty-fifth wedding anniversary vows in a tear-filled ceremony at Prince of Glory Church.

As mentioned earlier, Pastor Mark Hanson and I, in defining and clarifying ministry responsibilities, made our first priority teaching by serving as role models in our commitment to equally share pastoral duties. This meant intuitively understanding how to "cross lines" whenever necessary in our parish roles as community and social action issues evolved. During our time together we had many beautiful learning experiences, but I will mention only those I considered most significant to me.

My first challenge was getting to know and learn about the complex needs of people in the congregation relative to their mission in the Sumner-Olson and Glenwood public housing complex. Our ethnocentric concerns and personal experiences were a given fact, but we needed something more—the gift of spiritual discernment from God. I believe we both had this gift. We participated in the Glenwood Public Housing Resident Council, providing advocacy and leadership support where needed for people living in public housing. Prince of Glory, in consultation with other community leaders, initiated the process that gave birth to our public housing community radio station, UMOJA—Swahili for "community solidarity," later renamed KMOJ. To this day, the radio station continues to be on the air in Minneapolis. At its inception, the station's office for programming activities was located in one of the public housing units. The radio station's architect and engineering technician was Nolan Cramer, a white member of Prince of Glory Lutheran Church. Mark Hanson and I were original members of the radio station's board of directors. Because we felt that ownership of the radio station should be held by the public housing community, more residents were elected and began occupying important program decision-making positions on the station's board of directors. Prince of Glory remained supportive but was thereafter only loosely connected to the operation.

Pastor Hanson and I shared responsibility for all three senior-citizen public housing high-rise apartment buildings—one located on Olson Highway and the other two on Bryant Avenue. These buildings were considered an extension of our outreach ministry and became essential for both members and non-members living in the apartments. Church programs at all three locations consisted of weekly Bible studies as well as other supportive ministries.

Indicative of our ministry commitment in the Glenwood public housing complex was the request of a community social worker asking me to conduct a funeral at one of the senior citizen's buildings. She gave me all the background information, including the fact that the widower and his wife had no church or other family members. Space for the funeral was provided in a small meeting room on the first floor of the apartment building. When I arrived, the grieving widower, an older white man, was sitting in a chair next to the coffin sobbing uncontrollably. No one else was there, and the social worker had been unsuccessfully trying to comfort him. I could see she was glad I was there, and she quickly introduced me. Immediately, I realized why she was having so much difficulty in comforting the widower. He smelled of alcohol, and was slobbering and speaking incoherently. I began to work hard at listening to what he was saying. I heard a lot of self pity about what he had failed to do as a man and that now he was nothing more than a has-been. Now I understood how he was internalizing his sense of failure, guilt, and helplessness at not accomplishing more in life.

I proceeded with the funeral, struggling to speak and seek God's loving promise of resurrection for his deceased wife, while he continued sobbing and blabbering incoherently throughout the service. Then I remembered what this lonely grieving widower had said in our conversation and decided to use it. I said, "It's better to be a has-been than a never-been, because you wouldn't have been here for your wife." Suddenly he stopped crying, appeared to sober up and, wiping away his tears, shouted out a loud thank you to me. Startled, I could only pause for a moment and silently thank God. This was only one of many opportunities that connected Prince of Glory's ministry with the hopes of all the "has-beens" in our public housing community.

The concept of a Family Camp Church Vacation resulted from the congregation's awareness that many welfare recipients and residents of public housing never thought about taking vacations because they had few or no financial resources. The family camp was named Camp Knutson. It was located in Crow Wing County just east of Brainerd, Minnesota, on the shores of Cross Lake. To get to the family

Family camp was a great experience for families at Prince of Glory.

camp, we used the church's Sunday school bus as well as a couple of cars driven by families of the congregation, including the Branch family's auto. This gathering of the families in Prince of Glory congregation was beneficial in so many ways for the people who participated. They had an opportunity to experience one another in totally different ways than during Sunday morning worship services. Enclosed shower and toilet stalls were all unisex, creating an atmosphere where we learned how to share more and respect one another. The programs for the family camp were well planned by leaders of our congregation and the Camp Knutson director and staff. Camping orientation and shared responsibilities for maintaining the cabins, organizing worship services, counseling, and overseeing games, the beach, and water activities such as fishing, swimming, volley ball, water skiing, and boating, had to be completed before anyone could engage in activities. All the amenities for a good Christian family camp experience were provided by the leaders of our congregation, camp staffers, lifeguards, and instructors. It reminded me of all the fun I had at a Boy Scout camp when I was younger.

Two significant experiences occurred at one of our family camp outings. The first happened the night Doris and I had to sleep in a cabin that was infested with beetles and blood-thirsty wood ticks. These insects hid in the cabin walls, bunk beds, and mattresses, usually coming out only at night. This meant that we had to use flashlights to search our bodies for ticks that would burrow into our flesh. This activity kept us awake most of the night as we felt or imagined ticks crawling on us and sucking our blood. These nightmarish parasites took their toll on Doris, who after fighting off the ticks all night left the cabin very early in the morning without telling anyone. By the time I discovered she was missing and went looking for her, someone told me they had seen her out on the lake in a sailboat. I knew this could not be true because Doris could not swim and had a fear of being in the water. Nevertheless, I went down to the lake in time to see her with one of the camp staff pulling away from the dock in a sailboat. This was her first ride in a sailboat—maybe her first ride in any boat. As they pulled away she waved to me and loudly yelled that she had to get away from all the ticks and would see me later. It seemed that the wood ticks had cured Doris in her fear of being on the water.

The second experience occurred at one of our worship and prayer gatherings. I had established a counseling relationship with a biracial teenager in the congregation who was struggling with his identity and living without his father in a single-parent family. Time and again he had related how hard it was to deal with being labeled a "bastard" by his schoolmates and others in our neighborhood. At this particular worship and prayer service, I decided to share the young man's dilemma as a way of trying to heal his hurt and pain while maintaining his anonymity. Using myself as an example, I explained to the group that I grew up without a father in a single-parent family and that I too had been labeled a "bastard." In my own struggle to answer the question of why my father was not at home for me and my other siblings, I said that God had somehow strengthened me to realize that I had been given an opportunity to become the best "bastard" I could be by being a loving father to my own children. I hoped that my words would convey the message that we should not allow negative labels to limit us from being the best persons we can be. We are controlled and live out negative labels only as long as we give them power over us. Life in the family of Christ Jesus gives us strength to shed all negativity and live as God's cherished children.

Perhaps as the young man's pastor I should have handled his painful dilemma with more politically correct language and perhaps in a different context. However, he was hurting and had been struggling long enough. I believe that if I had used different terminology and not shared my story, it would not have had the impact on this young man and others like him living under similar conditions in our public housing neighborhood. In fact, there were many others like us present in our family camp gathering. Later, this young man and his white mother thanked me, saying, "We've been healed and strengthened to no longer feel alone, and we can handle the negative labels we've lived with for so long." Was I afraid? Of course! I had no idea how the young man's mother and others attending family camp would react to how I handled the situation. Notably, our friendship remains strong to this day. My courage goes only so far, but I cared enough to follow the road less traveled by demonstrating a risky love in struggling to be faithful to Jesus's love.

The congregation's racial and socio-economic diversity in no way limited or impaired our pastoral leadership. In fact, I believe it enhanced our ability to understand the complex nature of a ministry based on the gospel of love. I had many opportunities to learn how to discern and prioritize congregational, community, and family needs. As time passed, I realized how God had truly blessed both Mark and me in our leadership as role models for Jesus' mission. I especially enjoyed the fun and camaraderie that Mark and I had on our annual fishing trips for lake trout in Ontario at Rev. Robert Evans's cabin. Pastor Evans continued his friendship with Prince of Glory, and the trips were usually scheduled during the spring fishing season openers. Others pastors in similar neighborhood ministries were also part of our spring ritual. We used this time for rest and personal reflections on family and our ministry, but we were always focused on competitive fishing. My fishing buddies quickly discovered that I could fish with the best of them.

My work with Pastor Hanson ended in 1981 when he resigned following a year's sabbatical. After Mark resigned, I knew it would not be possible to fill both of our ministry roles in the congregation. But I was tired of moving from one geographical location to another and decided to remain as pastor of Prince of Glory. The congregation, with my initiative and the district's approval, called another white pastor. Working with him was "a trip," radically different than with Pastor Hanson. In fact, the environment was so filled with personal issues of pastoral responsibilities that it distracted the mission goals of our congregation. We never developed a sense of collegiality and camaraderie in team ministry. Our incompatibility and lack of concentration on the church's mission caused me to consider resigning. I did not have the wisdom or strength to help with his personal needs, because my first priority was to my family and the congregation. I was ambivalent, wanting to try to help him but in the end making a decision based on my understanding of the pastoral call as one aimed at the greater good of our congregation not its pastors. This turmoil created many sleepless nights which greatly concerned my family. I began to wake up every morning at 5:00, complaining of shortness of breath and fullness in my chest. Even though it was not an asthma attack, my shortness of breath reminded me of those days. Actually, my anxieties were causing me to have panic attacks and hyperventilate. Doris and Cheryl were always there in those early morning hours, praying and comforting me as best they could. Again, I felt a failure in guiding our congregation past this bump in the road and, even after prayer, I could not resolve these issues.

I have always believed that "the Lord makes a way out of no way." I decided to share my distress with a member of the congregation and good friend, Mike Bash, the son of Rev. Ewald Joe Bash. Realizing the seriousness of my situation, he phoned the synod office and asked the

Minneapolis Area bishop's assistant, Rev. John Fahning, to intervene. I did not tell Doris what I had done and that I was meeting with Rev. Fahning. I felt defeated and was too embarrassed at being unable to resolve the friction between me and the other pastor. By the time I finished sharing the story with Rev. Fahning it was time for lunch. After we finished eating, John spoke softly and slowly, trying to console me. I may have been crying and cannot remember exactly what he said. I probably shut him out because nothing he said made sense. It was only after he prayed that I finally heard him say: "Lonnie, we're fully aware, at the synod office, of what's happening at Prince of Glory and what you've been going through. Since Mark left you've done a good job. I can only think of one possible solution, and it's something I've never said to any other pastor, but why don't you just quit?"

It is impossible for me to accurately describe what happened next—it was a miracle. Raising my arms up as high as I could toward the ceiling, I opened my hands, shouting loudly and uncontrollably over and over again, "Oh, God, I quit!" I can only describe what happened next, but cannot explain it. As I repeatedly shouted the words "Oh, God, I quit!" I exhaled a lot of warm air from my chest. The air smelled foul, like the odor of stale tobacco, and my mouth tasted like tobacco. This was puzzling because I had not smoked for years. But now something extraordinary happened, I became totally calm and relaxed, as though everything hurting inside me had been exhaled with the odorous stale air. Immediately I became more alert and began to think with clarity. I did not second guess what I had to do, and I knew everything would be fine because I no longer was afraid of the consequences of whatever decision I made. For me it was another *kairos* moment—an answer from God to everyone's prayer! Rev. Fahning said he would follow up my decision to resign with supportive counseling provided by the synod Office for both of us pastors. After thanking him for his time and prayer, we shook hands, embraced, and I left. Following my meeting with Rev. Fahning I informed the new pastor of meeting with the bishop's assistant and my decision to resign. He responded with an expletive and ended his remarks by calling me a "snitch."

Now I was faced with the difficulty of explaining my unilateral decision to resign to Doris and other members of our family. After arriving home I asked Doris, who wanted to know where I had been, to go out with me to watch the sunset in Theodore Wirth Park. Parking the car in an area on one of the hillsides we got out and walked over to view the sunset. I felt guilty, wondering how to begin telling Doris about my decision to resign. I had no Letter of Call—which meant I had no job. In my heart of hearts I knew God had healed me in my troubles and would continue providing for the family I loved—even if it wasn't as a pastor. My confidence had been restored, and I was prepared for ongoing challenges, but I didn't want to lose Doris's trust and confidence. We had already gone through so many tough challenges, and she was always strong and understanding in the midst of all our experiences. Nevertheless, I was having a hard time finding words to explain why I left her and the family out of a decision that affected them. The sun had begun to set even lower in the sky when I finally blurted out my decision. I'll never forget the look of shock and hurt on her face. I felt her pain, I did not like myself, and I apologized. This was not the first time I had left her out of a family decision. Finally, I realized that it was not my ministry alone; it had always been the work of the Holy Spirit working in and through our family. With tears in her eyes, Doris forgave me, and we left the park agreeing to immediately begin family discussions about making another ministry move.

During this difficult time, I had several counseling sessions that helped me regroup, mentally focus, and cope with the many decisions and implications of resigning from my position as pastor at Prince of Glory. The congregational council was very supportive and for this I will always be grateful. The counseling sessions helped me focus more clearly on family priorities and continue my ministry in the church. Unexpectedly, I received support from the Rev. L. C. Kelly Jr., a black pastor, at Wayman African Methodist Episcopal Church (AME) who gave me a farewell sendoff with an invitation to speak at his church. Wayman AME Church was located in our community, and having their support was very encouraging.

Following my counseling sessions, I continued the recovery process by enrolling in a three-month work/study chaplaincy program in the summer of 1983 at North Memorial Hospital. I continued working part-time at Prince of Glory as well as serving as a chaplain at North Memorial Hospital. Two other Lutheran pastors whom I knew were experiencing similar problems in their ministries. It was really comforting to see that

I was not alone in my pain of feeling as though I was a failure as a pastor, husband, and father. Following my chaplaincy hiatus at North Memorial Hospital, our congregation granted me a six-month sabbatical with partial salary. I was given this time for renewal, reflection, and gathering information for transitioning to another ministry call. I used the sabbatical to serve as a chaplain at the Hennepin County Medical Center and University of Minnesota Hospital, spending three months at each hospital. Previously, I had completed seven years of clinical pastoral education in hospitals and correctional chaplaincy. I used my sabbatical to increase my experience in chaplaincy to obtain accreditation from the American Protestant Hospital Chaplaincy Association (APHCA). After completing the association's requirements, I was granted accreditation.

My sabbatical as a chaplain at the Hennepin County Medical Center was spiritually rewarding. There were two white women and two white men on the chaplaincy staff. We were all from varying denominational backgrounds and, as usual, I was the only black minister. We were assigned various locations throughout the hospital and given pagers to communicate with one another. Every week we met to discuss written verbatims of patient visits. At one of these meetings I prayed silently to be spared the kind of experience that one of my colleagues had described while assigned to night-call duty. This was a dumb, bone-headed prayer! In fact, I had already ministered in many crisis situations, but my courage had faltered.

The answer to my bone-headed prayer came sooner than expected when it was my turn on night-call duty. Usually this meant sleeping at the hospital in order to insure quicker responses to patient emergency needs. It also meant remaining at the hospital in the morning to work a double shift. Before going to bed that night, I might have even reminded God to remember my prayer for a restful, uneventful night. The room I slept in had a bed and table with a lamp and a phone. The room was so cold that I could not sleep until finding additional blankets in a small closet. Around 1:00 a.m., I was awakened by the phone; it was with a triage nurse asking me to meet her and a family in the conference room. A nineteen-year-old white woman had locked herself inside an automobile in the garage of their home and died from carbon monoxide poisoning. A doctor met me at the door of the family conference room, greeted me, and requested that I be with the family when they viewed the body. The parents of the deceased and two other daughters gathered around us as we entered the room. Speaking slowly and softly, the doctor introduced me as the hospital chaplain and explained how he had unsuccessfully tried to revive their daughter. The doctor explained what had medically happened and answered their questions. The young woman had two other unsuccessful suicide attempts.

The parents were told there would be a brief wait for the room to be cleaned before seeing their daughter. When the treatment room was ready, we all went in. So much for my earlier misguided prayer! I was now confronted with my fears of inadequacy to comfort this grieving family. Although these feelings were nothing new to me I feared the issues it might raise for the family's religious expectations and traditions. A nurse took us to where the body of their daughter was lying on an uncovered metal table. The body was clean and partially covered. The family stood huddled together with the doctor, while the nurse and I stood nearby. I was surprised to see that even in death the girl was beautiful, and I could not understand why this young woman had committed suicide. In the midst of tears and inaudible murmurs by the family, I remained speechless. The doctor and nurse left, and we returned to the family conference room. Once inside, everyone separated, seemingly looking for their own space in which to grieve. The father and mother stood huddled together nervously holding hands while observing their daughters. One daughter was pacing back and forth in a corner of the room, angrily expressing her grief by cussing and loudly asking, "Why did God let this happen?" She angrily shouted out at her deceased sister: "Are you satisfied now that you've finally succeeded in killing yourself?" I was afraid to say anything but noticed that the other sister was standing alone in another corner of the room weeping and sobbing but saying nothing. I was in the middle of the room desperately trying to come up with some way of comforting the family, but nothing came. All I could do was stand in silence, wait with the parents, and empathize with their terrible pain! The sister who had been venting her anger suddenly shouted out again, "Why? Why did she want to hurt us in this way? Why did she do this? She was my only friend, and now I'm all alone!" Saying nothing, the parents continued holding onto one another.

Finally, I responded to the angry sister's questions in a loud voice, saying, "God has not left you all alone! Look around, He's left you another friend—your sister who is here with you now! All this time, she's been alone and crying. You've been so hurt by your own grief that you haven't seen how much she's hurting. She needs you too!" Surprised and shocked, she turned around and angrily stared at me. Then she ran over and embraced her sister, crying out for forgiveness. When this happened, the parents and I walked over and hugged both sisters. Following a brief prayer, the parents thanked me and asked about my church affiliation. I told them I was Lutheran and found they were also Lutherans and belonged to a local congregation.

It was close to 3:00 a.m. when I left the bereaved family and returned to my room. A little later I woke up, dressed, and went back to work. Although I recognized my experience with this grieving family as another *kairos* moment when God came and healed all of us, my old fears returned. I unfairly compared myself to their pastor whom I thought was more capable of comforting them. We all have our personal demons that cling closely to us, and this was one of mine. The residual negative effects of racism will always elicit my need of God's presence and strength for deliverance. Later, the pastor of the grieving family phoned me, explaining why he had been unable to be with the family and thanking me for how well I handled their crisis.

From time to time, I face the demon of self-doubt but never doubt that Christ Jesus has called, enlightened, and empowered me to be there for people everywhere.

Following several attempts to secure ministry positions in the Twin Cities, including chaplaincy at the Hennepin County Corrections Facility in Plymouth, my ministry as pastor of Prince of Glory Lutheran Church ended after seven years. I had attempted to work with the new pastor for two years before resigning in 1983 to accept another pastoral call to an all-black congregation, Martin Luther Lutheran Church, in Mobile, Alabama.

CHAPTER 13

Martin Luther Church
1983-1989

The Lutheran Church—Missouri Synod (LC/MS) began its mission work with Negroes in Mobile, Alabama, at Martin Luther Lutheran Church on Davis Avenue, now Martin Luther King, Jr. Avenue sometime in 1922. A Christian day school was established and continued through 1937. Believing education to be a higher priority for Negroes, the Synod felt no need to establish a worshipping congregation and call a resident pastor. However, during these years song, prayer, and worship services were led by lay professional leaders of Martin Luther and missionaries from LCMS churches in the area. Rev. Richards, who was white, served from 1938 to 1940 as the first resident pastor of the congregation. In 1941 the Martin Luther Christian Mission School, which had been closed for three years, reopened, and the church called its first ordained Negro resident pastor—Rev. Louis A. Routte, a graduate of Augustana Lutheran Seminary in Rock Island, Illinois. He spoke fluent Greek and was an accomplished musician; he served as pastor of Martin Luther Lutheran Church from 1941 until 1970. Rev. Routte's long tenure of twenty-nine years at Martin Luther Church was primarily due to the lack of ministry calls for Negroes at white Lutheran congregations or in specialized ministries. After serving as pastor of Martin Luther Church, Rev. Routte accepted a call to the Lutheran Church of the Redeemer in Dayton, Ohio, to serve as associate pastor with Rev. Lawrence A. Stumme until his retirement in 1975.

Doris and I received airline tickets from Martin Luther Church to come to Mobile for my interview. This was my second pastoral call to a congregation, but the interview became an eye-opening experience for both of us. We were given the royal treatment, southern style! Indeed

God is good! After a difficult seven years at Prince of Glory Lutheran Church, we needed this kind of warm reception. The people of Martin Luther Church were in need, and so were we! We met with leaders of the congregation and toured the church sanctuary, building, and grounds. A man-sized mural of a black Jesus holding a shepherd's crook was painted on the wall behind the altar. After leaving the sanctuary we were ushered into a new air-conditioned building which included the pastor's office and space for several Sunday school classrooms. Later, we were given a brief history of the congregation and its needs. Stewart Memorial African Methodist Episcopal Church (AME) was located directly across the street from Martin Luther Church. Eventually, we would fellowship with this church in a number of church and community events.

Later that evening we were taken to a dog-race track for dinner and treated to a delicious meal of fried crab claws. This was the first time Doris and I had been to a dog-race track or eaten fried crab claws. The racing dogs were greyhounds or whippets, a breed of small, swift, long-legged slender dogs. They were trained to run after what looked like a large mechanical rabbit propelled around the railing of the racing track. While eating dinner we watched the dog races and observed a humorous incident. A middle-aged black man sitting nearby was really loud in anticipation of seeing the trainers get their dogs ready to run. Suddenly a bell rang, the gates opened, and the dogs were off chasing the mechanical rabbit. The crowds yelled and shouted, including the man sitting near us. Suddenly, as the dogs rounded a corner of the track, several of them skidded to a stop and walked off the track. The impetus for the dogs to run was the mechanical rabbit, and once they took their eyes off the rabbit they stopped running. A lot of groans came from the crowd, and the man near us shouted out loudly, "Hot damn, there goes all my money!" It was not a laughing matter for him, but we could not help hiding a few smiles.

My Sunday morning preaching debut was quite memorable. It was sweltering hot outside, and the humidity was extremely high when I stepped up into the pulpit. Looking down I saw small rays of sunlight shining through cracks in the sanctuary's front wall. Hurricane Frederick not only had caused cracks in the church walls but had also blown a capstone off the bell tower. In the middle of my sermon an elderly woman fainted and toppled over into her pew. Startled and concerned, with no idea what to do, I stopped preaching. I was relieved to see several people rush over to help. Shortly, I was told the heat and humidity had caused her to faint but that she was fine and I could continue preaching. This was not the only memorable incident of that day. While standing at the front door of the church greeting people leaving the service, a little girl who was with her parents asked me, "Are you Jesus? Will you come back and be our pastor?" Initially, I was shocked, actually blown away, because I had never thought of anyone thinking I was Jesus. What a day! First the elderly woman fainted, and now two penetrating questions were posed by a little girl! Looking embarrassed her parents intervened, trying to explain who I was and that I would let them know if I intended to come back. I quickly added my own response to the girl's question, "Thank you, but no, I'm not Jesus! Your parents will explain everything to you—and I'll have to think about coming back as your pastor." I wasn't totally truthful because I was still coping with a lot of "what ifs" and struggling with thoughts of not coming back. I needed a job, but my experiences that day had frightened me into not wanting to return.

Knowing the congregation was in dire need of a pastor made me ambivalent, but moving there would create a greater distance from our families in Chicago. Our strength was continually strained to the breaking point, and it was difficult for us to see how God was blessing us in all our moves. However, after a detailed discussion and prayer with our children, Doris and I were pleased to see how much they had matured. They engaged intelligently in the issues of change, accepting new responsibilities, and assuring us of having the strength and wisdom to handle everything. I believe Doris was more aware of their strengths and abilities than I was. Additionally, they reassured us of understanding our need for a less stressful ministry setting, and they encouraged me to accept the pastoral call to Martin Luther Lutheran Church. In so doing, I would follow the ministry of two previous white pastors, Rev. John Allen, a Wartburg Theological Seminary alumnus who graduated at the same time as I did, and Rev. James Cartensen, an LCMS pastor.

As the reality of separation drew near, our children made preparations to leave the nest; no one chose to come live with us in Mobile. Patricia was in Seattle with her family. Our oldest son, Terry, his wife, Arlene, and their infant son had already left Minneapolis for Austin, Texas;

Arlene's father and the rest of her family lived in Dallas. Cheryl left to complete her college education in Austin, traveling with her brother Keith and their cousin, Candace Hayes (Candy), who had flown into Minneapolis from Seattle to help them drive to Austin. Cheryl wanted to be with her oldest brother, Terry, and decided not to re-enroll as a student at Augsburg College, planning to complete her journalism degree at the University of Texas. David, our youngest son, and his dog, Sheba, remained in Minneapolis. Sheba would later be sent to Mobile. With our old Chevrolet station wagon in no condition for a long drive to Mobile, we gave the car to David. David decided to live with his brother Michael until he graduated from North Community High School. He continued his college education at North Hennepin Community College, then Augsburg College where he eventually graduated with a master's degree in social work. Our children had matured and were well able to make good decisions. The move to Mobile meant, for the most part, that parental advice and support would be done long distance. From my perspective Doris and I already received a glimpse of the true Land of Promise, seen in the lives our children! Although separated by geographical distance, we were blessed to still be a family.

Without faith it is impossible to please God or come to realize that wherever God sends us becomes a Land of Promise. In 1983 Martin Luther Lutheran Church sent me a letter of call, which I accepted, becoming their second ordained black pastor. After completing the six-month chaplaincy program at Hennepin County Medical Center in Minneapolis, Doris and I flew to Mobile, arriving shortly after Hurricane Frederick had struck the Gulf Coast. This was our second trip to Mobile but now I was coming as the pastor of Martin Luther Church. We landed at the city's small airport on a cloudy, hot sultry day with a soft, misty rain falling. The hot, humid air felt like we were in a steaming sauna. The airport was not equipped with the usual skyway connecting our plane at the gate, so we deplaned in weather that overwhelmed me with its humidity, causing some difficulty in my breathing. This dreary environment caused me to look up at the overcast sky and wonder if we had made the right decision.

But it was more than the weather. We both were still apprehensive about leaving our family behind in Minneapolis. I was not aware of how

Doris felt, but I was devastated because this was our first time having none of the children with us. A little later, Doris commented, "Moving so close to the Gulf of Mexico makes me feel like we've moved out of the United States." Her remark intensified my feelings of our having no control over the situation, and I was again overwhelmed by deep loneliness. The finality of our decision and geographical distance from our families continued to make me homesick. It seemed as if everyone was handling our move better than I was. As Doris and I walked down the portable stairs from our plane onto the wet airport tarmac, several attendants ran towards us carrying large umbrellas. They opened them to shield us from what was now a steadily drizzling rain and guided us to the baggage claim area. A member of Martin Luther Church greeted and assisted us with our luggage, and we were taken to our new home.

Because the church's parsonage was very small and could not accommodate our household goods, the church custodian was living there. We had to secure a new place to live before our household belongings could be shipped to Mobile. However, the congregation provided us a furnished apartment near the church. It was not much larger than the church's parsonage, but we had one bedroom, a kitchen with a refrigerator, and a small living room with a sofa and small black-and-white television set. The church van was provided as transportation until we could get our own automobile. The congregation had done a good job in planning for our transitional housing, but we had not anticipated fighting off large flying cockroaches in our apartment during the night and early morning hours. Regardless, our immediate needs were met, and we used an old church membership directory to contact members of the congregation. We lived in our apartment for eight months, until we sold our house in Minneapolis and borrowed additional money from a member of Doris's family for down payment on a new house. The house was located in West Mobile. Before moving from our apartment we discovered that a young black male teenager had been beaten and lynched, with his body hung from an oak tree directly across the street from our apartment complex.

Using information gathered from various sources, including official congregational documents, I compiled a fairly accurate history of the congregation's past ministry and sent it to the secretary of the American

Lutheran Church national archives in Minneapolis. I also included a copy of an old "model constitution" for Negro mission congregations of the LCMS. Martin Luther Church's congregational council deemed it of utmost importance to document the history of its struggles and ministry as a black congregation of the Southeastern District of the American Lutheran Church. As I worked with the congregation, I sensed a deep witness and determination to document their faithfulness and ability as a black Lutheran congregation to exist in the midst of oppressive Southern segregation and institutional racism. Indeed, it was a miracle that they had continued their relationship with the American Lutheran Church. Eventually the congregation's former ALC constitution was revised to reflect that of the new Evangelical Lutheran Church in America.

There were many priorities, but I began by identifying and updating congregational members listed in an old directory. Doris and I made many nightly telephone calls and endless home visits. However, we were pleased to have some members phone to welcome and invite us into their homes. Whenever visits were made, I was accompanied by a member of the congregation, directing me to the homes and making introductions. I was able to make some visits to the jobs of members. I was blessed in many ways by these visitations.

One day the Rev. James Cartensen, a former white pastor of the church, phoned to arrange a visit to the home of a member of our congregation while he was in town. Agreeing to the visit, we went to the home of Daisy Cyrus and her son, Carlos, who was home from college. Carlos's father was a maritime seaman who worked away from home on boats for most of the year. During our visit, Carlos explained why he was going to college, saying, "I want an education because I've got expensive tastes and need to be sure that I can afford them, but I also want to take good care of my mother." My immediate response was, "Carlos, that's not why you need an education—to spend money on your expensive tastes. There are more important reasons for getting an education than making money! It's good to hear that you're planning to take care of your mother, but you really need to think about other reasons for getting an education." Words cannot describe the look on each person's face. Daisy and Pastor Cartensen were silent and for a moment Carlos stared at me quizzically, then he said, "Thank you, I had never thought about education in any other way than making and spending money—not how to spend it!"

My pastoral relationship with Daisy grew, and on one occasion she attended a Southeastern District convention as a delegate from our congregation. After the convention ended, she made an unsolicited comment, seemingly coming from out of nowhere. In a soft but very explicit voice she said, "Pastor Branch, if someone were to ask me to describe your ministry at our church, I would summarize it as being one of encouragement. And I don't think you're even aware that it's happening." Her words deeply touched me as I realized that this was exactly what I was trying to do—challenge and encourage people to recognize the importance and value of their God-given gifts for ministry. It's true that "what goes around comes around." Later, another lady, Gladys Bradley, encouraged me even further by saying, "The most important thing I get from your sermons is that *we need one another!*" All these comments came when I most needed to hear them. Daisy Cyrus has since died, and I believe Mrs. Bradley is in a nursing home. The latest news I've heard about Daisy's son, Carlos, is that he completed college as well as medical school and is now a practicing physician.

Because the congregation had been without pastoral leadership for a long time, they were unable to work as a team and had little information about congregational ministry and even less of what was happening in the American Lutheran Church. Many whom Doris and I visited were glad to see their church leaders coming with us and showing us around the city. After identifying most of our members, I invited them to renew their commitment to the mission of the church. The next priority was to repair and renovate the church sanctuary. The building was already in need of repairs, but Hurricane Frederick had caused additional damage. Before my arrival the Southeastern District had designated and placed in escrow $10,000 for building repairs until the congregation called a new pastor.

Realizing this was not enough money to include central air-conditioning, the Southeastern District ALC Mission Partners program contacted Our Savior's Lutheran Church, my former congregation in Cedar Rapids, to ask for financial help. Hearing of our needs, the congregation eagerly looked forward to renewing their relationship with me and Doris. A mortgage-burning celebration was planned with a financial contribution to Martin Luther Church. Our Savior's made travel arrangements for us to come to Cedar Rapids and for me to preach at that Sunday's worship service. The congregation's outpouring of support was almost unbelievable—actually, it seemed more like a homecoming celebration than a mortgage burning. As Christians, it is not how financially well-off we are, but how faithful we are in using our resources to witness to loving relationships in Christ Jesus. Following the service, I greeted and embraced many of our friends, some who had tears in their eyes. This outpouring of love put everything in perspective, confirming that we are all members of the family of God. My use of racial distinctions is to describe this world's preoccupation with skin color. Actually the only state of mind needed was faithfulness to the mission of Christ Jesus! What a witness to the love of Christ by Our Savior's congregation and especially for those visitors who did not know us! I wept, knowing that we were truly missed and realizing how our leaving Cedar Rapids had brought blessings to Martin Luther Church. Following worship I received a $5,000 check designated for renovation of Martin Luther Church's sanctuary. The amount of money completely surprised me. I was unaware of how Doris had been affected because I could not stop crying. It was easy to thank everyone but extremely hard to say goodbye, so we thanked God for returning home with such a large gift. Yes, this was primarily a white congregation, but one anointed with the spiritual color of Christ Jesus, faithfully helping their family members at Martin Luther Lutheran Church in Mobile.

After returning to Mobile, someone remarked that I should seek a return visit to Our Savior's Church and preach another $5,000 sermon. Personally, I did not think my sermon was that good, but that it was family relationships in Christ Jesus that brought the blessings. Martin Luther Church council drafted a letter expressing our deep gratitude to Our Savior's, later sending photographs of our church building before and after the renovation. The gift from Our Savior's Church freed up the $10,000 held in escrow by the Southern District. A committee was selected to secure bids from construction companies and provide oversight for the project.

Soon, we discovered that no alterations could be made to the sanctuary's architecture that could cause Martin Luther Church's name to be removed from the State of Alabama's register of historical buildings. This included retaining our stained glass windows and following new requirements for installing central air conditioning. This brings to mind something that happened during one of our committee meetings. Although blessed in our fund-raising efforts, we did not have enough money for the air-conditioning unit and needed additional funds. A light-hearted, although somewhat tense discussion arose about raising additional money. Someone suggested we equally assess dues on every church member, which at first thought sounded good. However, one member of the committee passionately objected, saying, "Everyone in the congregation doesn't have the same amount of income, and it's not fair to ask those with less to give the same as those with higher incomes." Instead, he suggested that we ask our members to give what they could afford and increase our own fund-raising efforts. His analysis was accepted, and he won over the hearts of everyone when he said, "You can't turn the air-conditioning on or off based on who gave how much. If I'm gonna be cool, everybody's gonna be cool!" His remarks were hilarious but quite sensitive, causing a lot of laughter and unanimous approval to encourage designated gifts and more fund-raising to pay for the centralized air-conditioning.

Doris began to touch the hearts of many, moving them to name her the "First Lady of Martin Luther Church." She strongly resisted their suggestions, because it was not in neither of our church traditions. However, she could not put up much resistance when one of the women said, "This is our church—and nobody can tell us we can't have our own First Lady!" I wasn't concerned about Doris' abilities to handle the title because I knew she would use it not selfishly but as one who serves. As usual, her unpretentious personality and captivating smile made it relatively easy to work alongside the women. Her leadership increased their involvement in a variety of innovative congregational and Gulf-coast conference programs. Doris quickly recognized individual needs, especially those of the older women. She shared with me, "They're the ones working hard and long hours as day-workers [housekeepers and maids] in the homes of rich or well-to-do white people." She spoke with insight and empathy, "Our older ladies work just as hard at the church, and they seem to never take time for relaxation. Their income is the lowest in our congregation but they're more faithful in worship attendance and tithing. I think a good way for them to relax is to have our meetings away from the church once in awhile. In fact, I'm going to insist that we treat ourselves, at least once a month, to a dinner meeting at one of the downtown restaurants." I could remember a time when Doris was very concerned about her lack of qualifications in being a minister's wife. Perhaps now she was beginning to see that God knows our individual gifts, and all we have to do is use what God has given us. My wife realized she was in the right place at the right time! I thought it was a great idea but suggested that, unless it became necessary, she should not elaborate too much on reasons for the idea. In discussing her suggestion an elderly woman asked apprehensively, "Is it alright to eat and have our meeting at a downtown restaurant?" Although public facilities were desegregated, she was not quite sure it would all be acceptable. After being reassured, the women's organization decided to treat themselves once a month to a dinner meeting at a downtown restaurant.

Following Doris's election as president of the women's organization, there was a time of increased involvement with white Lutheran churches, working together in the mission goals of the ALC Gulf Coast Conference. There were more women in our congregation, and their organization was a vital part of our ministry, keeping us ecclesiastically and politically involved with other white congregations. Their work helped avoid our being isolated in the ALC Southern District. Our involvement was needed as a witness not only in our conference but in the district.

Improving relationships in our neighborhood became a priority. Martin Luther Church was strategically located, and we began reconnecting with the neighborhood through choir exchanges at Martin Luther Church and Stewart Memorial AME Church. I was elected to the board of Franklin Memorial Community Health Care Center, which was adjacent to our church parking lot. Initially, I sensed the reluctance of some members to wholeheartedly engage in reciprocating partnerships with our local churches. Most of the reluctance came from residual effects of past pastoral leadership and the fear of losing their uniqueness as Lutherans—which had somehow made them feel different, perhaps elite, and therefore separate from others in our neighborhood. Members of Martin Luther had lived in an environment of isolation from the neighborhood for so long that it had become a comfortable way of survival. So what's new in our struggles as black people? To strengthen Martin Luther Church's mission goals, we began reaching out to partner with a couple of white Lutheran churches in West Mobile. These gatherings consisted of joint choir celebrations and commemorative worship services such as Martin Luther King's holiday. Occasionally the agenda was to discuss concerns for our common mission as Christians in the ALC Gulf Coast Conference.

Martin Luther Church's women's organization sponsored a variety of fund-raising events, but the favorite and most effective was the Four Seasons Annual Tea. It provided great potential for evangelism as most churches in our neighborhood had no idea about our denomination. Tables were decorated to represent the seasons of the year—spring, summer, fall, and winter—and dinners were served. Families, friends, and other churches were invited to join in this annual celebration. There was a hostess at each table, greeting their guests and describing the symbolism of their particular seasonal decorations. The tea was quite competitive, with special recognition given to the table raising the most money. The hostess of the winning table received a small tiara or crown that was placed on her head in recognition that she was the current year's "Queen of the Four Seasons Tea." Doris participated, but always in a non-competitive manner. Various prizes were given away in raffles as well as door prizes. This was Martin Luther's biggest fund-raising event. Its intergenerational emphasis, especially in the "fashion and talent show" revealed many gifts of the young as well as others in the congregation. We persevered in our attempts to recognize everyone, knowing that the church's mission transcends all congregational programs. We cannot program love! Programs are transitory, but loving relationships endure the test of time. The essence of Christ Jesus' missional mandate has not changed: Go out into all nations (white and black neighborhoods, young and old) building relationships, not programs! Too much emphasis on programs can distract us from building spiritually motivated relationships. Building on our denominational heritage, Martin Luther Church began to have celebrative worship and neighborhood meetings with two other black LCMS congregations. Our work was productive because we did not spend time and energy with endless discussions of doctrinal differences. This was especially true when it came to the importance of our united witness in the neighborhood. It was helpful that I knew Rev. James Marshall, pastor in one of the churches, before coming to Mobile. He was one of several black pastors interviewed to come to Holy Family Lutheran Church in Chicago.

We were given an opportunity as black Lutheran pastors in the Southeastern District to unite for more effective ministry. The number of black pastors in our district was greater than in any other region of the country. There was one ordained black woman in our group, Pastor Alma Marie Copeland. We were separated by geographical as well as other barriers. We really did not know one another and knew even less about how to implement Christ Jesus' mission in our congregations and neighborhood. Recognizing this, we began scheduling open-ended agenda meetings to discern where and how God was leading us. Our first priority was to become more informed leaders, so we could intelligently articulate our concerns. These meetings resulted in creation of the Southeastern Lutheran Black Pastors Conference (SELBPC). Rev. Eugene Powell, the district president's black assistant, provided informational support and communication with the ALC Southeastern District president.

The ALC Southeastern Gulf Coast Conference consisted of only eight congregations, which I really appreciated because it was small enough to facilitate an awareness of our mutual needs. Regional directors from the ALC national office routinely scheduled visits to all American Lutheran Church mission churches to assist and support the congregation's ministry. One of few black regional directors assigned to the southeastern region of the ALC Division for Service and Mission in America and a white American Lutheran Church official came to visit Martin Luther Church. Both met with our congregational council to assess, support, and share information relevant to our ministry. At some point I became extremely concerned in how the white church official was speaking to the leaders of our congregation. I felt his remarks were condescending and directed at my pastoral leadership which did not encourage working as partners in mission. In fact he spoke as if he was our pastor, embarrassing me in the presence of council members. Obviously he ignored or had not read my monthly congregational progress reports. He appeared to be ignorant or disrespectful of Martin Luther Church's past historical struggles. I angrily said, "I don't think you know what you're talking about. Officially, I'm the pastor of this congregation, and if anyone here is going to be 'balled out,' that's my job, not yours!" Everyone was shocked, but I think this white church official learned a lesson on how and when to speak privately about his concerns, at least, with this particular black pastor. The members of Martin Luther Church had always shown respect to white officials of the American Lutheran Church and, money or no money, I expected the same respect from them. Sometime later at one of our Southeastern Lutheran Black Pastor's Conference meetings several disparaging remarks were made concerning the leadership of the regional director, especially his Christian witness. We were at an impasse on how to handle the situation, with no one willing to approach him with our concerns. Finally, I told the group that I was giving serious thought to contacting the national church office and applying for a position as regional mission director in our district. I really did not want the position because the time spent in traveling would separate me for long periods of time from my wife. I knew the regional director would eventually hear about my comment, and I soon received a phone call from him asking to put any concerns about him on our agenda for the next meeting. When we met, he confronted me about what I had said at our last meeting, inferring that I was going after his job. I explained our concern about his Christian witness on the job and its effect on his work as our regional director. The long and short of our conversation was that I was not interested in his job, but we all wanted him to take better care of himself and be aware of the various contexts in which others thought he was not giving a Christian witness. Initially, he had not shown much interest or given any validity to our meetings, but after this meeting he put us on his schedule and began to regularly attend.

The first organized effort at neighborhood outreach by Martin Luther Church's evangelism committee was a visit to the homes of black public housing residents near our church. Our visits were seen as a way of connecting with the neighborhood and answering the questions of some people who wanted to know whether or not we were Christians. I believe our presence may have been perceived by some residents as a socially elite white religion. Historically, the Lutheran Church was not well known to the black community, and Martin Luther Church,

Baptism at Martin Luther Church.

with its limited resources and lack of national church support, was no exception. Our evangelism committee formed teams of two or more people, including teenage members of our church, to visit the public housing complex. A very active member of Martin Luther Church's women's organization knocked on doors with me.

Armed with worship service bulletins, religious pamphlets, and newsletters of the American Lutheran Church, we began our visits early on a Saturday morning. We went from door to door, generally receiving warm responses with most visits which we intentionally made short in duration. However, the cordial responses quickly changed when we reached the door of one home. The main entry door was open but separated by a screen door. After knocking on the screen door for an extended time, a female voice loudly shouted at me, cussing and saying, "I'm sick and tired of all you goddamn Jehovah Witnesses knocking on my door, and I don't wanna talk to you!" Although she saw me, I could not see her and she never came to the screen door. I tried explaining to her that I wasn't a Jehovah's Witness, but she began cussing at me again, saying, "God dammit, I'm sick and tired of all of you church people coming around knocking on my door, bothering me. One of these days I'm gonna shoot somebody!" At this point the woman who had come with me became terrified and began pulling on my shirt, saying we should leave. As I backed away from the screen door, I apologized to the unseen lady for bothering her and assured her I would not return. I cannot explain why, but I was not afraid.

Following our visits, we met at the church to share our experiences while eating lunch. My teammate cried as she spoke about the lady who threatened to shoot us, saying, "I was really worried about Pastor Branch. I'll continue working on our committee but will never go on any more neighborhood visits." Later, she said, "I had forgotten what it's like living in some of the black areas of our neighborhood." The evangelism committee decided not to knock on doors in the public housing complex but occasionally to leave flyers and worship bulletins inviting residents to worship with us. Everyone concluded that the feedback revealed our lack of knowledge as to who these black people were and our need to reconnect with them. This was true in spite of the socio-economic diversity in our congregation. Somehow we had ignored or become blind in addressing the needs of those in our neighborhood. We were a black congregation, but there was a subtle, socio-economic, religious chasm separating and dividing us. Struggling for upward mobility, unwittingly we embraced neighborhood isolation to seek greater acceptance in the white church. Classism mingled with racism was alive and functional, distancing us blacks from one another. I clearly understand how the historical psychological ramifications of racial supremacy have blinded us in so many ways to our mutual socio-economic and political needs. That is our continuing struggle as black people against the psychological chains of slavery that blind and separate us, vis-à-vis the American dream. However, because we are an integral part of that dream's traditions, it is incumbent upon us to be assertive in changing it for the best. In other words, there is hope, and I pray that in trying to follow Christ's missional mandate that I have become a witness that positive change does happen.

The summer of 1985 was a really significant and refreshing year for me and Doris. In planning his vacation, our son Michael included a stopover in Mobile to visit with us and have our granddaughter, Michelle Amber Branch, baptized. Although she was only a year old, she insists that she remembers her baptism as well as that of another child baptized that same day. Another interesting thing happened this same year. Martin Luther Church's Sunday worship services were occasionally visited by "snowbirds"—white northerners, who vacation in the South during the winter to escape the cold and snow. I often received complements from them on how well we did our liturgical worship service. Many made comments on how surprised they were to find an all-black American Lutheran Church congregation. These conversations opened the door for informational dialogues about the rich, significant history of Martin Luther Church's ministry.

Sometime in 1985-86 I received a letter from Dorothy Green, a black coordinator for the American Lutheran Church's National Youth Gathering, inviting Doris and me to serve as hotel facilitators during the event in San Antonio. We decided this would be an excellent opportunity not only for us but also for our youth. It was an entirely new experience for them because there had been very few opportunities to participate in Lutheran church events outside of Mobile. Mrs. Green made arrangements to fly us to San Antonio early so we could participate in logistical orientation for program coordination, and also receive information on safety and security for youth attending the gathering. Similar orientations were given to youth groups from all congregations.

On the very first day of the gathering, following dinner, there was a knock on the door of our hotel room. Hotel security personnel had been instructed to bring a teenage white boy they had "busted" to our room. He seemed to be intoxicated, and they had caught him jumping from one balcony to another on the eighth floor of the hotel. He pleaded with us not to tell anyone about the incident. We told him that it was our job to decide how to report the incident and would talk about it with him before making any decisions. Doris participated in the conversation, but the young man soon asked to continue the conversation alone with Doris. Their conversation went on late into the night, so I went to bed. Later, Doris came and woke me up. The young man had confessed to smoking marijuana and was acting out a role he had created for himself as a jock with other young people in his congregation so he could feel accepted and fit in. Again, I wondered what had happened to Doris' past concerns about being a pastor's wife. We escorted the young man back to his room and found that his counselor, a young white female, had been out all night drinking and was now asleep. The following morning I made a phone call notifying his pastor of the incident and explaining the teenager's request to have counseling and confidentiality about what had happened. The pastor was somewhat aware of the problem and thanked us for our intervention, promising to follow up on the young man's request. Later we received a letter from the pastor, thanking us again and explaining how he had handled everything.

Another significant and potentially more risky event occurred one night between us and a teenage white girl who was inebriated and staggering down the hallway of the hotel. Doris and I had arranged to make late-night rounds on at least two floors of our twelve-story hotel either as a team or alone. Whenever it was necessary, I would be the loner. The plan was a good one because we quickly discovered that some youth counselors were doing their "own thing" instead of being responsible chaperones. On this particular night, Doris and I were making our rounds together. I had no idea what this young white girl had consumed, but she was staggering so much it appeared she was going to fall down in the hallway. Grabbing her by the arm, I identified myself as a hotel facilitator for the youth gathering and asked her to come with me and my wife to our room. There was no smell of alcohol on her, so I assumed she was on other drugs. As we escorted her to our room she began screaming out the name "Mike," scratching and digging her fingernails into my hand. That hurt, but I was not about to let her go. Doris became alarmed, cautioning me about the risk I was taking and telling me I should let her go. My reply was, "We're doing our job, and if any of our daughters were ever found in this condition I would hope someone would do what we're doing." The girl continued yelling for "Mike" to come to her rescue. Soon a young white boy poked his head out of a room and looked at us in the hallway. I told him to come to our room. I was determined to do the right thing and yelled loudly at him, identifying myself and asking him to come into our room. When he realized that I was not going to let the girl go, he came into our room, where Doris and I explained what was going to happen. After gathering enough pertinent information from both of these young people, Doris and I escorted them to a room where their pastor was sleeping. Awakened by the noise, he apologized for both of them sneaking out of the room and thanked us for what we had done. Later, we received a very nice "thank you" letter from him.

Faced with these negative experiences, Doris and I decided we had better check on the youth from our own congregation. What a pleasant surprise when chatting with our kids from Martin Luther Church!

They had not encountered any problems and were always in by curfew. However, we contacted their counselors to do a more extensive check on them. After all our experiences as hotel facilitators, Doris and I decided to stay up late on the final night of the gathering and dance with all the young people. We were, however, severely restricted in not having the kind of music we could dance to!

A very encouraging moment in our ministry at Martin Luther Church took place when the congregation decided to celebrate a special "worship service of recognition" to affirm my pastoral leadership. Money was raised by soliciting ads in our Sunday worship service bulletins and special deliveries of lunch and dinner plates consisting of fish, spaghetti, and coleslaw. The origin of this particular worship celebration to recognize pastoral leadership is rooted in Southern black tradition. In fact the tradition is so significant in affirming black pastoral leadership that it followed the exodus of Southern blacks to Northern cities. Of significance was that the recognition also included Doris, the "First Lady" of Martin Luther Church. We had never experienced this kind of recognition other than when we were leaving a congregation. The implications had an impact on the entire black neighborhood. In many ways it was like having a family celebration with friends and relatives. Reciprocity was assumed, that we would be supportive in similar celebrations at other neighborhood churches. We invited our family members up North to come to Mobile for this special honor, but none were able to come. When our daughter, Cheryl, realized no one would be there for our special day, she sent the following message via telephone:

> From all your children:
>
> Dear Mom and Dad,
>
> "Praise God from whom all blessings flow!"
>
> We thank God for the blessing of parents who stand behind their God and who taught us to do the same. We know that an Appreciation Day is secondary to the appreciation we all have for our God! We pray God continues blessing you two, in your ministry and the family at Martin Luther Church.
>
> "To God be the glory, for the things he has done!"
>
> Love always, your children!

I cried in realizing that time and distance had not and could not separate our family. This was another of many *kairos* moments, God's time: "And we know that in all things God works for the good of those who love Him and who have been called according to His purpose!" (Romans 8:28ff, NIV).

During 1985-87 I began participating, as did other black pastors, in merger meeting conversations with the American Lutheran Church (ALC), the Lutheran Church in America (LCA), and the Association of Evangelical Lutheran Churches (AELC). Rev. Les Weber, pastor of the Lutheran Church of the Atonement in Atlanta, was appointed by the Rev. Harold Skillrud, bishop of the American Lutheran Church's Southeastern District, to share information and dialogue with every black Lutheran pastor and congregation in the synod. Rev. Weber was very encouraging as he stressed the importance and inclusive nature of our contributions in the new church merger. I was extremely pleased to have Pastor Weber and Bishop Skillrud ask our organization, the Southeastern Lutheran Black Pastors Conference (SELBPC), to participate in forming the new Lutheran church. These churchwide conversations ended with the Closing Convention of the American Lutheran Church (ALC), held in Columbus, Ohio, in 1987. In January 1988 the ALC ceased to exist as it joined, along with the LCA and the AELC to form the Evangelical Lutheran Church in America (ELCA). The Lutheran Church—Missouri Synod (LCMS) declined to become a partner in this merger.

Prior to formation of the new church, while attending a Southern District convention, I was approached by Mary Winfrey, a member of the Lutheran Church of the Atonement in Atlanta, who asked if I was open to the possibility of a call to another congregation. The Rev. Les Weber, a graduate of Christ Seminary Seminex, which came into being because of a doctrinal schism within the LCMS, was her pastor. When Weber was called as the pastor to Mrs. Winfrey's congregation, the congregation had to reconsider its affiliation with LCMS. In June 1976, the congregation voted to leave the LCMS, and several months later was among the first black congregations to join the newly-formed AELC under the leadership of a black bishop, the Rev. William Herzfeld. When Lutheran Church of the Atonement left the LCMS, the synod demanded that the church pay off a $40,000 mortgage that was due the synod.

Through hard work and sacrifice, the goal was achieved in five years. I believe my name had been mentioned to Mrs. Winfrey by Pastor Weber for a possible call to the Lutheran Church of the Atonement because of my participation in church merger conversations. I was very comfortable at Martin Luther Church in Mobile and had not thought of leaving that congregation, so I really was not interested in seeking another pastoral call. However, I sensed this might be an opportunity for me and Doris to move geographically closer to our families.

In response to Mrs. Winfrey's inquiry, I invited Martin Luther Church's council president and convention delegate, Robert Williams, to share in our conversation. I really felt good and must confess to having ulterior motives in requesting his presence. I wanted him to hear that there were other Lutheran congregations interested in having me as their pastor. Mr. William's response was very gracious as he said, "We're satisfied with our pastor. Pastor Branch is a very good pastor, and our membership has grown in many ways because of his leadership. We don't want him to leave, but wouldn't hold him back if he wanted to leave our church." I was equally pleased to have Mrs. Winfrey hear this positive endorsement of my work at Martin Luther Church.

Later I received a phone call to come to Lutheran Church of the Atonement in Atlanta for a pastoral interview. I felt strangely peaceful and comfortable prior to and during the entire call committee interview process. In fact, after noticing that there was not an opportunity on the agenda for me to ask questions of the call committee, I respectfully requested time for me to interview the committee. Walter Stublefield, chairman of the committee, assured me I would be given time to respond to comments and ask questions. Having become more knowledgeable through the years about usual congregational concerns and needs and the dynamics of dialogue in call committees is another reason I felt comfortable. Also, I had no extraordinary ministry problems that might necessitate my seeking another pastoral call.

The congregation's call committee specifically asked, "What would you change if you became pastor of the church?" I quickly responded, saying, "I have no idea if any changes are needed but would always be guided in making changes in the context of discussions with the congregation." Later, I learned of the reason behind the question. During a previous interview with another pastor he had spoke of having Holy Communion every Sunday instead of once a month. When asked about my strengths and weaknesses, I said, "My weaknesses are the same as all of us in this room, prayerfully hoping that God's forgiving love has us on his radar screen. However, I do believe my strengths can best be seen in my love for people. At the same time, I realize that in some ways this could possibly be a weakness, but it's a weakness I'll have to live with."

Until writing this memoir, I had not given much thought or fully understood these words spoken by God to the Apostle Paul but now believe that they also apply to me: "My grace is sufficient for you . . . for my power is made perfect in weakness" (2 Corinthians 12:8-10, NIV). Usually all pastoral interviews include preaching, which I did, but cannot remember anything about it. Nevertheless, the call committee recommended to the congregation that a letter of call be sent to me. I accepted the letter of call from Lutheran Church of the Atonement and was installed as their pastor in 1989. Following my acceptance of the call, Edgar Glass, a member of the call committee, said that I had become his "love pastor" because none of the pastors previously interviewed had mentioned love as one of their strengths.

I became very emotional, in ways that surprised me, when I informed Martin Luther Church of my leaving. Our youth presented a petition signed by members of the congregation requesting that I remain as pastor of the church. Mr. Williams, who had told Mrs. Winfrey that he did not want me to leave, assisted them in writing the petition. Truly, this was unexpected and occurred following the closing of a Sunday worship service. As I listened to several positive critiques of my leadership by youth in the congregation expressing their love, tears welled up in my eyes. I knew that there were others who did not feel the same as the youth. The petition, signed by over eighty adult and youth parishioners, is truly a ministry keepsake which I have kept safe in my files. Such positive appreciation of pastoral ministry is rare, especially coming from church youth. I had instructed and nurtured most of these teenagers through two years of confirmation preparation with a number of study retreats in our home. This petition left me emotionally humbled with a grieving heart because I knew they had all become my family. I realized that we had gone through many personal struggles together, but I had never considered how the spiritual impact of my ministry touched them.

I was leaving as the church was still growing, with a membership roll of 100 people. The Sunday worship service attendance averaged ninety members and the choir had grown numerically, attracting new people to our worship services. With our increased community involvement, Martin Luther Church had begun receiving its share of people from the community into membership. I was leaving the congregation with sadness but thanking God for allowing me and Doris to have shared our lives with such a loving family of Christians. It is difficult to explain my feelings but "praise God from whom all blessings flow," they have all become family to us!

A very significant spiritual experience occurred that can only be described as my parting "peace conversation" with a member of the congregation, Eva Antone. On my last Sunday a "goodbye banquet" was given in recognition of our ministry together. Following the meal I greeted several people, including Mrs. Antone, with whom I had experienced a few disagreements. I noticed that she was lingering alone in the church's kitchen and decided to go in and personally say goodbye. I had not thought about what to say but made the following comments, "Eva, I want you to know that although we had our differences I love you; in fact I love all the people here at Martin Luther Church. I'm going to miss all of you, but Doris and I were always planning to move closer to our families in Chicago." As she wiped tears from her eyes, Eva said, "I love you too and will miss you and Doris." Leaving the kitchen, I noticed that the former president of our church council, Prince Colley, had seen us talking and Eva crying, so I explained to him what had happened. He said, "Even though you two didn't get along, I knew she didn't want you to leave. We all feel the same way!" Eight years later, on October 19, 1997 Doris and I returned to Mobile to celebrate the congregation's seventy-fifth anniversary. Doris, who had become a proficient designer of worship banners, made a special one for the momentous occasion.

CHAPTER 14

Lutheran Church of the Atonement

1989-1996

In March 1989, our move to Atlanta seemed like *déjà-vu* as Doris and I had to live in another leased apartment, the Landrum Arms, located on Landrum Avenue in Atlanta. As was the case in Mobile, it was raining when we arrived, but this time the rain was not misty—it was frigid. While helping the mover bring some of the smaller household items into our apartment, I got soaking wet and chilled, developing flu-like symptoms and asthma. My illness delayed beginning work at the church, with the cancellation of two Lenten worship services. The moving van driver had to hire another man to help him unload our furniture. Various boxes containing our household goods cluttered every room in the apartment, and it took months for us to unpack everything. Once again, our dog, Sheba, came with us, becoming the only family member accompanying us wherever we moved. The dreary weather was not the only thing affecting our arrival in Atlanta. We were still trying to find time to unpack our household goods and settle down in the apartment when David asked us to come to Minneapolis and to officiate at his marriage to Rebecca. Sadly, I had to refuse his request because of my illness and the immediate pastoral needs in our new congregation.

There was a death in the family of a member of the congregation and, realizing there was no time to rest, I hit the ground running. Helen Thomas was a member of the congregation whom I had not yet met, but I understood the needs of her family. Even though we had just arrived, she phoned to notify me of her husband's death. She was very nice, apologizing for asking my help after my recent arrival and wanting to know if I could do his funeral service. Her concern was that he was not a member of the congregation, and she wondered if there would be a problem in having his funeral at the church. I assured her that I saw no problem, that our ministry was to her family, and the funeral would be done at the church. Later I received "a heads-up" phone call warning me that there may be some negative fallout because of my decision. I am sure the warning was meant to help, but it raised a number of concerns because I did not want to get off to a bad start this early in my new ministry. I immediately phoned Isaac Freeman Jr., a retired U.S. Army colonel and honored leader in the congregation. I had met and briefly chatted with him during my pastoral interview and was now seeking his wisdom. Following the Lutheran church mergers, Colonel Freeman, who had previously served as vice president of the Southeastern Synod Council, had been elected as the first black president of the ELCA Southeastern Synod. I informed him of my conversation with Mrs. Thomas and my decision to have her husband's funeral at our church in spite of the warning I had received. I explained my thoughts about the funeral as our congregation's ministry to a grieving widow and her family, and explained that I was not asking his permission, only his support. He said, "I'm glad you called because I wasn't aware of Mr. Thomas's death. But I'm a little peeved that you've been bothered about using the church for the funeral." He said that it was possible that some of our members didn't understand rules regulating use of the church building but confirmed Mrs. Thomas and her family's membership and their faithfulness to the ministry of the congregation. He firmly stated, "As pastor of the church, you've made the right call, and I support your decision."

Following my conversation with Colonel Freeman, Mary Winfrey, the council president, drove me and Doris to the bereaved widow's home to plan funeral arrangements. Mrs. Thomas lived in Lithonia, a suburb of Atlanta, and when we arrived she was surrounded by a large number of family members. Mr. Thomas was the father of Laura Thomas Lindsey, who later became council president. Laura's husband, Charles Lindsey, served as a church deacon. Many family members belonged to the congregation and, as I discovered later, were also actively supporting the church's ministry. It was comforting to have Mrs. Winfrey there to introduce us to the family and assist in the funeral arrangements.

Everyone assisted in making funeral arrangements, and it was at this time that I discovered there would be deacons of the church to help in the funeral. The service was held on Good Friday, which was unusual because I had never conducted a funeral during Holy Week. Not being fully recovered from my illness added to my discomfort in trying to pull the service together, and I wasn't feeling very well on the day of the funeral. However, I listened well enough to gather enough information about the deceased and his family to write a sermon-eulogy outline. Everything went fine, the funeral service was well attended, and I received no negative feedback.

Nine months later, Colonel Isaac Freeman had a heart attack while driving home following completion of some work at the church. He was discovered in his car, which he had been able to park along the side of the road. His death deeply saddened his family and many in the congregation because of his leadership and work in the church. During my pastorate he never served on the church council, but he was often present at our meetings as a member of the congregation. On December 21, 1989, I officiated at his funeral, assisted by Southeastern Synod Bishop Harold Skillrud, other clergy, and official representatives of the U.S. Army. Colonel Freeman was buried with full military honors at the Lincoln Memorial Cemetery on Simpson Road, not far from our church. This was the most prestigious funeral I had ever conducted. Some in our congregation felt that with Colonel Freeman's position as the first black president of the Southeastern Synod, Bishop Skillrud should preach the sermon. I discussed their thoughts with the bishop, offering him the opportunity, but he declined, explaining that I was Colonel Freeman's pastor and should do the sermon. I understood the wisdom of his words and felt, as always, his strong support of my pastoral leadership. On the day of Colonel Freeman's funeral the church was filled with members, neighborhood residents, clergy and lay representatives from other congregations representing the Southeastern Synod. Following Colonel Freeman's death, the church's community room was named the Freeman-Holland Conference Room, in memory of Colonel Isaac Freeman and Mr. Richard Holland. Both men were respected leaders and faithful servants of the congregation.

Shortly after being installed as pastor of the church, another black pastor informed me that he had been the congregation's first choice as pastor but had returned the letter of call. Later I discovered he had indeed been their first choice but returned the call because of failure in salary negotiations. In retrospect, I know that God is good and I was truly blessed to be the congregation's second choice because it resulted in my becoming the first black pastor of Atonement Lutheran Church—with an increase in salary. Yes, I was the second choice but now had become God's first choice! There were many firsts: For the first time in eighteen years I became the pastor of a congregation with a little over 300 members, including a large number of black men with a men's chorus. This was my first financially self-supporting congregation. Thanks to the long-suffering patience of our women's choir director, Mary Holloway, I learned to chant the liturgy for our worship service.

Another first was to have a Deacon's Board with ten men and two women, all elected to assist in worship and the spiritual care of the congregation. Each deacon was assigned approximately twenty-five members of the congregation. They met monthly with me to discuss membership visits, and to identify and prayerfully articulate spiritual needs in the congregation. I also shared with them my own visits which were made to mostly sick and homebound members. During these visits I always received Sunday service offering envelopes. Whenever I missed one of these home visits, I received a phone call asking me to come and pick up an offering envelope.

There are a number of deeply spiritual pastoral visits I made, but none more challenging than those made to Alice Dixon and her paraplegic son, Leroy, who occasionally attended worship services in a wheelchair. Leroy's paralysis was the result of a diving accident when he hit his head on a huge rock, severely injuring his spinal cord. All his limbs below the neck were paralyzed. It was amazing to see how well Leroy could feed himself. He really liked fried chicken; whenever I visited him, I would stop at a local restaurant and buy fried chicken. Eventually I contacted the ELCA Men in Mission program in Atlanta and asked them to help build a wheelchair ramp for Leroy's visits to the hospital. On the day the ramp was built, we all had a big fried chicken dinner party. On the last visit Doris and I made to the Dixon's home before we left Church of the Atonement and returned to Minneapolis, Ms. Dixon gave us a farewell gift of $100. Knowing how hard they struggled with their meager income and the extent of their poverty, I initially refused the gift.

However, after seeing the look of hurt and disappointment on both their faces, I relented and accepted what I knew was their "love offering" to us. I had never felt so humble in my life!

Among other significant visits were those made to the home of Dorothy Grayson, a member of the congregation who was a widow and diabetic. Once when I arrived at her home the door was ajar and Ms. Grayson was lying on the floor in a coma. I called the paramedics, and she was taken to the hospital. Usually, this happened when she had not eaten or taken her medication. My visits were short and extremely difficult because of the severe dampness in her home. A leaking roof had caused severe deterioration to the walls, resulting in rotten rugs, carpeting, and floors. Mold and mildew was everywhere, and my visits to her home triggered asthma attacks. Hoping to help her, I contacted her former pastor, Rev. Les Weber, who informed me that after her husband's death there were no family members to provide care and help her with the house. He told me she had been ripped off several times by roofers and had finally given up hope of ever getting the roof repaired. However, he suggested that I contact Resource Service Ministries to see if their "Take a Home and Receive a Blessing Program" might help. I contacted them. What started out as the repair of a leaky roof resulted in a total renovation of Ms. Grayson's home, including electrical rewiring. She received a new furnace, hot water heater, and refrigerator. The labor was provided by volunteer prison inmates on work release, parole, or probation. The women of our congregation provided daily lunches, prayers, and good conversation for all the volunteers. The house was in such bad shape that it took a year to get all the supplies and volunteers needed to complete the project.

During the next seven years I was faced with a number of important decisions concerning our family. David, our youngest son, married Rebecca Kosnopsal in 1989 at St. Olaf Lutheran Church in Minneapolis. Doris attended the wedding, but I was unable to go because it came soon after my arrival at the church. In 1990, two years into my pastorate at Atonement Lutheran Church, Michael and his wife, Debra, divorced. This was a very sad and painful time for our family, but especially for our grandchildren who were devastated by the separation. As often as possible, Doris and I traveled to Minneapolis to provide whatever comfort and support we could to our now-broken family. We had been married thirty-seven years, and this was a new experience for us. However, there was a break in the sadness when our youngest daughter, Cheryl, graduated from the University of Texas in April 1990 with degrees in journalism and marketing. Doris and I traveled to Austin for the graduation. What a wonderful time it was to see our daughter receive the college diploma she had worked so hard to get! But the roller-coaster ride plummeted down, reminding us of our own vulnerabilities. Sadly, three members of my family in Chicago died, and as the oldest member of the family as well as an ordained minister, I was expected to conduct all three funerals. I did not mind the role, but it was very hard putting all the pieces together in preparing for the funeral while going through my own grieving process.

My mother, Rebecca Kershaw, died on September 23, 1990, due to medical complications related to Alzheimer's. I'm truly thankful for the loving care given her at home by my family in Chicago. They were caregivers par excellence! During our vacation and whenever possible we traveled to Chicago to give whatever support we could to our families. Providing loving care for Mama was extremely stressful. I thank God for the cooperative spirit and coordinated efforts by everyone in the family. I am sure there were some in the family who felt that I should have done more. However, the issue was resolved as it became apparent that I did not have the financial resources or time to help resolve the problems connected with her health care. I could not leave my church responsibilities in Atlanta. However, frequent phone conversations helped ease tensions to help us provide good care for the matriarch of our family. For me, the last piece of the puzzle was put in place when I officiated at my mother's funeral. In pain she welcomed me into this world, and now in pain and joy I ushered her soul into the loving care of God.

Following my mother's funeral, Lutheran Church of the Atonement gave a service of recognition for my work as their pastor. Over 112 members of the congregation signed and gave me a very large greeting card. The front of the card had a picture of Daffy Duck saying, "I like you a lot. I mean. . . more than average. I think of you as special. I mean . . . we're talking LOVE, Baby!" What a spiritual uplift this was during these hours of sadness in our family! But the roller-coaster ride continued its downward spiral.

A year later, on November 8, 1991, my stepfather, Elbert Kershaw, died. I truly loved and respected him as a father. I returned to Chicago to conduct his funeral, and was very proud of my brother, Loyal David Kershaw, as I listened to the words he spoke at our father's funeral.

In December 1991 my oldest son, Terrance, and his son, Lequent Tyrel Branch, moved from Austin to Atlanta because he and his wife, Arlene, had divorced—the second one in our family. Terry was so devastated that he resigned his job as a computer operator at the Veteran's Administration Hospital in Austin and came to live with us in Atlanta. But God's manifold blessings were always omnipresent in every roller-coaster ride of our odyssey. Before the year ended our granddaughter, Sydney Marie Branch, was born in Minneapolis on December 3, 1991, to Keith Branch and Jeannette Sledge. And in that same month I received a very special Christmas present from our daughter Cheryl. I don't think she realized how significant it was to me. It was a beautiful framed picture of two young black boys playing together. One was riding the back of the other—which some call piggy-back riding, but which we Southern youngsters call horsey. The picture, a print by artist Brenda Joysmith, is still hanging on the wall in our home and is entitled, "He's My Brother." Cheryl wrote a note to me on the back of the picture saying that this picture "speaks to me of two things—your ministry and our family." I wept as I read it, not only because of what she had written but also because the picture reminded me of those earlier days playing with my younger brother George, when I carried him on my back. But these were tears of joy, not pain!

Soon after arriving in Atlanta, Terry and Tyrel became members of the Lutheran Church of the Atonement, actively participating in worship and other programs of the church. I instructed Tyrel in how to be an acolyte, and he assisted me in many Sunday morning worship services. Our church was a congregation that opened its doors to the surrounding community in various supportive ministries. One evening during a community drug awareness program held at the church our son, Terry, took a microphone and said, "I'm a recovering crack cocaine addict! And I know there are a lot of people out there hurting, just like me. In my heart of hearts, I know that I'm better than what I've been doing." What a shock it was for us to hear him make this open confession! We didn't know about his addiction—and were not embarrassed, only surprised. As a matter of fact, we were proud of his revelation and later participated with him in family counseling at the Veteran's Administration Hospital.

One evening when returning home from the church, I found Terry sitting in his mother's rocking chair. Doris was not home, and it was getting dark outside. The lights and television set were not on, which was unusual, but I could see Terry slowly rocking back and forth in the chair. He did not say anything until I walked into the room. Then he spoke with conviction and determination. "Daddy," he said, "I've been praying, and God has given me an answer. I didn't get in this shape in one day, and it's going to take more than one day for me to get out of the trouble I'm in." I sensed that he had a religious experience. It definitely became a turning point in Terry's recovery not only from addiction but also from his wayward, irresponsible ways. Terry had money when he came to Atlanta, but he was now without a job and had bad credit. The realization of having all our prayers answered was powerful. Terry said, "I haven't been much of a positive role model as a father for my son." At this point he began crying. Again, I was surprised at how God had guided us into this moment. Cheryl, who lived in Austin during Terry's addiction, had given a lot of loving support to her brother and nephew, to whom in many ways she had became a surrogate mother. Everybody at some point in their life needs somebody to turn to for help, and—thank God—no matter what has happened to us we have always been supportive of one another as a family! On his road back to recovery, Terry began working at all kinds of odd jobs. He worked as a janitor, cleaning various offices until transportation became a problem. Later, he worked with a member of the church, Pete Turner. They became close friends, and Terry began working with Pete setting up office cubicles for employers in the region. Pete was a member of the congregation's male chorus, and later Terry joined the men's chorus too, on one occasion singing the National Anthem at the Atlanta Braves baseball game in Fulton County Stadium (renamed Ted Turner Field). Eventually he worked at the U.S. Post Office, and later I officiated at his second marriage to Vivian Scott, a single parent with two children.

In 1992, I was blessed to have the honor and privilege of baptizing two of my grandchildren. Patricia, Michael, Cheryl, Keith, and David planned their vacations so they could visit Atlanta at the same time. The gathering was the Branch family reunion. As the children's grandfather, I baptized both of them at our church: Keith's daughter, Sydney Marie Branch; and David's son, Joseph Lee Branch. After the baptisms our choir director, Mary Holloway, invited us to have dinner at her home.

In April 1994 Doris and I flew to Minneapolis so I could officiate at Michael's marriage to Patricia TeBrake in Maple Grove Lutheran Church. It was very good to see Michael move on with his life after a very painful divorce from his first wife. His pastor and congregation were very supportive of the biracial marriage. The wedding was well attended, including the bride's parents, John and Judith TeBrake, who lived in Brooten, Minnesota. Michael's fishing buddies stood by him at the altar during the ceremony. Doris and I had stayed over after Michael's wedding so we could attend our youngest son David's graduation from Augsburg College. David received his second degree, this one in a master of social work. We thank God for his wife, Rebecca, who sacrificed much in assuming extra family responsibilities to help with David's two extra years of study. We will always remember with gratitude the support and guidance given him by his student advisor, Mary Lou Williams, who was also present at his graduation. David

Celebrating David's graduation from Augsburg College.

is currently employed by the Minneapolis School District as the principal of North Senior High School Academy.

In 1995, Lutheran Church of the Atonement welcomed its first black seminary intern. What a fight I had in securing her internship! Realizing that internships were limited, I mailed my required paperwork to the national church office on time and was promised an intern for our congregation. However, while I was on vacation, the internship was rescinded without warning and given to another congregation, St. Paul's Lutheran Church in Decatur. Only after making a rather angry phone call to the ELCA director of internships, threatening to visit the church office in Chicago, did I receive another seminary internship for our congregation. Rebecca Templeton, in spite of a series of financial struggles, graciously accepted a one-year appointment at our church. There's more to this incident than I care to write about, but this I will say: If you don't stand up for your rights, no one is going to give them to you. And personally speaking, I'd rather get knocked down than lie down!

The downward spiraling roller coaster rides continued. My brother Elbert Leonard Kershaw Jr. (Stuffy), a real fun-filled guy, died in his sleep on January 9, 1995, from high blood pressure. Traumatic and deeply painful family losses were escalating. I seemed to be constantly asking when something else bad was going to happen in our family. The sadness about Stuffy's hypertension was that no one knew he was ill. Once again I traveled to Chicago and officiated at a younger brother's funeral.

During my pastorate in Mobile, I was a member of the newly structured Southeastern Lutheran Black Pastors Conference (SELBPC). When I moved to Atlanta I became president of the organization. As the pastor of Lutheran Church of the Atonement in Atlanta where the ELCA Synod office was located, the bishop's office was more accessible. In fact, the synod office was quickly utilized as a centralized location for all our meetings.

Conferring with Bishop Harold Skillrud at an SELBPC meeting.

Bishop Harold Skillrud usually attended our meetings, but when he was unavailable the bishop's assistant, Rev. Eugene Powell, a member of our organization, substituted for him. During one of our meetings at the synod office an angry exchange took place between me and a white regional mission director, Rev. Richard (Dick) Gant. The incident occurred because of paternalistic remarks he made to Rev. Eric Campbell, a black pastor from Tuskegee. His remarks and voice inflection implied that, because of his experience as a white parish pastor in an all-black congregation, he knew more about the needs and aspirations of black people than Rev. Campbell when he said, "Show me proof of your success with increased membership, and I'll give you more financial support." Looking rather embarrassed and hurt, Pastor Campbell listened quietly and never responded. However, I did, saying, "Your previous ministry with black people, no matter how many years, doesn't make you an expert on their needs! Pastor Campbell was born black, and you were not. Because his congregation is struggling to grow and is hurting financially doesn't give you the right to speak to him like this. Don't ever, in my presence, let me hear you bawling out another black man as though you know more about our needs than we do!" Rev. Gant did not respond, though he turned a little red in the face. For me, this was another one of those "whoops, there I go again" moments. My only concern was that this time my comments happened in the presence of a bishop of the church. No one else spoke, and the silence in the room was deafening, adding to my feeling that maybe I was in trouble and should not have spoken this way in the presence of the bishop. But it was hurtful to hear how Rev. Gant had spoken to Rev. Campbell. It was as though there was no respect or encouragement given to this black pastor by his white mission director.

I felt good about my relationship with Bishop Skillrud but was now worried that my angry outburst had put it in jeopardy. Later that same day I received a phone call from the bishop's black assistant, Rev. Powell. He said that the bishop's only concern was whether my comments were appropriate and legitimate. His response to the bishop was that "for some time there has been a need for someone to say what Lonnie said, and he spoke for us all. We all supported his comments." Rev. Powell concluded his phone call by saying, "Lonnie, don't worry about it. You're still in good standing with the bishop." I breathed a deep sigh of relief! My friend and colleague Rev. Eugene Powell has since died. This incident gave more credibility to significant participation in the synod through the Southeastern Lutheran Black Pastors Conference. Having served for two years as president of the Southeastern Lutheran Black Pastors Conference I resigned in 1996, receiving a gavel engraved with my name and the dates I served as president. The incoming president, Rev. O. Dennis Mims, presented the gavel to me. During my tenure as pastor of the Lutheran Church of the Atonement I also served on the Southeastern Synod Council.

Sometime in 1996, Mary Lou Williams, a member of Prince of Glory Lutheran Church in Minneapolis, phoned me with information about a correctional chaplaincy position opening in the Greater Minneapolis Council of Churches (GMCC). Mary Lou was aware that Doris and I wanted to return to Minneapolis to be with the family we had left behind. I had applied for this position fourteen years ago earlier, before accepting the call as pastor of Martin Luther Church in Mobile. Mary Lou apologized for being late in getting me the application and hoped that I could get it in on time. I immediately called my friend Rev. Thomas Van Leer, who was on the correctional chaplain staff of the GMCC. Tom knew of my experience in correctional chaplaincy, and he advised me to fill out the application, include a résumé, and mail it as soon as possible. Additionally, he added that he would try to delay any final decision until I could be interviewed. Following our conversation I quickly submitted my application and résumé. Soon I received a phone call from Rev. Sue Allers-Hatlie, who had oversight for correctional chaplaincy in the GMCC. She was attending a seminar in Atlanta and scheduled a brief meeting with me to discuss the position. Our meeting was not an interview, only an opportunity to meet one another. Our discussion was encouraging and promising, because Rev. Allers-Hatlie made several positive remarks about my correctional chaplaincy experience compared to that of other applicants. Following our meeting, I contacted the Minneapolis Area Synod, notifying Bishop David Olson that I needed his recommendation and endorsement. Later, I flew to Minneapolis to be interviewed by the director of GMCC, Gary Reierson. All went well, and I was hired and assigned to the Hennepin County Adult Corrections Facility as one of the staff chaplains from the GMCC. The position gave me oversight and responsibility for development of the correctional facility's interfaith religious program.

Doris and I felt that our pre-retirement move back to Minneapolis was very important because we saw our presence as grandparents to be strengthening our family relationships. Moving to Minneapolis was both timely and "age friendly," because we were younger than most grandparents. Our roots were already established in the city including a small part of its history and it was geographically closer to our families in Chicago. More important, family needs had increased in the North and, in particular, Doris and I needed to be with the younger members, especially our biracial grandchildren and the white members of our extended family. This was an excellent opportunity mutually to share racial histories and traditions. For the past twenty-five years our family ties had been stretched almost to the breaking point by financial and geographical limitations. Moving from a nomadic family lifestyle and returning to a more centralized location became vitally important for all of us. Feelings of homesickness had always tugged at our hearts. The overwhelming need to be closer to family made my decision to accept the chaplaincy staff position a priority.

I was more emotional than usual when leaving Atlanta. Our southern odyssey had bestowed God's gracious love on us by his people everywhere! It was as difficult to leave Atlanta as it had been to leave Houston, Anamosa, Minneapolis, and Mobile. These ministries were forever etched into my mind when ten members of Martin Luther Church in Mobile, led by William Prince Colley, former church council president, came to Atlanta to bid us farewell. They were determined not to let us forget the love we had experienced as the family of Christ Jesus in Mobile. Prince, as he was called by everyone, knew how important it was to see us one last time. Our needs were reciprocal, because Doris and I were strengthened by their loving presence to continue serving God's purpose in our lives. Their visit was a witness of God's power of love. A member of our congregation remarked, "Pastor Branch, for so many people to travel this distance to say goodbye to you and Doris, they must have loved you both! This is the first time I've ever seen this happen." My heart is always deeply touched whenever I see the end result of the gospel as love!

Tears welled in my eyes again as I realized, perhaps for the first time, why I have always become emotional whenever positive things are said about me. Somewhere and somehow, perhaps all my life, I have swallowed hook, line, and sinker that, because I am black there is nothing I could ever do to measure up or amount to anything. But now I have no need to measure up to anyone's expectations but those of a most benevolent, gracious God! As I write, I'm painfully aware of how many other black people may feel the same way. And now here I was faced with these loving people from Martin Luther Church, confirming what God had done for God's people in mission! We had all "measured up" to everything given us by Christ Jesus and God had made us all "somebodys"—God's own children. We received a lot of farewell cards with cash or checks enclosed. The messages recalled our time together and prayed for God's continuing blessings in our future. Gregory Love, a member of the Lutheran Church of the Atonement, the son of Deacon Willie Love, highlighted the farewell service by giving a brief homily and recalling some of my most significant ministry accomplishments at the church. Church members, visitors, and others filled the pews, heightening an already deeply emotional farewell. Later, Gregory sent me a copy of the videotaped service. Doris and I will forever give thanks and praise to God for God's people, the church, in every place!

CHAPTER 15

Hennepin County Adult Corrections

1996–1999

Retirement was never a foregone conclusion when it came to my work in God's ministry. God's call to serve is not finished until God says it is finished! The eyes of my heart have been opened to understand the purpose of my life in these words of Jesus: "No one who puts his hand to the plow and looks back is fit for service in the kingdom of God" (Luke 9: 57-62, NIV). My determination is as strong as ever to continue following the missional mandate of Christ Jesus. I've complained at times, but never looked back or retreated from where God has sent me. I embraced my life as the epitome of what it means to work towards a ministry of reconciliation.

Cheryl flew to Atlanta from Austin to help with our long drive to Minneapolis, with a stopover in Chicago. Feeling a deep need to be geographical closer to our family, she had planned to move after finding a job at the University of Chicago Press. Cheryl seemed to be always there, at the right time, whenever we needed help in driving to new ministry locations. While enroute we stopped in Louisville, Kentucky, for a night's rest at a local motel. Although we awoke that morning to see a lot of heavy blowing snow, we continued our drive to Chicago. We remained in Chicago for a couple of weeks, visiting with our families there as well as in Gary, Indiana. As usual, we stayed at "our favorite motel," the home of Doris's sister, Maxine, and her husband, Ernest McShan. Cheryl remained in Chicago, renting one of the McShan's apartments, and we lost our relief driver. Doris and I continued our drive into Minneapolis, arriving at our son Michael's home in Maple Grove at night, in the middle of a swirling snowstorm. We lived with Michael and his wife, Patricia, until we could get our own home. Both assured us that we were not crowding them out in any way. However, when the moving van came and unloaded our furniture, we could not help feeling a bit uncomfortable in storing the furniture in their basement. We lived with them for six weeks before moving into our own home in Brooklyn Center. Michael's fishing buddies helped move us. Eventually, they also became my fishing buddies. We selected Brooklyn Center because it was centrally located to facilitate visits to the homes of David in North Minneapolis, Keith in New Hope, and Michael in Maple Grove. Since David, Rebecca, and their children were all members of St. Olaf Lutheran Church, we joined their church.

My final correctional staff chaplain interview with Gary Reierson, executive director of GMCC, went very well. Rev. Sue Allers-Hatlie and Rev. Thomas Van Leer participated in the interview. I was encouraged to see my friend again and enthusiastic to have the opportunity of working with him. Rev. Allers-Hatlie had oversight for the GMCC correctional chaplaincy program, and had an office located at the Juvenile Detention Center (renamed Juvenile Justice Center) in downtown Minneapolis. Chaplain Tom Van Leer worked at the Hennepin County Home School in Minnetonka. My ministry work was at a medium-security facility at the Hennepin County Adult Correctional Facility (formerly known as "The Workhouse") in Plymouth. The facility housed between 300 and 400 men, in addition to a women's unit housing more than sixty females. The work-release center provided limited space for inmates to serve their time while still employed outside the facility. An industry workshop was also available where the inmates could work to earn money. I had oversight in structuring interfaith religious programs for the facility and worked closely with the coordinator of volunteer services who performed criminal background checks and orientation sessions to the volunteers. I provided new inmate orientation, weekly and special worship services with Holy Communion once a month, Bible studies, individual and group counseling to men and women units. I visited cell blocks, isolation cells, and the work-release center as needed. Occasionally I ate with inmates and other correctional staff in the mess hall.

Other responsibilities included providing an imam for Islamic inmates or a rabbi for Jewish inmates. For obvious reasons, religious volunteers were not allowed to provide communion services. I made frequent unannounced visits to monitor volunteer activities, observing what was being taught and the interaction between inmates and volunteers. Sometimes it was necessary to remain after regular working hours to monitor these groups. This brings to mind a visit I made to a volunteer Bible study group. When I arrived, an older white volunteer, nicknamed Buster, was teaching his group. The study went well until shortly before the end, when inmates began to verbally witness to their new faith in Christ Jesus. A young black inmate was speaking about how God had blessed him. He told everyone that he was a recovering drug addict and would soon be released. His testimony went something like this: "Thank the Lord, I've found a new life and way of living. I don't have to do drugs anymore. I'm leaving here in two weeks, and I need all your prayers. I'm going to find a church and join it as soon as I get out and go to church every Sunday. And I'm going to move into the suburbs where there're no drugs." I waited patiently for a response from Buster, the volunteer Bible study leader, but he never spoke. When he continued to allow other group testimonies, I asked for permission to speak. In an affirming way I thanked the inmate for his testimony but cautioned him on assuming that there were no drugs in suburbia, saying, "Drugs are everywhere, but most of them come out of suburban communities into the cities. No matter where you move, drugs will be there! You can't run away from them. I'll guarantee that when you move into the suburbs, you'll find just as many drugs there as in the city. When your Bible study is over I'll recommend some churches and pastors you can talk with." After the Bible study ended I provided him with information on several support groups and churches.

Another perhaps more spiritually significant event took place only two weeks before I resigned my position at the facility. I received a phone call from a correctional officer who said that an inmate wanted to speak with me before leaving the facility. Ordinarily I could have had a private room outside the cellblock, but since I was leaving for the day I requested the use of an unoccupied cell in this particular cellblock where we could talk. When I entered the cellblock there was a lot of loud cussing, but I had not paid much attention to the noise until the officer brought the inmate into our cell. We sat down and tried to talk above all the noise but found it impossible. This was when I became acutely aware of a particular voice loudly yelling above us on the second tier, shouting vile words. The profanity was incessant and became louder. Finally the noise reached the point where I needed to act. I stepped outside our cell into the middle of the cellblock, telling the young inmate who was with me to wait until I returned. There were three tiers of cells in the cellblock, and sometimes the inmates threw feces or other objects down onto the first level. And this was where I was now standing. The next thing I did was even more surprising. Raising both arms in an upward motion, I shouted out as loudly as I could, "Praise God! Praise God! Praise God! Thank you, Jesus!" Suddenly, the entire cellblock became silent. Hearing no further noise, I returned to the cell where the young inmate was waiting for me to return. Speaking to him, I said, "That's better. Now we can talk." However, before we could begin talking the same voice softly spoke, saying, "F— you." The unknown voice spoke only once; we never heard it again. I spoke to the young inmate saying, "At least he's quieted down and stopped all the cussing." In retrospect I believe his shouting had initiated all the noise in the cellblock, because everyone was quiet now.

After completing my conversation with the inmate I left for home. As far as I was concerned, this was the end of the matter until several days later. While saying my nightly prayers I was interrupted by the sound of a soft voice saying, "F— . . . you!" I was able to complete my prayer but had to keep beginning over and over again. My mother had taught me the Lord's Prayer in childhood which I had never forgotten. But now this soft voice had now followed me from the workhouse, continuing to disrupt my prayers night after night. Again and again I prayed for the Lord to remove the voice so I could say my prayers in peace, yet the voice continued interrupting my prayers with the same softly spoken words, "F—you. F— you!" I didn't tell Doris what was going on, fearing what she might think. Although it spoke softly, the voice was consistently disruptive. I was confused and at my wits end. I didn't know what to do. However, for some inexplicable reason I had the strength and determination to continue praying. One night while I was praying, the voice spoke the same words again, but this time another voice interrupted all the cussing and said, "I'm God Almighty. Don't worry about the words you hear, I don't hear them. I only hear what you're saying to me!" I was immediately relieved and completed my prayers without hearing the voice. Although from time to time that same soft voice continues trying to creep in and disrupt my prayers, it doesn't bother me anymore. "When the devil had finished all this tempting [distractions], he left him until an opportune time" (Luke 4:13, NIV).

In 1996, while visiting family in Chicago I baptized my sister-in-law, Nadine White, at her home in Gary, Indiana. Nadine was struggling with cancer and requested that I baptize her at home. The baptism was witnessed by her husband, Jimmie White; her daughter, Wanda; and Nadine's two sisters, Doris and Maxine. Nadine died on February 1, 1997. Doris had gone to Chicago to visit her sister but was unable to get to Gary, Indiana, before she died. This was devastating to Doris because she had gone to Chicago to see Nadine. Later, we drove in a caravan of family cars to Gary for Nadine's funeral.

In 1999 I baptized my grandson Noah Raymond Branch at St. Olaf Lutheran Church. Later, in October of that year, Doris and I flew to Atlanta to drive with Terry to the wedding of his son, Lequent Tyrel Branch, and Rayquel Duffie in Garland, Texas.

My work as a correctional chaplain at the Hennepin County Adult Correctional Facility ended with my retirement in 1999. Correctional

Living in the Minneapolis-St. Paul area allowed more frequent family gatherings.

staff at the facility gave me a farewell party. Doris, Michael's family, Keith, and David attended the event. Rev. Sue Allers-Hatlie and Rev. Thomas Van Leer were there from the GMCCs to give their well-wishes. A similar gathering followed, given by the Minneapolis Area Synod in recognition of my retirement. As usual, I was emotionally affected at both events. The correctional staff at the facility gave me a clock encased in a small wooden, hinged book that could be opened. Inside it was a gold-tone engraving that read, "Remember Our Time Together—March 31, 1999." These words had a profound meaning as it represented the time we served together in our work at the correctional facility. During the synod's recognition retirement gathering, it was a church family event, including recognition of Doris's dedication to our spiritual odyssey in God's various Lands of Promise. I was extremely glad to see that she was recognized because of her many contributions in ministry and the vital role she played in God's plan. As kind words were said about her, I reminisced about the days when she struggled with my becoming a minister and the time she reluctantly became "First Lady" of Martin Luther Church in Mobile. I love her so much and am so proud of everything she accomplished as my wife, the mother of our children, and especially through her service in God's church.

Doris, pictured here with a great-grandchild, was a true ministry partner throughout our spiritual odyssey.

CHAPTER 16

St. Olaf Lutheran Church

2000-2002

After officially retiring in 1999 I was called to a part-time position to work with Rev. Dale Hulme as the visitation/community pastor at St. Olaf Lutheran Church. The position seemed to place more priority on congregational visitation than in the community. Nevertheless, I was able to handle visitations and bring a few new members into the church. The new century highlighted the birth of two more grandchildren: Devante Alexander Branch was born on March 7, 2000, to Keith Branch and Cindy Morin. Eliana Rebecca Branch was born March 14, 2000, to David and Rebecca Branch. Our first great-grandson, Jarek Malachi Branch, born on April 4, 2000, is the son of Nicole Marie Branch. Jarek, with his mother's consent, was legally adopted by her father, Michael, and his wife, Patricia. I was blessed with the honor and privilege of baptizing Eliana at St. Olaf Lutheran Church in May 2000 and Jarek on October 22, 2000, at Maple Grove Lutheran Church. I have baptized seven grandchildren and one great-grandson.

In 2000 David became assistant principal at Lincoln Middle School in Minneapolis. He immediately enlisted me in the "Big Brother/Big Sister" program, mentoring and tutoring a black student for the next two years.

My brother George Vanderbilt Branch who lived

With my "brother" in the Big Brother program.

254 | Reflections of Light

in Peoria, Arizona, was a heavy cigarette smoker suffering with severe emphysema. Hearing from his family that he had been hospitalized, Doris and I flew to Phoenix and were immediately driven to the veteran's hospital. We were at his bedside with his wife, Rosie, and other family members when he died on December 1, 2001. George was sixty-six years old. It is impossible to fully describe our emotional needs because the pain of George's loss seemed unrelenting. Doris and I moved from one grieving family member to another, doing what we could to console and comfort them. The family scene seemed somewhat chaotic until I realized that none of us, including doctors and nurses, had the answers that would keep our loved one from dying. We did not have the power or ability to control life's final situation. Sometimes alone and at other times together, we prayed in coping with George's impending death. And with God's help we found answers when embracing and comforting one another in our own unique ways during our death watch at the hospital.

Doris and I returned to Minneapolis following George's death, later flying to Atlanta, renting a van, and driving to Chattanooga, Tennessee, with our children Terry, Cheryl, and Keith for the funeral at Taylor's Funeral Home. As usual I was the family pastor and officiated at my brother's funeral service. The funeral was well attended with a large number of relatives present, almost like a family reunion. George's burial service was held at a small outdoor military chapel located just outside the gates of Chattanooga's National Veterans' Cemetery, accompanied by a military honor guard. This is where my brother's body was interred.

On our way to the cemetery I had a very interesting conversation with the funeral home's limousine driver. He began the conversation by saying, "Your family had provided another minister as a back-up just in case you weren't able to complete the service, but you did a good job, especially in how you did the eulogy." He asked about my education, pastoral background, and the churches where I had been the pastor. When we returned from the cemetery, a meal was served at the church where my brother's mother-in-law, Bettye Paine, was a member. After praying and blessing the food and those present, I encouraged my nephew Tor Branch to represent our family in thanking everyone for their prayers and support. Tor felt inadequate, saying he was unable to speak well enough to say the right things, whatever that meant. I explained to him the importance of maturity in sharing leadership in the family and that it was time for him to lead. My brother's oldest son was in prison, so it was truly Tor's time to stand, and it was also my time to assure him that his speaking would honor his dad. Even though I had resigned myself to being the family pastor, I could not agree to be responsible for doing it always. Tor did an excellent job, and I believe he knew it because of the applause and accolades he received afterward. I was very proud of him, and I know his daddy would have been even prouder!

Numerous unresolved family issues surfaced prior to and following the funeral, which of course meant that as the eldest in the family and family pastor, I had to do some brief but intense individual counseling. Numerous photographs of the family that were taken serve as a reminder of that time. Most of the pain came from what I consider years of normal relationships of a black family struggling for equilibrium in the midst of life's brokenness. It was par for the course when looking for your family identity within the instability of a racist society. We have all been through this, from slavery until this day, making it seem impossible to escape. As family, we must embrace it and move on—as our parents did. We need to see that in the end it was the power of forgiveness that moved us ahead and that the future is now in our hands. Nevertheless, pain and loss of identity and belonging is as real as death, which cannot be ignored.

CHAPTER 17

A Continuing Odyssey

2003-2009

As time passed I continued to accept my role as the family pastor. It happened again when I drove to Brooten, Minnesota, to officiate at a reaffirmation of wedding vows for Michael's in-laws, John, who was recovering from a stroke, and his wife, Edith TeBrake. I also gave the sermon/eulogy at the funeral of David's mother-in-law, Ivy Lee Quist. Indeed, this was a sad time for us, as our families comforted one another in the loss of a loved one who had suffered with cancer.

In 2004, when principal of Anne Sullivan Communications Center School in East Minneapolis, David continued to keep me busy in ministry. He asked me to be the guest speaker at his school's celebration of African-American History Month on February 12, 2007 (Lincoln's birthday). The event celebrated the National African-American Parent Involvement Day, and the auditorium was filled with students, parents, and teachers. Although knowing that Doris never liked being in the spotlight I was glad when David insisted that she sit up front with me. When introducing me as the speaker he called on me to recognize his mother and have her stand next to me. Everything went fine, but in my remarks I had an occasion where I felt it was appropriate to use the word "nigger" to have a more truthful and effective impact on what was happening at the time. The impact was more than I expected. David, who was comfortable with everything, asked me to meet with him and three white teachers in his office to discuss my use of the word. I had no idea that one of the teachers was married to a black woman. Before meeting with David and the teachers, I was surprisingly encouraged by a young black female student, a member of the school band, who came up and greeted me saying, "Thank you. I really appreciated what you said and how you applied it to our educational needs." My discussion with David and the teachers went well and ended with my driving one of them home.

In 2007, David was assigned by the Minneapolis School District to be the principal at Lucy Craft Laney Elementary School in North Minneapolis. He coaxed Doris and me into working as a team to tutor students at his school. During this time we decided it was a good idea to become volunteers in the Community Tutorial Program of the Plymouth Christian Youth Center (PCYC). I would be the chauffeur and Doris would be the navigator; I would be the disciplinarian, the tough guy, and she would be the nice lady she always was to our students. For two years it was an exciting new learning experience. Currently David is the principle of North Senior High School Academy.

One of many pleasurable family experiences was baptizing my oldest sister, Lenora Flemons, in Chicago at the home of Doris's sister, Maxine McShan. The baptism took place in 2009, and was attended by my younger sister, Roberta Kershaw-Jones, and Lenora's daughters, Rebecca Effinger and Robin Ewing. Lenora has since had surgery for lung cancer and is living in a nursing home near her son Richie Battle.

Throughout my missional odyssey the following Scripture text has guided and strengthened me in the way:

> "The words of the wise are like goads [motives], their collected sayings are like firmly embedded nails . . . given by one Shepherd [Jesus Christ]. Be warned, my son, of anything in addition to them. Of making many books there is no end, and much study wearies the body *(mind)*. Now that all has been heard; here is the conclusion of the matter: Fear God, and keep his commandments; for this is the whole duty of man. It is God who will bring every deed into judgment, including every hidden thing, whether it is good, or evil" (Ecclesiastes 12:11-14, NIV).

> "And surely I will be with you always, to the very end of the age! (Matthew 28:20)"

Having faith in these promises of God has guided our families through it all.

EPILOGUE

Glowing Lights

All these people were still living by faith when they died! And didn't receive all the things promised; but they still saw them from a distance and welcomed them, embracing the truth that they were aliens and strangers here on earth. *People who live like this show their faith, in that they're looking to Jesus Christ for a different land* (Hebrews 11:8-10, 13-16, Life Application Bible, NIV, italics mine).

I've moved away from looking for Lands of Promise and closer to the Promise Keeper! Swift transitions in life have made it difficult, but not impossible, to understand why I am still alive. Why me and not younger members of our family? Perhaps the answer is in the writing of my memoir—and the angel spoke: "Not by might nor by power, but by my Spirit,' says the Lord Almighty" (Zechariah 4:6, NIV).

I pray that your hearts have been opened to see beyond earthly circumstances to acknowledge God's love in our family: "My ears had heard of you, O God, but now my eyes have seen you! Therefore I despise myself and repent in dust and ashes" (Job 42:5-6, NIV Life Application Bible).

Hallelujah, God for giving me an opportunity to write about my life as being meaningful. The many Lands of Promise have shown me a common human need for all people to unite in God's love. The sin of racial superiority continues to blind blacks and whites, making us all victims!

In 1985 a movie entitled *Back to the Future* told the story of a typical American teenager living with his dysfunctional family. Using a time machine and a modified sports car he and his friend go back to the year 1955. *Having lived in the 80s he has a hard time coming to grips with never having lived in the 50s.* His mistakes are many, one of them costly, when he accidentally interferes with his parents' courtship. Realizing the damage he has done to his family and that *if he doesn't change things his own future is in extreme jeopardy,* he immediately takes responsibility to get his parents back together before time destroys his own future forever. In going back to our future: Can we take responsibility to correct past mistakes to ensure a better future for our families? This young teenager's problems are characteristic of our own. What were his motives—your guess is as good as mine. Perhaps it was simply to find the innate love inherent in what it means to be a family. Nevertheless, it was vitally important for him to return to his past to see what he could do to correct mistakes he had made that would terminate his own future. This is precisely why I have written a story about the particular struggles of my life.

All our lives are filled with questions that may never be answered, and because of this truth we give up or ignore our potential as family. The question for us is this: Will we take the time we have to "time travel" back into the past looking, perhaps for the first time, at where we've interfered, maybe even screwed up our relationships with the family we love? If so, will we be responsible for rectifying past mistakes that have damaged the future of our family and that of our posterity? The answer to these questions is between you and God! We make many choices throughout life, and this choice is yours alone. Today, more then ever, we are smothering in the fear and smell of death, insidiously being drawn into family separation, into an ethos of selfish individualism and "survival of the fittest."

Sadly, this same fear and incipient distrust in God has become intensified in our churches. Is it possible to trust God to renew a new Christian family renaissance in us? Can we make time to come together and resolve damaging mistakes of the past for the benefit of our posterity? With God's loving countenance, Jesus looked at them and answered: "With man this is impossible, but with God all things are possible!" (Matthew 19:26, NIV). If our parents had not done the best they could with what they had, we would not be alive today. Now it is our responsibility to go "back to the future" and return to our present time with a renewed vision of family love, even though we still carry the scars of past failures!

"Once having been asked by some Pharisees when the kingdom of God would come, Jesus replied, 'The kingdom of God does not come visibly, nor will people say, Here it is, or There it is, because the kingdom of God is within you'" (Luke 17:20-21, NIV). I pray that our family will come to realize that the kingdom of God is within each of us in our baptism into Christ Jesus who said: "Listen to what the unjust judge says, and will not God bring about justice for his chosen ones, who cry out to him day and night? Will he keep putting them off? I tell you, he will see that they get justice, and quickly. However, when the Son of Man comes, will he find faith on the earth?" (Luke 18:4-8, NIV).

Every land becomes a Land of Promise when we faithfully follow God's call to obedience! With the resurrected Christ living in us, we have the strength to live in all the Lands of Promise.

APPENDIX

Researching Family Roots

As allowed by law, census data becomes public after seventy-two years (Title 44, United States Code, section 2108). After that time information can be used for family histories and other historical research. For additional information look at the 1900, or earlier census family names: Fleming, Carter, Branch, Aycock, Bentley, Kershaw, Ward, and Wilkerson (Dutch population in Pennsylvania). Geographical research areas include Arkansas, Louisiana, Mississippi, and for Branch and Wilkerson, in Tennessee and Pennsylvania.

A recent photo of the Lonnie and Doris Branch family.

Acknowledgments

"We Christians have no veil over our faces; we can be mirrors that brightly reflect the glory of the Lord" (2 Corinthians 3:18, The Living Bible).

My lovely, intelligent wife of sixty years, Doris Jean Hayes, is truly a feminine woman whom God has endowed with a beautiful and captivating smile. In the early days of our marriage, God gave her the strength and wisdom of love to raise our fledging family to maturity and responsibility.

Our oldest daughter, Patricia Lynn Branch is married to Pierre Humphrey I, and lives in Seattle, Washington, with their two sons, Pierre II and Nicholas Tyrone.

Until his death, Doris' brother, Ralph Cletus Hayes, lived in Seattle with his wife, Elaine Ishikawa, and their four children. Ralph shared his work with me on family genealogy and his research of black pioneers in the Northwest Territories. Following his death, Elaine assembled his work and published a book.

Our oldest son, Terrance Branch, served two years in the U.S. Air Force and is employed at the U.S. Post Office in Atlanta, Georgia. After divorcing Arlene Smith-Joyner, he remarried and lives in Morrow, Georgia, with his second wife, Vivian. Arlene remarried and lives in Dallas, Texas. Terry's only child, his son Lequient Tyrel, also lives in Dallas. Tyrell, a divorcee, has two biracial daughters, Bria and Hailee Michelle Branch. Bria was our first great-granddaughter.

Michael Anthony Branch lives in Maple Grove, Minnesota, with his wife, Patricia (Patty) TeBrake, and their adopted grandson, Jarek Malachi Branch. Jarek is the son of Michael's oldest daughter, Nicole Marie, and is our first biracial great-grandson. Nicole Marie Branch is unmarried and lives in Coon Rapids, Minnesota. Jarek's birth has great significance for his great-grandmother Doris who cut the umbilical cord following his birth.

Michael's youngest daughter, Michelle Amber lives in Plymouth, Minnesota. Michelle has given birth to our second great-grandson; Brody Michael Korpics was born on April 9, 2013. Michelle's brother Michael Jeffrey lives in Crystal, Minnesota. Debra Robinson-Mreen the mother of all three children has remarried and lives in Cedar Rapids, Iowa.

Our son, Keith Branch, lives in Minneapolis and is unmarried with two children. His oldest child, Sydney Marie, lives with her mother, Jeanette Sledge. His youngest child, a biracial son, Devante Alexander, lives with his mother Cindy Morin.

Our youngest daughter, Cheryl Elaine Branch, is unmarried and lives in Brooklyn Park, Minnesota. She works closely with me by providing much needed technical assistance and other resources in writing my memoir. I will always be thankful to her friend and mentor, Margaret Fisher Dalrymple, who lives in Reno, Nevada. Margaret was very helpful in using her editorial skills, comments, and suggestions in my memoir.

Our youngest son, David Alan Branch, lives in North Minneapolis with his wife, Rebecca Lee Kosnophal. Their oldest sons, Matthew Alan and Joseph Lee, are unmarried and continuing to pursue college educations. Joseph is now the father of our third great-grandson, Jackson Rebel Branch, born on October 26, 2013. The two youngest children are Noah Raymond, now in high school, and Eliana Rebecca, in junior high school.

My oldest sister, Lenora Branch-Effinger-Battle-Flemons, has survived three marriages. Rebecca Effinger and Robin Ewing, her two daughters, and her only son, Richie Battle, live in Chicago.

My youngest sister, Roberta Kershaw-Jones, also lives in Chicago. She has two sons, Arnel Jones and Otis Mixon. Both sisters have provided helpful information for the writing of my memoir.

Realizing that our families lived in Memphis, Tennessee, during the same time I was born, my brother-in-law, Ernest McShan, Sr., has given me additional data about the lives of blacks living in the city.

Words cannot express the love, respect, and gratitude that our family has for the members of Holy Family Lutheran Church and Rev. Fred J. Downing, whose witness exemplified God's call to mission in Cabrini-Green. The vision given him by God was not to look for certainties but see possibilities in the lives of those oppressed by the principalities and powers. His gentle persuasion helped me to understand why the American Lutheran Church needed me as an ordained minister. My dear friend, Pastor Downing, died on October 4, 2011, in Fredericksburg, Arizona. Our family will always remember and give thanks for our friends at Holy Family, Ida Lockett and Ruth Harris. Ida comforted us with her prayers and abiding love in those trying times of our congregation's ministry. Ruth saw my need to have a history of our congregation, and I'll always thank God for her husband, James, and his leadership in Holy Family Church's time of crisis.

I thank God for Renetta Ludgood, Martin Luther Lutheran Church in Mobile, Alabama, and Betty Jinks, Lutheran Church of the Atonement in Atlanta, Georgia, for providing information about my pastorates in those churches. I am thankful to Rev. Thomas H. Van Leer, a black pastor of the African Methodist Episcopal Church. Tom has published his own memoir, *From Promise Land to the Promised Land*. Without his encouragement to see the larger picture, ignoring my excuses, I do not think I would have began writing. We were born in February, one year and two days apart—Tom in the city of Promise, Tennessee, and me in Memphis. I am truly grateful for another friend, Marsha Jarvela, who encouraged me to join a writer's workshop group in North Minneapolis. George Roberts, the group's director, is a retired white schoolteacher from North Community High School. A black woman, Debra J. Stone, is the group's co-facilitator; her writing expertise uses the idiomatic language indigenous to black and white communities.

Theatrice Williams became one of my mentors relative to his work in the Conference of Inner City Ministry (CICM) of the American Lutheran Church. "T" and his wife, Mary Lou, are remembered for their hospitality when assisting and supporting my arrival at Prince of Glory Lutheran Church in Minneapolis, Minnesota. Melvin Brown and his wife, Bettye, are the godparents of our first granddaughter, Nicole Marie Branch. Mel has died, but his prophetic utterances about Prince of Glory's mission will always echo in my ears, reminding me of those difficult days of our ministry.

Holy Family Lutheran Church and our family are forever grateful for the love shown by Charles and Jean Sweet and Midvale Lutheran Church in Madison, Wisconsin, for their support of our ministry. Jean's letter to the Rev. Dr. Frederick Schoitz, president of the American Lutheran Church, pleading for his intervention to rectify the injustices foisted upon us by the ALC Illinois District is etched in our memory.

My thanks are endless for God's people everywhere; especially those who think they may have done too little. God has seen you and accounted your faith and sacrifices as priceless. God's memory never fails and, even now, is blessing each of you with God's love!